Muybridge

MUYBRIDGE
Man in Motion
by Robert Bartlett Haas

University of California Press   Berkeley, Los Angeles, London

SOURCES FOR THE PHOTOGRAPHS

Bancroft Library, University of California, Berkeley: 10, 11, 13, 16-21, 23-26, 28-44, 50, 59, 64-67
California Historical Society: 5, 12, 72 **California State Library:** 14, 22 **Chicago Historical Society:**
15 **Eastman House:** 118, 121, 122, 128, 129, 132a and b, 133, 135, 152 **Robert Haas Collection:**
48, 49, 69, 70, 113, 119, 120, 154, 155 **Kingston-upon-Thames Museum and Art Gallery:** 99, 100
Leroy F. Krusi Collection: 68 **Mrs. Janet P. Leigh,** Odd Fellows Home, Saratoga, California: 48
The National Archives No. 165-m m-1624A: 51 **Oakland Museum:** 60 **Beaumont Newhall Collection:** 58 **B. J. Partridge,** Public Library, Kingston-upon-Thames: 4 **Philadelphia Museum of Art:** 96
Rodney Rulofson: 6, 71 **Norma Selfe Collection:** 1, 2, 3, 153 **Science Museum,** London: 109
Smithsonian Institution: 92, 94, 134 **Stanford Museum of Art:** frontispiece, 8, 9, 56, 73, 74, 75, 90,
97, 98, 101-109, 111, 112, 114, 121, 136 **Stanford University:** 15, 27, 47, 49, 50, 61, 77-89, 110,
126 **Stanford University Archives:** 52-57 **Stanford University Library:** 72, 76, 115, 123, 124, 125,
126, 149 **Frank Tietjen Collection:** 148 **Title Insurance and Trust Company,** Los Angeles: 7
United States Patent Office: 91, 93, 116, 117 **University of California at Los Angeles:** 62, 63, 131,
147, 149, 150 **University of Pennsylvania Library:** 130 **University of Southern California Library:**
137-146 **University of Texas:** 127 **Stephen White Collection:** 45, 46.

A NOTE ON THE SIZES OF MUYBRIDGE'S PLATES

Before his trip to Paris in 1881, Muybridge used the wet-plate process of photography, with the following plate sizes: 20 x 24 inches (*mammoth*), 8 x 10 inches (*full*), and 3½ x 8½ inches (*stereo*). After his trip to Paris, he began using the dry-plate process: 1 x 19 inches (*Philadelphia plates*). The plate sizes for his later work, in the form of lantern slides at the Museum of Science, London, is unknown. The subjects covered Canada, the Eastern seabord, Yellowstone Park, and the World's Columbian Exposition in Chicago, 1893. It is possible that many of the "official" views of the Exposition were taken by Muybridge on commission for the Exposition photographer.

The kind of plates used for photographs in this book follow. *Mammoth:* 59, 60, 61, 62, 63, and 72.
Full plates: 28, 29, 30, 40, 41, 42, 43, 52, 53, 54, 55, 56, 57, 76, 77, 78, 79, 80, 81, 82, 83, 84, 85,
86, 87, 88, 89, 90, 101, 102, 103, 104, 105, 106, 107, 108, 112, 120, and 126. *Stereo:* 8, 10, 17, 18,
19, 20, 21, 22, 23, 24, 25, 26, 27, 31, 32, 33, 34, 35 36, 37, 38, 39, 44, 51, 66, and 67. *Philadelphia
plates:* frontispiece, 137, 138, 139, 140, 141, 142, 143, 144, 145, and 146.

University of California Press
Berkeley and Los Angeles, California

University of California Press, Ltd.
London, England

Copyright © 1976, by
The Regents of the University of California

ISBN 0-520-02464-8
Library of Congress Catalog Card Number: 73-78542
Printed in the United States of America

Design and layout: William Snyder

FOR PETER AND ROBIN HAAS

Contents

PART FIVE: Creative Expansion

PART SIX: Elaboration and Public Acclaim

PART SEVEN: Retrospection and Retirement

PART EIGHT: Man in Motion

Preface

In the last years of the nineteenth century a new form of instruction and entertainment came into being which today we call the motion picture. It came about when, through the ingenious work of many men, a practical machine was developed for projecting, upon a screen, images that had been sequentially registered on a continuous, flexible strip of transparent material by means of instantaneous photography.

This combination of elements in a single machine was not the accomplishment of any one person. The concept had been "in the air" all through the second half of the century. When the time was ripe, in the 1890s, for moving forward into practical production, a number of persons in different parts of the world arrived at workable solutions almost simultaneously. Before long, motion picture production grew to be one of the most spectacular industries of the world. The educational film, the documentary, the story film, and the art film, even the motion picture film on television, became a major resource for education and diversion for people everywhere.

Among the many experimenters whose work led up to the modern motion picture, none stands more in the vanguard than Eadweard James Muybridge.

Muybridge reached the peak of his fame before the commercialization of the motion picture. His was a one-man show. He carried instantaneous, sequential photography to its peak in his time. He developed a machine for projecting sequential photographs in apparent motion. These he showed before audiences over the western world between 1879 and 1895. Making his living by this means until his retirement, which coincided with the rise of the film industry, he was his own underwriter, producer, scriptwriter, cameraman, director, processor, editor, exhibitor, narrator, advertising man, and distributor. In addition,

he showed motion pictures, for a time, in the first theater specifically built for that purpose.

In the scramble for precedence and commercial advantage which characterized the motion picture industry in its earliest years, many were ready to underplay and undervalue Muybridge's pioneering efforts. Motion picture history of the first half of the twentieth century more often reflects this than not. Now, following the hundredth anniversary, in 1972, of Muybridge's initial work in instantaneous photography for his first great patron, Leland Stanford, the time has come for a clearer assessment of his contribution.

Although as a private person Muybridge remains a somewhat shadowy figure because of persistent quirks and gaps in his biographical record, the tangible legacy of his work remains. In that legacy we find one of the great monuments of nineteenth-century scientific and artistic endeavor. Its prophetic character still influences artists and scientists today, a century after Muybridge's first endeavors to penetrate the secrets of rapid motion.

To only a few are given the capacity to see beyond the surface of things — as Leonardo penetrated the inner life of nature, as Rembrandt penetrated the psychological truth of his subjects, as Turner penetrated natural appearances in his revolutionary work. To Eadweard Muybridge was given the capacity and the commitment to go beyond the static world and enter into the fleeting world of movement.

The scientist in Muybridge *analyzed* this world; the artist in him *returned* that world to motion. Like all great guides he takes us with him, and after the journey we can never see things in the old way again. Far more important than his contribution to the modern motion picture is his contribution to our vision. He tips us into the twentieth century, with a philosophical readiness for novelty, change, and flux.

The sources upon which I have drawn are varied. First, there is Muybridge's own scrapbook, now at the Public Library, Kingston-on-Thames; it contains clippings and memorabilia that Muybridge wished to preserve; after his death, additions were made by the borough librarian, Benjamin Carter. A second source is the collection of correspondence and Muybridgiana assembled by the late Janet Pendegast Leigh and bequeathed to me. Third, I have had access to the Muybridge files of the George Eastman House, made available by the distinguished photographic historian and former curator of Eastman House, Beaumont Newhall. A fourth source is comprised of the body of material that I have turned up here and abroad: printed articles and newspaper accounts, related secondary sources, and information supplied in letters and interviews by numerous persons such as Muybridge relatives, librarians, photographic and film historians genealogists, local historians, and friends who undertook specialized research in my behalf.

Acknowledgments

Many people helped me to gather together the documentation on which this book is based.

In England I was cordially aided by two generations of Borough Librarians at the Public Library, Kingston-upon-Thames: Mr. Harry Cross and Mr. F. John Owen.

In America I was similarly aided by staff members of various institutions: the Bancroft Library, California Historical Society, California State Library, Eastman House, New York Public Library, San Francisco College for Women, Leland Stanford Jr. University, the Libraries of the University of California at both Berkeley and Los Angeles, and the University of Pennsylvania.

Friends and associates who have helped in immeasurable ways are: Dr. David Bershad, Mr. Joseph Davis III, Mrs. Margaret Duncan Greene, Mr. Sol Lesser, Dr. Kenneth Macgowan, Mr. and Mrs. Beaumont Newhall, Mr. Rodney Rulofson, Mrs. Norma C. Selfe, Mrs. Vicci Sperry, Dr. D. B. Thomas, and Mr. Robert Weinstein.

Five close collaborators are hereby acknowledged for their guidance of the present book through the several stages of writing: the late Mrs. Janet Pendegast Leigh who encouraged me to believe I could tell the Muybridge story; William and Mary Hood, whose generous sharing of their photofile of copy negatives made possible the first draft of the book; Mr. Thom Andersen, whose parallel project of creating a film about Muybridge provided me with necessary critical interchange; and Mrs. Anita Ventura Mozley, whose magnificent revival of Muybridge through her 1972 Exhibition of his work at the Stanford University Museum of Art and its accompanying Catalogue made her the spiritual colleague in the last and most important stages of the book's completion.

Seldom has an author had such fortunate editorial help. Mr. Ernest W. Callenbach Jr., sponsoring editor of the University Press, and his able associates, William H. Snyder and John Enright, dealt creatively with both the book's production and its writer.

The final word of gratitude and admiration must go to Mr. Jesse Phillips whose extraordinary editing of the text was, in itself, a whole course in teaching authors how to write.

Five generations of my own family in California have been conservators of original Muybridge materials given by Muybridge himself to my great-grandfather, William Chauncey Bartlett. Appreciation and gratitude are hereby expressed to him and to the succeeding generations who cared for their preservation: Emma H. Bartlett, Ethel Bartlett and Alice Bartlett Haas, Tomi Kuwayama Haas, Peter and Robin Haas.

1. The earliest known photograph of Eadweard J. Muybridge, born Edward James Muggeridge in 1830.

PART ONE:
Early Travels and Provisional Career

1. Kingston-upon-Thames (1830-1851)

Eadweard Muybridge, whose name and achievements were one day to make a stir in the world, was born on April 9, 1830, in the ancient Surrey town of Kingston-on-Thames, not far upriver from London. As the parish register of All Saints' Church shows, the name given him at baptism was Edward James Muggeridge, which in later life he was to change more than once.

His father, John Muggeridge (1797-1843), was well established, on a small scale, as a grain, coal, and timber merchant. Several members of the Muggeridge connection lived in or near Kingston, where the family had some renown for eccentricity.[1] Eadweard's mother, Susannah Smith Muggeridge (1808-1874), was a native of Hampton Wick, just across the Thames from Kingston. She came from a prosperous and numerous local family engaged in the business of carrying by barge.[2] Four sons were the issue of the marriage of Susannah Smith to John Muggeridge. Eadweard (1830-1904) was the second son, preceded by John (1827-1847) and followed by George (1833-1858) and Thomas (1835-1923).

The Muggeridges lived comfortably at 30 High Street, formerly West-by-Thames, or Town's End, in Kingston.[3] On the ground floor were offices and the great, gaping entrance-way through which wagonloads of fuel and provender passed in and out. On the two floors above were the living quarters, paneled in

oak that dated back to the eighteenth century or before. The rear windows looked out upon John Muggeridge's yards and docks, and upon the Thames, which stretched out lazily and beautifully here in its upper reaches.

Eadweard grew up in a world of parents, grandparents, uncles, aunts, and cousins. The hub of this domestic life was his maternal grandmother, Susannah Norman Smith (1782-1870). This powerful woman, left a widow in 1818, carried on her husband's barge business successfully until her sons were old enough to take it over. A memoir by a granddaughter describes her and pictures the setting of Eadweard's boyhood:

My mother's mother, Susannah Norman Smith, was a remarkable woman. In these days when we read in novels of the women of former times who swooned on the smallest provocation, and according to tradition were helpless and useless when work was needed, it is pleasant to record the work of a woman who was otherwise. My grandmother was left a young widow. Her ninth child was born after her husband's death. His business is now almost unknown in these days of steam. He owned barges on the Thames, and many men, as well as many horses, were needed for the work. When he drove in his gig to London, to buy wheat or coal, he took under the seat of his gig, a carrier pigeon, and in his pocket a quill or two, and when he bought a cargo, he wrote on a small piece of paper the number of barges he needed, put the paper in the quill, tied it under the wing of the pigeon and set it free. Someone watching for the bird's arrival unfastened the quill, took the message to the barges, and they started. . . .

All the varied work connected with this business, the young widow took over; her two eldest sons were able to help but

---

[1] Norma C. Selfe (second cousin of Eadweard Muybridge), Normanhurst, New South Wales, Australia, to Robert Bartlett Haas, March 14, 1963. Letters from Mrs. Selfe are hereafter cited as Selfe correspondence.

[2] Selfe correspondence, February 12, 1963.

[3] F. John Owen, borough librarian and curator, Kingston-on-Thames, Surrey, England, to Haas, June 9, 1961.

2. *Right*, Muybridge's mother, Susannah Smith Muggeridge (1808-1874).

3. *Below, right*, Muybridge's influential maternal grandmother, Susannah Norman Smith (1782-1870).

4. *Below*, Muybridge's birthplace in Kingston-upon-Thames (formerly West-by-Thames), 30 High Street.

little when their father died, but school education was not then deemed so necessary as nowadays and they soon were taken from school, and well tutored by their mother, began the different education of business. . . .

My grandmother had no vote, she had, i am sure, never thought of such a business. She was not what we now call "well educated," but, for all that, [was] a notable woman. Left a widow, with nine children, one born after her husband's death, she carried on his business as well as he had begun it. His barges still went down river to the docks and brought back the cargoes the town desired. His horses still walked, sleek and well fed, along the towpath and the men who did the varied work of the barges were well content. . . . They lived in two rows of cottages at the back of the garden. My grandmother knew their wives, and the name of every new baby. She knew also more sometimes than they suspected and did not refrain from giving advice when she thought it was needed. She was a benevolent despot and every man, though only a bargee, listened respectfully when she spoke.[4]

The four boys in the Muggeridge household grew up in the shadow of this remarkable grandmother. Their education fell under her scrutiny. Indeed, family affairs were mostly directed from the deep armchair in the parlor at Hampton Wick, where she sat half hidden by the tapestry frame which stood before her, working the pictures in silk and wool cross-stitch that she gave to each of her many children and grandchildren.

Toward Christmas, Grandmother Smith, dressed in creaseless satin, a great cap of white silk ribbons and roses on her head, a diamond winking on the band of velvet which kept her "front" in place, sent out a clarion call to her daughters that her kitchen and her maids were ready for them and that the long preparation for the feast must begin:

This message was the harbinger of Christmas; and all the preparation, which lasted for weeks, was much more delightful than the feast itself, for it meant stoning raisins [and] washing currants, chopping peel, cutting up apples, and all the excitement of packing mincemeat into great stone jars and hanging rows of puddings on the rafters in the scullery; and withal, the warm fragrance of the kitchen, and the walk home along a snow covered path with my mother.

Christmas was the one great festival of the year. . . . With the dawn of the great day a few trusty messengers came through the garden, entering silently by the little gate near the conservatory, and each one was given a basket, the Christmas gift of my grandmother. . . . To each [household] according to its size a plum pudding, or an immense mince pie, flavored by the etceteras for a Christmas dinner and accompanied by a bottle or two of homemade ale, was sent with a messenger of good will and an enquiry after the health of the family, from the woman who held in trusted hands the welfare of the little community. . . .

My grandmother made Christmas time a season for family reunion. . . . The producing of good things to eat was not only an excuse for a display of good will to all who prospered by her management, but also an opportunity for considering all that related to the well being of her own descendants. After Christmas dinner, at which every son and daughter was expected to be present with even the latest grandchild (and there were always a few highchairs), each grandson or daughter was expected to stand before the family autocrat (in family order) to recite, or tell of work done, or answer pointed questions on varied subjects. Before the time came preparation was made in every family, preparation which included every detail [of] health, conduct and dress which might attract the careful oversight of the head of the clan.

As I drew near the door that hid me from her sight, I heard a strange deep voice say, "Who's that walking so slowly as if she was afraid?" [I answered,] "It's me, Grandma." As I entered the room the same telling voice went on, "Then come in and say what you have to say. Only thieves and rascals are afraid! Hold up your head and speak out!"

In this matriarchal environment of Victorian middle-class virtues, comfort, and prosperity Eadweard Muybridge learned his sternest values. He, too, stood in his turn before his hostess and recited or read, and then heeded the comments of the listeners before he received his grandmother's gift and retired to give place to the next of age. The little ones were taught to say, "Your good health, Grandma." The older ones were taught to admire the shining silver and glistening crystal — all bought "when the barges paid" and a monument to Susannah Norman Smith's industry and solid belief in family possessions. Such family gatherings were both an education and an ordeal.

Eadweard's mother was "more tender and outwardly loving" than was his demanding grandmother.[5] She caressed her children and comforted them. She had pet names for them. Her nephews and nieces were always delighted when "Aunt Muggeridge" asked their parents whether she might have them for a week or two in her home.

Of Eadweard's father we have no comparable knowledge. In 1843 the parish register noted his death: "John Muggeridge of Kingston, age 46, buried 5th March." What influences he had on his sons we do not know. But now Susannah Muggeridge was left to support and educate them. From a Kingston directory entry of 1850, "Susannah Muggeridge, Corn and Coal Merchant, West-by-Thames," we know that she carried on her husband's business for some time after his death. It was ultimately managed for her by a Smith brother when none of the four sons showed a disposition to carry it on.

[4] Maybanke Susannah Anderson (cousin of Eadweard Muybridge), "My Sprig of Rosemary," unpublished memoir, 1915, in the possession of her daughter, Norma C. Selfe; hereafter cited as Anderson memoir.

[5] Selfe correspondence, n.d.

At the time of the father's death, John Muggeridge was on his way to becoming a doctor. A somewhat mysterious figure, he changed his surname to Wybridge, and by this name he was known until his death in 1847.[6] Eadweard and George no doubt attended Queen Elizabeth's Free Grammar School in Kingston. Thomas, the youngest Muggeridge son, was sent up to London, to Christ's Hospital, in 1843. He remained there, a "Bluecoat Boy," until 1852.[7]

Of Eadweard at this crucial time of life, the memoirist recalled:

My mother's sister had four sons, one of them was an eccentric boy, rather mischievous, always doing something or saying something unusual, or inventing a new toy, or a fresh trick.

To a quiet little girl, much younger than himself, he was a sort of hero. I was always willing to listen, or to render small services to Edward, fetching and carrying for him, even though I sometimes had a misgiving as to the wisdom of the business.

Some sense of the man he was soon to become is present in this vignette. Both the positive and the negative aspects of his individuality emerge — his inventiveness, his ability to command attention and cooperation, his capacity for undertaking unusual projects, on the one hand; on the other, his mischievousness and this impulsive behavior, which often aroused misgivings.

From the upper rooms of the house on High Street, Eadweard Muybridge could have seen, across the Thames, the great gardens of Hampton Court palace; upriver was Windsor Castle (where one day he would lecture on "The Attitudes of Animals in Motion"), and below were Walpole's "Strawberry Hill," Richmond, Kew, Chiswick, Putney, Fulham, and then London, heart of the Empire. Along with the other Kingston lads, Eadweard must have roamed beyond the family environment to experience the verdant beauty and historical character of his native place. Its relics reached back to Roman times. The early Saxon settlement on the spot was called Moreford, or Great Ford, because the Thames was fordable here. Like the river and the Kingston bridge at the center of the town, the market place was a focus of excitement. To the Kingston market produce of all kinds was brought, and cattle and horses were herded there for sale or barter. The thriving trade, the movement of the animals, the bustle of the market-day crowds were part of the boy's experience. As he matured, he looked beyond Kingston. Small

coastal vessels from European ports found their way up the Thames and filled him with wanderlust:

There was nothing worth doing in Kingston, sleepy hole. He wanted adventure, the world was wide, and he wanted to see it. The home of his mother . . . gave him nothing of interest to do and at last he announced his intention of going away. But where to go? That question, he could not, or wouldn't answer. No persuasion prevailed.[8]

London was his first proving-ground away from Kingston. Muggeridges had been stationers and booksellers there since the eighteenth century.[9] In the 1850s, Muggeridge, Sprague and company were wholesale stationers at 61 Queen Street in Cheapside.[10] Eadweard Muybridge's later interest in developing patents for a "plate printing apparatus" suggests that he may have found employment with this firm.

A cousin, Edward Smith, had now established a business in America. His stationery store, at Second Avenue and East 49th Street in New York City, sold also "toys, musical instruments, games, candy," and the like, and he had a printing press for small jobs.[11] It is not surprising that Eadweard began to look for some kind of work that would get him passage across the Atlantic to New York:

He wanted to see the world and "to make a name for himself" and at last he came to say "good-bye." He was going to America. That was all we were told.

When he went to say farewell to his grandmother, she with her usual kindliness put a pile of sovereigns beside him and said, "You may be glad to have them, Ted." He pushed them back to her, and said, "No, thank you, Grandma, I'm going to make a name for myself. If I fail, you will never hear of me again."

Hard words for his mother, but he meant them, and in a day or two he was gone.[12]

But he took something from his native town: a new spelling for his name. In 1850 the "Coronation Stone," upon which seven Saxon kings had been crowned, was rediscovered in Kingston. With due pomp it was installed there as a public monument. On its plinth the names of two kings appeared as "Eadweard." Edward Muggeridge, perhaps in some inward act of identification, now

---

[6] Fay Muridge Olson (granddaughter of Thomas Smith Muridge), Tacoma, Wash., to Haas, November 24, 1962.

[7] Selfe correspondence, February 12, 1963.

[8] Anderson memoir.

[9] Graham Pollard, *The Earliest Dictionary of the Book Trade,* London: The Bibliographical Society, 1955.

[10] The *Post Office London Directory,* London, 1852-1856, and information from Mrs. Margaret Greene, Mill Valley, Calif.

[11] Selfe correspondence, September 14, 1967.

[12] Anderson memoir.

chose "Eadweard" as the spelling of his Christian name. At the same time or soon afterward, "Muggeridge" became "Muygridge." The "muy" may have reflected the belief in an infusion of Spanish blood in his ancestry, by way of Flanders, in Tudor times.[13]

Thus adorned, he set out for the United States, watched by three English widows — his grandmother Susannah Smith, his aunt

Rachel Smith Wyburn of London, and his mother. He left behind a country mourning for William Wordsworth and betook himself to one electrified by the publication of *Uncle Tom's Cabin;* a country trying to right itself economically on the optimism generated by the Great Exhibition of 1851, for one already throbbing with excitement over the discovery of California gold.

[13] Information supplied by Fay Muridge Olson.

2. Commission Merchant in America (1851-1855)

New York in the 1850s was a restless city. Horace Greeley counseled the youth of the day to go west, and companies of gold seekers, following his advice, were setting out daily for California. They sometimes left steady jobs and anxious families behind them, convinced that they would be able to pick out of the "diggings" more in a week than they earned at home in a year. Some succeeded in doing that. Even the down-and-outers, returning beaten and bankrupt from the gold regions, failed to discourage the rising generation of Easterners or to deter the immigrants from Great Britain, Ireland, France, and Germany who poured through the city, hardly stopping long enough to buy their copies of the *Emigrant's Guide.*

One might expect to find "Eadweard Muybridge" among those for whom New York was only a point on the way west. Yet for a few years he resisted the pull. The East Coast was the arena of his first independent professional work.

As a commission merchant for the London Printing and Publishing Company, Muybridge arranged the importation of unbound books from England and their binding, sale, and distribution in the United States.[1] (He later became also a business agent for Johnson, Fry and Company, a publishing firm with offices in Boston, New York, and Philadelphia.)[2] Traveling between New York and the principal ports along the Atlantic and Gulf coasts, he was often in the southern states, particularly in Louisiana.[3] By the time he was twenty-five years

old he had achieved more than a modest financial security. The New York daguerreotyper Silas T. Selleck, one of his earliest American friends, said of Muybridge during these years: "His disposition was good, his manners [were] genial; he was a good business man, sound and vigorous of health."[4]

Selleck appears to have been of a family engaged in printing and bookbinding, and he may have met Muybridge in the course of business, but his real enthusiasm was for daguerreotypy.[5] To Selleck's studio came an unending round of "sitters" who expected each picture to be a miracle, no matter how plain their faces might be. He practiced the mysteries of "sun painting": the silvered sheet of copper was sensitized by iodine vapor, the plate was exposed to the action of the sun's rays reflected into the camera, the latent image was developed with mercury and secured with sodium thiosulfate, and the brilliant, mirror-like picture was carefully mounted in a little embossed-leather snap case all its own. His friend's enthusiasm for the new art may initially have encouraged Muybridge to experiment with it. In letters home at this time he mentioned "working at photography."[6]

Muybridge may also have met other members of the photographic profession through Selleck, who was a close friend of Matthew B. Brady. This "prince of photographers" had learned

[1] Anderson memoir.

[2] Inferred from an advertisement issued by Muybridge in San Francisco (n.d.; probably about 1856), found in the back cover of a copy of J. A. Spencer, *History of the United States from the Earliest Period to the Administration of James Buchanan,* in the California State Library, Sutro Branch, San Francisco. Johnson, Fry and Company appears for the first time in the *Boston Directory* for 1859, although members of the firm are listed as early as 1855.

[3] See his *Animals in Motion,* p. 69 (in Dover edition, New York, 1957;

originally published by Chapman and Hall, London, 1901); hereafter cited as *Animals in Motion.*

Visits to New Orleans and "other shipping points in the United States" are mentioned in a clipping of March 28, 1902, preserved by Muybridge in his scrapbook, at the Public Library, Kingston-on-Thames; hereafter cited as Scrapbook.

[4] Selleck made the statement in testimony at Muybridge's trial in 1875. He also affirmed that he and Muybridge were friends in New York in the 1850s. *Daily Register,* Napa, Calif., February 5, 1875.

[5] The *New York City Directory,* 1854, lists "S. T. Selleck, printer, 8 N. Moore, N.Y."

[6] Anderson memoir.

E. J. MUYGRIDGE,
113 MONTGOMERY STREET, SAN FRANCISCO.

AGENT FOR

THE LONDON PRINTING AND PUBLISHING COMPANY,
LONDON, EDINBURGH, DUBLIN, AND NEW YORK; AND

JOHNSON, FRY AND COMPANY,
NEW YORK, BOSTON, AND PHILADELPHIA.

PUBLISHER AND IMPORTER OF

ILLUSTRATED AND STANDARD WORKS.

Has on hand a larger assortment of handsomely gotten up Illustrated Works
than any other house in California; comprising some of the most valuable and
magnificent Works ever issued from the English or American Press, bound in
various styles of elegant and superb bindings, and offered for sale at low prices.

TO GENTLEMEN FURNISHING LIBRARIES!
BOOK PURCHASING AGENCY.

Works upon the Fine Arts, Law, Medical, Scientific, Theological, Architectural,
Mechanical, Civil Engineering, Agricultural, and Miscellaneous Books,

PURCHASED ON COMMISSION

through our Agencies in London, Paris, and New York, and delivered in San Francisco at the published price, with addition of established rates of commission.

Express charges to the interior of the State to be paid by parties ordering. A
deposit of twenty-five per cent. on value of work required in all instances, the
balance to be paid on delivery.

E. J. MUYGRIDGE,
163 CLAY STREET., SAN FRANCISCO.

5. A San Francisco advertisement for the London Printing & Publishing Company, circa 1859.

his daguerrean skills from the American artist and photographic pioneer Samuel F. B. Morse, and was in the 1850s introducing the ambrotype and the paper photograph to the public and to other photographers in New York. A lucrative new field was being opened. To the professional photographers it brought an enormous increase in gallery business.

Muybridge undoubtedly was aware of the new technique of wet-plate photography and printing on paper from a glass negative, which now made possible an unlimited number of prints of a single photograph. Yet it was to be a decade before he turned to photography as his profession.

Meanwhile he watched Selleck wrestle with gold fever. Selleck's insurance against failure as a prospector was to be the camera. When Selleck eventually struck out for the Far West and established a successful photographic gallery in San Francisco, Muybridge must have considered the feasibility of following him. When it became certain that the city had room for other enterprising merchants, he resolved to go there and open a bookstore. If California had no need for books, photography was open to him, too, as an alternative.

For several months, however, he continued his work on the east coast. On voyages and during long periods in port, he made observations of animal life and natural wonders which prefigured the scientific preoccupations of his later career. On shipboard he began to study with particular interest the flight of sea birds, and to reflect upon aerial locomotion.[7] A quarter century later, this interest led him to correspond with the French researcher in animal locomotion, Etienne Jules Marey, and to send instantaneous photographs of gulls in flight to him. Ashore, the wilds of the southern states were nearly as they had been when John James Audubon roamed there, a somber world of swamps and forests, prairies and bayous, abounding in alligators, snakes, eagles, buzzards, turkeys, and other free creatures of land, water, and air. Muybridge recalled later how he had "watched a buzzard wheeling around, at various elevations, for the space of an hour, without the slightest apparent effort of motion."[8]

His observations of human reaction, during the same period, showed an impulse toward analysis and a flair for interpretation:

My work frequently required me to visit the levees to oversee the shipment of books. Steamboats from up river country discharged their cargoes of cotton and other merchandise, each bale, barrel, or box being marked in black with some distinguishing symbol of the shipper or the consigner, such as a diamond, a cross, a circle, or with both symbol and letters all plainly recognizable at a glance to the ordinary run of white man.

I was fascinated to discover that the unschooled slaves who discharged these cargoes were entirely incapable of distinguishing the difference in form between the various symbols. . . .

It being necessary to segregate the shipments to each consignee from each shipper into separate lots on the levees, clerks were employed to mark each package with a distinguishing color. For the purpose six or eight pots of different paints were employed, and either one or two dabs of paint of one or two colors were roughly impressed on the packages.

This I was delighted to discover, the laborers were easily able to discriminate.[9]

[7] *Animals in Motion*, p. 69.
[8] Ibid.
[9] Clipping (see n. 4), in Scrapbook.

The scene of these informal experiments in perception is recorded in his photograph of the river-boat *Whisper*. Bales and boxes stand around the lower decks, and the laborers carry aboard great sacks, each marked for easy identification.[10] Later, in California,

[10] A photograph of the *Whisper* which I found in 1962 among Muybridge's lantern slides, in the Science Museum, London, has been reproduced in Kevin McDonnell, *Eadweard Muybridge: The Man Who Invented the Moving Picture,* Boston: Little, Brown, 1972.

Muybridge observed that the Indians of the Yosemite Valley, while almost entirely lacking the ability to distinguish form and shape in a drawing or photograph, had no difficulty in correctly sorting pieces of variously colored paper.

Business success had come to Muybridge quickly, guaranteeing his basic survival and his creature comforts. Now new intellectual interests and new geographical environments attracted him.

3. California Bookseller (1855-1860)

The unruly and flamboyant new state of California had forged its character, such as it was, in the raw heat generated by the gold fever. After James W. Marshall discovered gold nuggets in the sawmill tailrace at Coloma in 1848, Easterners and Europeans came pouring in to pursue their "uproarious, single-minded search for El Dorado." San Francisco became a tent city overnight. Two years later, California had been admitted to the Union and its population had risen from perhaps 20,000 to a total approaching 100,000. Then, after the Gold Rush peak of "disorder, speculation and high living," things slowed down a bit. More money was being lost than made in the mines, and a sobered population began to realize that "fortunes could be won in California only in the same hard terms as elsewhere."[1] Clarence King, who described the state in the fifties as barbaric, by the sixties would concede that it had made a "vast, inspiring stride from barbarism to vulgarity."[2]

During the first half of the fifties, San Francisco was alive with business and prosperity. Money was superabundant. Houses of brick and mortar succeeded those of lath and canvas on the hills above the Bay. The commercial section of the city took on a look of permanence. Toward the end of 1855, however, and about the time that Eadweard Muybridge arrived there, the city suffered a financial collapse. It could no longer survive on a Gold Rush economy, nor could it survive the open-faced crime. Concerned citizens formed the Vigilance Committee, taking the law into their own hands, but thereby forcing a reform of public morals and local politics.

Despite these parlous times, Muybridge moved into the life of the community and did very well for himself. He established a

bookstore and general salesroom at 113 Montgomery Street, an excellent location.[3] On the floor above he maintained a separate office in the name of his suppliers, the London Printing and Publishing Company. From these two locations he provided culture-hungry Californians with books of law, medicine, science, theology, architecture, engineering, literature, and agriculture. In the style of the times he may have supplemented his stock with such related items as magazines, legal forms, playing cards, sheet music, "philosophical toys," drawing instruments, and artists' materials. In an advertisement he claimed to have on hand "a larger assortment of handsomely gotten up Illustrated Works than any other house in California; comprising some of the most valuable and magnificent Works ever issued from the English or American Press, bound in various styles of elegant and superb bindings." He also undertook book purchasing on commission (for "gentlemen furnishing libraries") through his cooperating agents in New York, London, and Paris.[4] A copy of a book from his store carries the name of "The London Printing and Publishing Company, London and New York," with the locally added imprint "E. J. Muygridge, San Francisco," showing that Muybridge was still using the intermediate form of his surname.[5]

Muybridge was soon known to the local literary and Bohemian crowd. They were a cosmopolitan lot — lawyers, editors, painters, capitalists, actors, photographers, physicians, and politicians, many of whom were destined for prominence in the rapidly growing city. Muybridge served on the board of the Mercantile Library Association, an institution with these laudable

[1] Joseph Henry Jackson, ed., *Gold Rush Album,* New York: Scribner, 1949, p. 185.

[2] Clarence King, *Mountaineering in the Sierra Nevada,* ed. Francis P. Farquhar, New York: Norton, 1935, p. 312.

[3] Robert Earnest Cowan, *Booksellers of Early San Francisco,* Los Angeles: Ward Ritchie, 1953. Cowan's earliest date for Muybridge in San Francisco is 1858, but he appears in directory lists as early as 1856, and may well have arrived the year before.

[4] Advertisement cited in chap. 2, n. 2.

[5] In the collection of Rodney E. Rulofson, Fairfield, Calif.

THE

HISTORY AND TOPOGRAPHY

OF THE

UNITED STATES OF AMERICA:

EDITED BY

JOHN HOWARD HINTON, A.M.,

ASSISTED BY SEVERAL LITERARY GENTLEMEN IN AMERICA
AND ENGLAND.

Illustrated with a Series of Views,

DRAWN ON THE SPOT AND ENGRAVED ON STEEL EXPRESSLY FOR THIS WORK.

FOURTH EDITION, BROUGHT DOWN TO 1850.

VOL. II.

PRINTED AND PUBLISHED BY

THE LONDON PRINTING AND PUBLISHING COMPANY,
LONDON AND NEW YORK.

E. J. MUYGRIDGE, SAN FRANCISCO.

6. Muybridge's stamp appears on the title page of a book he sold for the London Printing & Publishing Company in San Francisco.

7. A contemporary drawing of a Butterfield Overland Mail Company coach, the kind of vehicle in which Muybridge had his accident in 1860.

purposes: "To withdraw youth in particular from the haunts of dissipation, and to give to persons of every age and occupation the means of mental improvement, and a suitable place for passing their leisure hours." Besides providing a library of several thousand volumes, the association sponsored "occasional lectures on interesting topics, literary and dramatic essays and readings, and frequent public debates on political and other subjects of the day." Muybridge, along with other self-improving and literary-minded men, made the Mercantile Library his substitute "for a portion of the comforts of a home," which were not easy to come by elsewhere in San Francisco.

During this period Muybridge described himself as an "athlete." His interest in sports was a Kingston heritage. In San Francisco, clubs devoted to boating, rifle shooting, cricket playing, and gymnastic exercises were open to him. His physical strength and abundant energy, commented on by Selleck, had brought him halfway round the world, and he continued to expend them lavishly in business travel and sight-seeing jaunts.

As he prospered, he brought his brother George from Kingston to San Francisco. Probably the younger man was expected to give him more freedom for contacts with new libraries and bookstores over the state. But George Muggeridge (listed in a San Francisco directory in 1858 as George Muygridge, a clerk in his brother's store) was not a well man. He had tuberculosis, and the family's hopes for benefit from the climate were disappointed. He is believed to have died in San Francisco in 1858.[6]

Eadweard then sent for his youngest brother, Thomas (who now also briefly called himself Muygridge). Tom was twenty-three years old. He had started training to become a ship's officer at Christ's Hospital, but before completing his studies he left the school. He was, however, in the merchant navy from 1852 until 1856.[7] In getting Tom to come to California, Eadweard was not only supplying himself with a new helper whom he could trust, but also carrying on his role of responsible elder brother, as he had sought to do with George.

Now free to leave the store again for work and travel about the state, he explored the varied resources and natural beauties of California, still largely unknown to the outside world. Beyond

[6] The Muggeridge family tree indicates his death year as 1858. Selfe correspondence, August 5, 1967. Whether George died in California is conjectural; he was not buried in Kingston.

[7] Information from A. W. Robinson, clerk, Christ's Hospital.

San Francisco, which was building up the slopes of its sand hills, lay "fertile valleys, mountain heights and desert plains," as he wrote, and beyond these were the "extravagant hunting grounds" of the northern and southern mines, and the Yosemite Valley.[8] In 1859 the Yosemite Valley was being photographed for the first time, by Charles L. Weed.

This vast frontier of grandeur and freedom fired Eadweard Muybridge's imagination along new lines. Portrait photography had never held his attention, but the camera could be used for documenting the rich, flamboyant life and scenery of this frontier and for making it known to the rest of the world. The landscape photography of Weed, Robert Vance, and Carleton Watkins was being offered for sale in local galleries with success. The idea of bringing the panorama of California before the world on a grand scale (which the repeatable photographic print made commercially feasible) suggested a new endeavor to Muybridge. He now proposed to make an extensive photographic record of his adopted state. He no longer toyed with photography as an avocation, but began to regard it as a possible second profession.[9]

In consequence, he put the bookstore into the hands of Matt Gray, a music publisher and seller of musical instruments, and left the offices of the London Printing and Publishing Company under the direction of Tom. With plenty of money at his disposal, Muybridge set out in the summer of 1860 for a combined vacation and business trip to Europe, planning to devote part of the time to preparing for a photographic career and seeking commercial outlets for the photographs that he would take in California on his return.

He chose an arduous mode of travel, preferring to see new regions of the United States rather than enjoy the comparative ease of an ocean voyage to the East Coast. The Butterfield Overland Mail Company had been carrying the mails and a few "brave and hardy souls travelling overland" since the fall of 1858. Travel was continuous, day and night, over a route stretching nearly 3,000 miles from San Francisco to the Mississippi River.

There were Concord coaches for the passengers and Celerity wagons for the mails, each drawn by a four-horse team. From San Francisco the route lay south, through difficult terrain. Between Los Angeles and Fort Yuma it crossed vast expanses of desert. Between Fort Yuma and Tucson, scattered mountains broke the desolate plain. Horses, drivers, and passengers alike suffered from the heat, and water had to be conserved carefully. From Tucson to El Paso, and from there to Fort Smith, Arkansas, was a long, hot ride of several days, the latter part across Texas and the Indian Territory. Travelers were prey to great anxiety on account of the Indians, who were known to be troublesome along parts of the route.[10]

Between the Brazos and Red rivers, in Texas, the rolling prairie was intersected by the Lower Cross Timbers, a stretch of wide woodland like a vast orchard of post oak. Horses were changed at every way-station, and the wilder the teams were, the more relentlessly they were driven. Mustangs and wild mules, who had been broken but recently, pulled the coach along through the alternating prairie and woodland. Suddenly the coach in which Muybridge rode was careening along at breakneck speed, and it became apparent that the driver had lost control of the team. Passengers scrambled to brace themselves for a crash. Muybridge tried to cut his way out through the back of the coach with a knife. One of the passengers jumped from the door and was killed. When the coach overturned and broke up, Muybridge was thrown headlong against a boulder and knocked unconscious. Hours went by before Butterfield scouts discovered the wreck and gathered the injured out of the broiling sun.[11]

For days Muybridge lay in a hospital at Fort Smith, ill and unidentified. When he regained consciousness, his eyes had separate vision; he could neither taste nor smell the food that was offered; and his blond hair and beard, he claimed afterward, had turned an ashen gray. When he could travel again, he went on to New York. Here he instituted a suit against the Butterfield company for ten thousand dollars. Medical treatment meanwhile proving unsatisfactory, he soon went on to London and put himself under the care of the celebrated Sir William Gull at Guy's Hospital.

[8] Prospectus for Muybridge's "Panorama of San Francisco from California Street Hill," September 1877; in Scrapbook.

[9] According to the *California Hydraulic Press,* North San Juan, Calif., June 4, 1859, "fine photographic copies of paintings" could be seen at "Muggeridge's bookstore." Information from William and Mary Hood, Twenty-nine Palms, Calif.

[10] See Waterman L. Ormsby, *The Butterfield Overland Mail,* San Marino, Calif.: Huntington Library, 1955.

[11] Details from newspaper accounts of Muybridge's trial; for example, the *Chronicle,* San Francisco, February 6, 1875.

4. Lost Years (1860~1866)

Sir William Gull was the leading diagnostician of his day. Although he did not report on Muybridge's case in his extensive medical writings (so far as we know), the patient himself later described symptoms which suggested that the effects of his injury may well have been serious and long lasting. "His head was confused and [it] ached. He had double vision — that is, where there was one man he could see two." His senses of taste and smell were "impaired," and he was "very deaf."[1]

Since "natural therapy" was frequently prescribed by Sir William Gull for his patients, it is likely that for Muybridge he recommended a long period of rest to be followed by a course of steadily increasing outdoor exercise. In the early months of 1861, however, Muybridge returned to New York to proceed with the suit that he had lodged against the Butterfield Overland Mail Company. It was settled for a quarter of the sum he had asked. Back again in England by late summer, he wrote to his uncle Henry Selfe in Australia that he would shortly leave for the Continent, "on business that may detain me some months."[2] Where and how these next months, or indeed years, were spent, we do not know. The forwarding address given to the uncle was "E. J. Muygridge care of Mrs. Wyburn, 6 St. Johns Villas, Adelaide Road, St. Johns Wood," in London. Meanwhile Eadweard's mother, who had been living in London with her sister, Rachel Wyburn, returned to Kingston-on-Thames to share a house with her unmarried brother, John Smith. Perhaps Eadweard, seeking recuperation, was often there with them. Certainly he was in contact with his Kingston relatives and friends, and photography was providing him with a therapeutic outdoor activity. Within three or four years he was able to pick up the threads of his energies and pursue systematic photographic work.

Just as Selleck had interested him in daguerreotypy and early paper photography in New York, now a Kingston friend aided his development. The friend was Arthur Brown, whose eccentric but inventive schemes strongly suggest a temperament to which Muybridge would be drawn. The memoir by Eadweard's cousin states:

At this time the art of using the sun as an assistant to portraiture was in its infancy. Daguerre had succeeded in taking portraits on a polished plate, and [some photographers] were making experiments in using glass instead of the polished plate on which daguerreotypes were taken. Mr. Brown was one of these, and from day to day he was busy preparing glass to compete in an exhibition soon to be held in London. To take a portrait not only a camera and a prepared glass plate as well as chemicals were needed, they were no use without a subject and my first understanding of the reason why Mr. Brown was always pottering about, and earning no money, as my mother said, was obtained when he came to see my mother. He told her he could not go on without subjects for his work, and then after some explanation of what was wanted, he asked her permission to take me out of school, sometimes, so that he might stand me on a chair and take a picture of me. . . .

My brother, Harry, Mr. Brown said would also be a good subject, and he might be taken as he came home from Grammar School. So the experiment was launched and we were the first of Mr. Arthur Brown's sitters. . . . One [picture] of Harry was sent to an exhibition in London where the new process was discussed and prizes offered for the best examples of it, and Harry's picture took a prize because the medium tones were exceptionally well developed.[3]

Brown's influence is apparent in some of Muybridge's schemes of this time. In the aforementioned letter of 1861 to Henry Selfe he describes a machine for washing clothes and other textile articles, referring to himself as being "in legal point of view *the inventor*, and entitled to all the rights and privileges of a patent therefor," and suggesting that the uncle undertake to introduce the machine into Australia. Along with the letter he sent a set of plans outlining what were essentially his own improvements on previous machines. These, he believed, would produce a new apparatus which would be much appreciated "if its merits and labor-saving qualities were known." He speaks also of an earlier proposal having to do with the "plans and specifications of the new process of, and apparatus for, plate printing," which he suggests his uncle hold in abeyance because he has discovered that Australian and English patent law differ as to how the "inventor" may be defined.

Muybridge's letter reveals familiarity with legal terminology and issues, particularly English and American patent law. "I am in *fact*, and I think I would be so considered in law, the inventor of *both* machines as laid down and described. And I think were a patent granted me, I could sustain any action for infringement on the principle I might bring against subsequent applicants." He goes on to review for Selfe every patent granted in England relevant to his proposal from 1780 to the close of the year 1860. He is

[1] *Chronicle,* San Francisco, February 6, 1875.
[2] August 17, 1861; collection of Norma C. Selfe.

[3] Anderson memoir.

very convincing. The ability to think in legal terms was to reappear in many forms in his later life.

Concerning the washing machine, he writes: "I have drawn the plans to a suitable scale, for ordinary sized domestic machines; not being a practical draughtsman, the plans are not as accurate as might be desirable; and certain technicalities may be omitted, and inappropriate terms used in the description; I have however I think given them with sufficient disinterestedness, to enable any carpenter, a machinist, upon reference, to construct one without difficulty."

The terms upon which he offered his idea to his uncle seem almost equally "disinterested." They were that Selfe should take out patents in Sydney and Victoria at his own risk and cost, while Eadweard did the same in England. Selfe would have full permission to promote the washing machine in the Colonies, but Eadweard offered no legally binding document to support his contention that he would "at no future time make any *demand . . .* for rumuneration, or expenses." As a friendly, but perhaps legally eccentric afterthought, he says: "Should however you realize 'something handsome' from the undertaking (of which I am almost fully persuaded you can), or should I at any time be in *need* of money, some mutual understanding may then perhaps be arrived at."

At thirty-one Muybridge shows himself capable of initiating rather sensible and useful schemes, and of carrying them to a certain independent stage of realization. Although no patent for his washing machine seems to have been granted, we see him becoming able to combine the practical and the visionary in a unified endeavor, conceived and carried out in his own terms. In subsequent years many patents and copyrights were in fact granted to him, both in England and in the United States.

During Muybridge's seemingly lost years a new device based on photography was claiming public attention. The stereoscope had come into fashion.[4] This was an optical instrument for viewing two small photographs, taken from slightly separated points of view and mounted side-by-side so that the images fused in one's vision and gave the illusion of solidity and depth. Before long it became the *pièce de résistance* of every well-appointed parlor. Families vied to possess collections of stereoscopic cards, photographically illustrating remote places, little-known peoples, and natural or man-made wonders. In an era of commercial expansion and insatiable curiosity about the world, stereoscopic scenes provided welcome mementos for the traveler as well as entertainment for

[4] For the development of the stereoscope and its effect see Robert Taft, *Photography and the American Scene,* New York: Macmillan, 1938, chap. 10; also Helmut and Alison Gernsheim, *The History of Photography,* rev. ed., New York: McGraw-Hill, 1969, chap. 20.

8. A photographic card for the stereoscope.

9. Brewster's lenticular stereoscope, a popular device for viewing such double photographs.

the stay-at-home. To meet the demand, enterprising photographers bought stereoscopic cameras and went into action to secure the desired "representative views." By 1858 one firm, the London Stereographic Company, was advertising "a stock of 100,000 different photographs of famous buildings and places of interest in England and abroad."[5] The owner of the firm, George Swan Nottage, acquired great wealth through the sale of stereoscopic cards and eventually became Lord Mayor of London.

The promise of new photographic markets in the United States motivated Muybridge in his return to the West Coast. With the strange mixture of business acumen and desire for travel and new experience which had served him well as a commission merchant and bookseller, he packed up the finest stock of photographic equipment that his money could buy and prepared to travel back halfway round the world. As he did so, he altered the spelling of his surname again, calling himself at last Eadweard Muybridge. He must have held some belief in the magical power of words to change things either in himself or in the attitudes of others. Presently he took on also the pseudonym "Helios," perhaps seeking the ambiance of the sun god for his role of photographer and planning to shed his light over the world through pictures.

[5]Gernsheim and Gernsheim, op. cit., p. 257.

PART TWO:
West Coast Photographer

5. Helios and the Flying Studio (1867–1873)

The Civil War had sobered the United States during Muybridge's absence. Now, after a period of convalescence and gloom, the country was coming alive again. The new optimism was closely related to the construction of the first transcontinental railroad, which fired the hope that an unprecedented era of prosperity would follow upon the joining of the rails, then being laid simultaneously westward from the Missouri River and eastward from Sacramento, California. Construction moved ahead as rapidly as the laborers could be driven, for government subsidies became available only as track mileage was completed.

Leland Stanford, the "War Governor of California," worked while others slept, to get the Central Pacific's lines across the Sierra Nevada and on toward Utah Territory. He and the others of the "Big Four" — Charles Crocker, Henry E. Huntington, and Mark Hopkins — managed to solve the formidable engineering and financial problems of the project with a pooling of determination and sleight of hand. Their goal was to beat the westward-moving Union Pacific in the construction dash to the Salt Lake Valley. The race created the greatest excitement in California since the Gold Rush.

In 1869 the joining of the rails made the old sea and land routes obsolete. Now the material wealth of California could move to eastern markets economically, while a swift flow of tourists would bring in new wealth. Times were already changing in San Francisco, where the population was approaching 200,000. Clarence King, who had noted the barbarity of the first decade

after the Gold Rush and the vulgarity of the second, found that the city was softening a little, as if it were beginning to be aware that it "stood on the threshold of greatness." "Polite literature, scientific research, and the mellowing influence of art" were beginning to surpass "money making" as the main interest of the citizens. Ambitions were growing more refined. Intellectual pursuits were supported "not by the select few, but by the masses." At any rate, this was the way San Franciscans of the sixties and seventies liked to hear the story told.[1]

This was the San Francisco to which Eadweard Muybridge returned with his newest dream of photographing the Far West for all the world to see. He descended on the unsuspecting city with a new name, new photographic skills, and renewed energy and purpose.

The bookstore, left in the hands of his brother half a decade before, had long since been given up. Thomas Muggeridge had quit California and become a dental surgeon in New South Wales, whence he wrote complaining of "lack of clients, poor furnishing of room by late owner, only a dental chair and sofa, dullness of the town and having 'the Blues.' "[2] Through the convenient alchemy practiced by the Muggeridge brothers, he was now known as "Dr. Thomas Muridge."

Eadweard Muybridge plunged immediately into six productive

[1] *Mountaineering in the Sierra Nevada* (cited in chap. 3, n. 2).
[2] To Elizabeth Selfe, April 23, 1867; collection of Norma C. Selfe.

13

and strenuous years of photography, which were to culminate in publication of the *Catalogue of Photographic Views, Illustrating the Yosemite, Mammoth Trees, Geyser Springs, and Other Remarkable and Interesting Scenery of the Far West, by Muybridge,* a résumé of his work to 1873.[3]

The views listed in the catalogue comprise some 2,000 photographs, grouped into several series. By far the greater number are in stereographic form, intended for mounting and sale on cards, but some are offered in larger sizes for framing or for album collections.[4] Muybridge apparently arranged the listings and wrote the descriptive text himself. The fact that the numbering of the sequences is not continuous may mean that he wished to mark the existence of photographs that he had assigned to other publishers.

San Francisco Views

For the first year or so after his return, Muybridge made his professional headquarters with his old friend Silas Selleck, at the Cosmopolitan Gallery of Photographic Art, 415 Montgomery Street. He identified himself from the outset as a landscape photographer, not a gallery portraitist. As he built up the corpus of his early San Francisco pictures, he moved about the city in a smart, light horse-drawn vehicle, labeled "The Flying Studio."[5] Any notion that he was merely Selleck's "outside man" was dispelled when he marketed the sterescopic cards through the Cosmopolitan Gallery under his "Helios" pseudonym and indicated his copyright with the notice, "Entered according to Act of Congress, 1868, by E. J. Muybridge."[6]

The series of local views presumably was begun in 1867 and compiled in large part during the next five years, to be continued sporadically until he left San Francisco in 1881. Muybridge must have taken nearly a thousand photographs in San Francisco and around the Bay. Many of these, whose titles are known, have not been discovered.

Two bound volumes, possibly Muybridge's studio sample books, are our major source of information about the "San Francisco

Views." Each contains about 400 half-stereos, mostly numbered and titled by hand. They comprise most of Muybridge's early stereoscopic photographs of the city and its vicinity, and show the scope of his work and the range of his documentation to 1873.[7]

A preoccupation with San Francisco Bay is evident in such views as "Sunlight Effect on the Bay," "Moonlight on the Bay," "Sunset over Mt. Tamalpais," "The Golden Gate from Black Point," the Golden Gate at different times of day and under different weather conditions, "Richardson's Bay," and "Yachting on the San Francisco Bay," along with many other views incorporating this most spectacular topographical features of the region.

Prominent buildings and street intersections in San Francisco, showing the city's booming commercial life, find an important place in the series: "St. Mary's College," "Pacific Bank, Sansome Street," "Merchant's Exchange, California Street," "Montgomery Block," "Odd Fellows Hall," "Bank of California," "Maguire's Opera House," "Trinity Church, and Jewish Synagogue," "Mercantile Library, Interior," "The Cliff House," "Montgomery Street, North from California," "California Street, West from Montgomery," "Russian Hill from Telegraph Hill," "Montgomery and Market Street, Fourth of July," "City Front from Long Bridge," and "A Street on Telegraph Hill." In addition there are single views of the city from its prominent hills, as in "San Francisco from the top of California Street," and a segmented six-plate "Panorama from Rincon Hill."

Other views show governmental and military installations at the Presidio, Fort Mason, Black Point, Fort Point, and North Point, and on Alcatraz Island and Yerba Buena Island (then known as Goat Island); ships, yachts, and wharves on the city's waterfront; the Bay View, San Francisco and San Jose Railroad, and the Central Pacific; the Chinese in San Francisco; and Woodward's Gardens. There are a few topical scenes, such as "French Admiral Clové and staff at Alcatraz Island" and "House Moving in San Francisco"; a portrait of the deluded "Norton,

---

[3] Published by Bradley and Rulofson, and printed by Francis and Valentine, San Francisco, 1873; hereafter cited as *Catalogue*.

[4] The larger prints were 5½ x 8½ inches, 7 x 9 inches, and 17 x 21 inches.

[5] Several stereoscopic prints exist showing the photographic cart with the Flying Studio name prominently displayed.

[6] Muybridge preferred to operate in his gallery associations as an independent outdoor photographer rather than as a gallery partner. For most part, he published his photographs independently, even though they were distributed through various outlets. The *Catalogue* photographs, published by Bradley and Rulofson, were a major exception.

[7] Stereos 1-278 are not listed in the *Catalogue*. The two volumes are uniquely valuable for identifying them. The volumes are in the Bancroft Library, at the University of California, Berkeley, which acquired them in 1971 from the collection of Monsignor Joseph M. Gleason at the San Francisco College for Women.

Gleason was a pastor at Palo Alto, California, from 1909 to 1928. He may have obtained the volumes from the family of John Doyle, Muybridge's lawyer in San Francisco, who lived near Leland Stanford's "Palo Alto Farm." Muybridge left some belongings at the farm when he went to Europe in 1881, and correspondence in 1893 indicates that he never succeeded in reclaiming them (see chap. 28). Presumably the belongings were given to Doyle later, including the two volumes.

Emperor of the United States," shows a noted human feature of the city and sometime source of comic relief.

Interspersed among the scenes of geographical wonder and civic pride are a small number of views which play upon the delicate and transient aspects of nature and reveal the lyrical side of Muybridge's skill with the camera. These portray sunsets, "moonlight effects" and "sunlight effects" on water, groups of trees, and cloud formations. While revealing no particular technical innovation on his part, they indicate considerable technical competence and, more importantly, counterbalance the documentary nature of most of his work. Muybridge's atmospheric effects seem to bear a conscious relationship to the poetic brushwork of the English painters Constable and Turner, or to the proto-impressionists, including Whistler, as if he were seeking photographic equivalents for their experiments in paint.

Other San Francisco photographers, stationers, and booksellers advertised and sold views of local scenery. We do not know to what extent they took their own photographs or used "outside men." If they bought certain of Muybridge's plates, as we suspect, they were entitled to issue them without identifying the work as his.[8] It has been thought that some of Muybridge's San Francisco photographs, like some in subsequent series, may have been published in the eastern United States and in Europe without mention of his name. At any rate, the local views that he entered for American copyright in 1868 were sufficiently popular to be marketed actively by him or by his agents in San Francisco for a decade or more. Stereoscopic cards from the series have had a high rate of survival, and many are in public and private collections over the world. Less frequently found are the larger views of some of the same subjects, seemingly made for framing.

[8] For example, a stereograph of Yosemite Valley listed in the *Catalogue* as no. 1377, "Tisayack, from Glacier Point," and published by Bradley and Rulofson in San Francisco as a view by Muybridge, was also published by E. and H. T. Anthony and Company, New York, as "Glories of Yosemite Valley" without credit to Muybridge as the photographer. On the other hand, a similar stereograph by Muybridge was also published by Bradley and Rulofson with the same number and title. The identity of the separately published stereographs was discovered by William and Mary Hood.

Photographic scholarship has not yet dealt with the practices of nineteenth-century photographic publishers nor determined the circumstances in which some photographers retained their identity on publishers' trade cards and others did not. As large collections of copy prints are beginning to be compared and cross-filed in special collections and reference libraries, it may be possible eventually to make definitive attributions of many photographs whose authorship is now uncertain, including some which Muybridge probably took.

Yosemite Valley and the Calaveras Grove of Mammoth Trees

Muybridge continued his documentation of the Far West with a series of photographs of the Yosemite Valley, as yet relatively unvisited but already a much described wonder of the world. He writes of it in the *Catalogue:*

This wonderful valley, with its lofty peaks, its stupendous precipices, its majestic waterfalls, and innumerable points of beauty, is now so universally known as the scene of Nature's most marvellous creations, and has been the theme of so many works by the poet and the artist, that it is entirely unnecessary to mention, excepting in our Catalogue, the names even of its many attractions. It was discovered in 1851, is situate in the County of Mariposa, about 250 miles from San Francisco, and is about 4,000 feet above sea level. In 1864 it was granted by the United States Government to the State of California, for the free use and recreation of the public for all time to come.

Some of the pictures were taken on commission for John S. Hittell, an early immigrant with literary aspirations who was currently putting together the first guidebook for the valley and wished to have it illustrated by photographs "because no engravings could do justice to the scenes or convey perfect confidence in the accuracy of the drawing of such elevations."[9]

The distinction of being the first to photograph the amazing valley belongs to Charles L. Weed, whose work has been almost forgotten. Weed arrived in the valley on June 17, 1859, with a party from San Francisco led by James M. Hutchings. Among his first subjects was Yosemite Falls in a view from the base, creating the illusion that the three waterfalls were one. Weed returned to San Francisco with at least 20 large plates, 10 x 14 inches, and 40 stereos, which his employer, Robert H. Vance, quickly advertised for sale.[10] Several of these views appeared as engravings in *Hutchings' California Magazine.*[11]

The second photographer known to work in the valley was Carleton E. Watkins. He had been an employee of Vance's branch gallery in San Jose, but by 1857 had acquired his own gallery in

[9] John S. Hittell, *Yosemite: Its Wonders and Its Beauties, with Information Adapted to the Wants of Tourists about to Visit the Valley,* San Francisco and New York: H. H. Bancroft and Co., 1868, p. iv.

[10] Bill and Mary Hood, "Yosemite's First Photographers," in *Yosemite: Saga of a Century, 1864-1964,* Oakhurst, Calif.: Sierra Star Press, 1964, pp. 44-52; Mary V. Hood, "Charles L. Weed, Yosemite's First Photographer," *Yosemite Nature Notes,* June 1959, pp. 76-87.

[11] Also in James M. Hutchings, *Scenes of Wonder and Curiosity in California,* San Francisco: Hutchings and Rosenfield, 1861, and *In the Heart of the Sierras,* published at the "Old Cabin, Yo Semite Valley" and the Pacific Press Publishing House, Oakland, Calif., 1886.

10. Muybridge's "Flying Studio" in the Yosemite Valley, 1867. A portable dark-tent, chemicals, and the hat used for covering and uncovering the camera lens are all part of the outdoor photographer's paraphernalia.

San Francisco. Watkins entered the valley for the first time in 1861 and brought along a view camera capable of taking 18 x 22 inch glass negatives. He returned again and again, until his name became indelibly associated with the valley. Mount Watkins bears his name today. Some of the 8 x 10 inch photographs that Watkins took in 1864 and 1865 were incorporated in the reports of the Geological Survey of California, headed by Josiah Dwight Whitney, state geologist from 1860 to 1874.[12]

[12]Watkins' photographs were used to illustrate the second report, *Geology, Volume I* (published by authority of the Legislature of California and printed at Philadelphia in 1865); in *The Yosemite Book,* New York: Julius Bien, 1868; and in a later book incorporating the work of the survey but published independently under the auspices of Whitney, *Geology, Volume II: The Coast Ranges,* Cambridge, Mass.: John Wilson and Son, 1882.

In *The Yosemite Book* original photographic prints were attached on linen hinges (republished from 1869 to 1874 without the photographs as *The Yosemite Guide-Book*). In *Geology, Volume I* the photographs were reproduced as woodcuts; in *Volume II* as heliotypes. These works are described in Francis P. Farquhar, *Yosemite, the Big Trees, and the High Sierra: A Selective Bibliography,* Berkeley: University of California Press, 1948, pp. 29-34.

It was in the spring of 1867 that Muybridge made his first trip to the valley — an arduous and expensive outing which required the unpacking and repacking of his elaborate equipment at several points on the journey.[13] From San Francisco to Stockton, the trip was made by river steamboat. Then a jouncing stagecoach or rented wagon carried the traveler south on the stage roads by way of Murphys to Jacksonville, on the Tuolumne River. Muybridge's stereos reveal that he first visited the Big Trees, or giant sequoias, of what is now known as the Calaveras Grove, sixteen miles beyond the town of Murphys. Here he secured 25 views. With his cumbersome equipment — small view camera, stereoscopic camera, cases of glass plates, bottles of chemicals, darkroom tent, tools, camping gear, food, and firearms — he next had the choice of two routes, one ending at Black's, on Bull Creek, and the other a few miles beyond Big Oak Flat. By one or the other, entrusting his precious possessions to a guide and a string of half-wild mules and mustangs, he completed the last leg of the journey and got his first glimpse of the breath-taking valley from the spot frequently designated by early travelers as the "Standpoint of Silence."

He seems to have established himself on the valley floor at Hutchings' hotel, or near by. He photographed the hotel, took part in the play of the Hutchings children, and adopted Hutchings' practice of using the ponderous Indian names for the places that he photographed. With the hotel as a center, Muybridge worked slowly about the valley that spring and summer, photographing from the chief vantage points as light, weather, and rough trails would permit. With the view camera, using 6 x 8 inch plates, he took the pictures that, in reduced size, became illustrations for Hittell's valley guidebook, *Yosemite: Its Wonders and Its Beauties.* With the other he obtained scenes for the popular stereographic series.

The photographic work was an exacting and unwieldy process. After arriving at a chosen destination, Muybridge had to spend some time choosing the viewpoint from which his pictures would be taken and calculating the best time of day for the exposures. Guides and horses would have been dispatched ahead with equipment and supplies, and a camp prepared if the wait was to be a long one. The cameras, tripods, lenses, and chemicals were unpacked. Then the darkroom tent of the "Flying Studio" was pitched. As the work began, the chemical sensitizing of the wet plates went on in the tent. Exposures were made, and the sensitized plates were developed immediately afterward. A half dozen successful views in a day would be considered a productive result. When these operations were combined with mountain climbing, irregular weather, and the transporting of heavy equipment, Muybridge had need of all his athleticism and a commanding patience besides.

The larger photographs appear to have been taken in the spring, and the stereos in the spring and summer.[14] It would seem that Muybridge did not number the pictures as he took them in the field, but arranged them later in a sequence fitted to a typical tourist's itinerary, beginning with the north side of the valley at the foot of the Mariposa Trail and progressing as follows:

In the Bridal Veil Meadow Area: Moonlight Rock, Bridal Veil Fall, Cathedral Rocks and Spires, El Capitan from the west, and the Three Brothers
In the El Capitan Meadow Area: Yosemite Fall, base of Eagle Cliff, Sentinel Rock, El Capitan from the east, The Domes, and views of the Merced River
In the Sentinel Meadow Area: Sentinel Meadow, Rocky Point, Sentinel Rock, and Yosemite Fall
In the Stoneman Meadow Area: Stoneman Meadow and Mirror Lake[15]

On one excursion, 700 feet above the valley, in the area usually visited last by tourists because of its difficult access, he obtained another series:

In the Canyon of the Merced Area: Illilouette, Happy Isles to Vernal Fall, Wildcat Valley, and Nevada Fall

Several strenuous trips around the rim of the valley, high above the floor, produced a remarkable series:

Rim of the Valley Area: Inspiration Point, Taft Point, Sentinel Dome, Glacier Point, base of Upper Yosemite Fall, Union Point, Panorama Rock, Clouds Rest, Mount Watkins, and top of Upper Yosemite Fall

On the public acceptance of this six months' labor Muybridge staked his professional future. He was more than justified by the technically excellent and pictorially distinguished photographs that he brought back to San Francisco. First, he had not been content to repeat views that had been chosen by his predecessors.

[13] Mary V. Jessup Hood and Robert Bartlett Haas, "Eadweard Muybridge's Yosemite Valley Photographs, 1867-1872," *California Historical Society Quarterly, XLII* (March 1963), pp. 5-26. Parts of this article are used by permission in the following account.
[14] Compare, for example, stereos 56 and 57 in the Gleason volumes.
[15] Here and in the next two listings I use the modern place names and the ordering supplied by Mary and William Hood, who from their knowledge of the valley have deduced Muybridge's probable vantage points, and who have checked their attributions by photographing the same scenes from these locations and comparing the results with his pictures.

YOSEMITE:

ITS WONDERS AND ITS BEAUTIES.

WITH INFORMATION ADAPTED TO THE WANTS OF TOURISTS ABOUT TO VISIT THE VALLEY.

By JOHN S. HITTELL.

Illustrated with Twenty Photographic Views

TAKEN BY "HELIOS,"

AND A MAP OF THE VALLEY.

SAN FRANCISCO:
H. H. BANCROFT & COMPANY,
609 Montgomery St., and 607-617 Merchant St.,
NEW YORK: 113 WILLIAM STREET.
1868.

11. Title page of Hittell's *Yosemite, Its Wonders and Beauties,* for which Muybridge supplied and tipped into the text original prints of twenty photographic views.

EDW. J. MUYBRIDGE

Has now ready for sale the most comprehensive and beautiful series of Photographic Views, illustrating the wonderful

Scenery of the Yosemite Valley

ever executed. They comprise

260   VIEWS

of the various falls, precipices, and most picturesque and interesting points of sight in the valley.

100, 6 x 8 inches, mounted on tinted boards, 14 x 18 inches, price, $1.25 each, or $1. each in quantities of 20 and upwards.

160 Views for the Stereoscope, - - - - - price, $4.50 per dozen.
    "   Card size for the album, - - - - - " 2.50 "

All of these can be had unmounted, for the convenience of those wishing to forward them by mail. A complete series of the same various sizes, illustrating the most noted

MAMMOTH TREES

in the State.

These views are by HELIOS, and are justly celebrated as being the most artistic and remarkable photographs ever produced on this coast.
[See criticisms.]

Also preparing for publication, a complete series of

SAN   FRANCISCO   VIEWS!

and a series illustrating MINING SCENES, and the Principal Places of Interest on the Coast.

HELIOS is prepared to accept commissions to photograph Private Residences, Views, Animals, Ships, etc. anywhere in the city, or any portion of the Pacific Coast.   Address, care of EDW. J. MUYBRIDGE,
                                    Cosmopolitan Gallery of Photographic Art,
                                        415 Montgomery St. San Francisco.

Opinions of the Press.

At the regular monthly meeting of the PHOTOGRAPHIC SOCIETY OF PHILADELPHIA, held March 4th, 1868, the Vice-President, J. W. HURN in the Chair, on motion of MR. GUILLOU the following resolutions were unanimously adopted:

"*Resolved,* That this Society take great pleasure in attesting their high appreciation of the artistic skill in the selection of these views, and the eminent talent evinced in their photographic reproduction."— *The Philadelphia Photographer,* April, 1868.

MAY, 1868.

12. The brochure of his 1867 Yosemite series, which Muybridge issued from Selleck's Cosmopolitan Gallery of Photographic Art, 1868.

The usual "vantage points" suggested by Hutchings or the valley guides, or previously photographed by Weed and Watkins, were only his starting places. He sought variations, returning to his own favored spots at different times of day and even in different seasons, recording the changes as if for his own gratification. Second, having chosen the natural beauty of the valley as his primary subject-matter, he went still further and explored, as he had begun to do in the San Francisco views, the transient aspects of nature — moonlight, mist, shadows, reflections, broken light, and rainbow effects. A preoccupation with rushing and falling water foreshadows his later interest in the portrayal of motion. In this he achieved a highly personal mode of expression. The touch of the romanticist penetrates his landscapes, not merely that of the topographical realist. Third, he often extended the expressive value and tonal variety of his pictures by adding cloud effects which were printed from negatives of clouds photographed especially for this purpose.

Thus he was able to add a harmonious and clouded sky in the printing room to control the mood of his pictures.[16] At about the same time he invented and patented the "Sky Shade," a device for holding back the sky areas in his negatives, to prevent their becoming overexposed and washed out, while giving full exposure to the other areas.

By February 1868 Muybridge was planning the sale of a series called "Scenery of the Yosemite Valley." In a brochure issued from Selleck's gallery he announced himself as the publisher, but still hid the authorship of the pictures under the name "Helios."

I am now preparing for publication twenty views of our world-renowned Yo-Semite Valley, photographed last year by "Helios." For artistic effect, and careful manipulation, they are pronounced by all the best landscape painters and photographers in the city to be the most exquisite photographic views ever produced on this coast, and are marvelous examples of the perfection to which photography can attain in the delineation of sublime and beautiful scenery, as exemplified in our wonderful valley.

Upon my list of subscribers for the series — among the names of nearly all our best known connoisseurs and patrons of art — are those of Messrs. C. Nahl, Keith, Wandesforde, Norton Bush, Jewett, Kipps, Denny, Van Vleck, Bloomer, etc., Artists: Messrs. Wm. Shew, Rulofson, Selleck, A. Nahl, Edouart, White, Vaughan, and other photographers.

The size is most convenient for transmission abroad, for binding, or the portfolio: 6 x 8 inches, mounted on tinted background boards 14 x 18 inches.

The price at which they will be issued ($20 for the series), placing them within the reach of those having only moderate resources, will probably command for them a sufficiently extensive sale to remunerate me for the great expense attending their production.[17]

Artists and the press were invited to an advance showing at the gallery, and the pictures immediately won local commendation:

Watkins' splendid Yosemite series has long challenged admiration, and has made certain points of the wonderful valley widely known. A new Yosemite series has been taken by a photographer of this city, who hides his name under the significant classicism of "Helios." These views, 20 or 30 in number, are taken from fresh points,

[16]The Skyshade was described by Muybridge in a letter, (under the pseudonym "Helios," in the *Philadelphia Photographer,* May 1869, pp. 142-144.
[17]Brochure in Scrapbook and in the collection of the California Historical Society.

selected with a nice regard to artistic effect, and illustrating the valley and its cliffs and falls more variously than any previous series.[18]

The views surpass, in artistic excellence, anything that has yet been published in San Francisco, resembling, as they do, the absolute correctness of a good sun picture after nature, with the judicious selection of time, atmospherical conditions and fortunate points of view. In some of the series we have just such cloud effects as we see in nature or oil painting. . . . The publisher of the remarkable series of portfolio pictures seems to have the best names of San Francisco Art-Critics on his subscription books, and will probably find that our people encourage meritorious home art.[19]

Muybridge also sent 125 prints from the Yosemite series to the *Philadelphia Photographer* for review. By March, the Photographic Society of Philadelphia had seen the pictures and its members were moved to put their feelings on record: "Resolved, that this Society take great pleasure in attesting their high appreciation of the artistic skill in the selection of these views, and the eminent talent evinced in their photographic reproduction." This resolution, printed in the April issue of the journal, aroused such curiosity that the editor, Edward L. Wilson, requested the loan of four or five of Muybridge's negatives, from which prints were prepared for a later "Picture of the Month." A review in the November issue compared "Helios" to "the great Wilson of Scotland," establishing his national reputation among photographers. Local fame increased with the publication of Hittell's guidebook, which carried 20 prints of photographs by "Helios" (reduced from 6 x 8 inches to visiting-card size and mounted in the book).

An excellent publicist, Muybridge kept San Francisco's arbiters of taste informed about his work. For example, on May 14, 1868, he presented a number of prints to the directors of the Mercantile Library with the following letter:

Accompanying this are a few photographs of the Yosemite Valley, published by me and of which I beg your acceptance.

Some of the members of your board I know to possess considerable discrimination and a very refined taste in artistic matters, I shall therefore be pleased to receive [an] expression of the boards opinion respecting the merits of the prints.

Your worthy ex President whom I believe to be considerable of a connoisseur expressed a desire to have them framed and placed in some desirable place in the new building, [and] should this be concurred in by the rest of the board I shall feel highly flattered.[20]

By May, also, Muybridge was advertising for general sale, his "Scenery of the Yosemite Valley," a series of 260 photographs comprising 100 in the 6 x 8 inch size and 160 small views for the stereoscope.[21] These he sold in vast quantity from Selleck's gallery (and no doubt other photographic outlets in San Francisco) and through Wilson, Hood and Company, of Philadelphia, who now became his Eastern agents.

Vancouver Island and Alaska

By 1868 Muybridge was established as one of the outstanding landscape photographers in San Francisco. Ambitious to become the leading one, he announced through advertisements that he was "prepared to accept commissions to photograph Private Residences, Views, Animals, Ships, etc., anywhere in the city, or any portion of the Pacific Coast."[22] Soon he had a commission that took him an unexpected distance from the city and in a new direction. He was, as he later put it, "appointed to accompany General Halleck for the purpose of illustrating the Military Posts and Harbours of Alaska."[23]

It was only in 1867 that public attention had been drawn to this territory, when Secretary of State William H. Seward accomplished its purchase from Russia for $7,200,000. This "largest real-estate deal since the Louisiana Purchase" put an end to Russia's holdings on the continent of North America. It also brought Seward excoriation in the press for acquiring with public funds what was assumed to be a frozen wilderness and popularly termed "Seward's Folly" and "Icebergia."

Photographic documentation was needed for Alaska's potential to be believed. Major General Henry W. Halleck, in command of the Military Division of the Pacific, was made responsible by the War Department for gathering information about the commercial value and strategic usefulness of the territory. In a telegram to Secretary of War Edwin M. Stanton, Halleck reported that he had learned from a recent visitor to Alaska that its worth was greater than had been supposed. Stanton then ordered him to transfer men and materials to the Military Department of Alaska, with headquarters at Sitka. By the spring of 1868, seven regiments had been posted to the new department, under Major General Jefferson C. Davis. As favorable information began to trickle back to the Military Division of the Pacific in San Francisco, Halleck himself undertook a trip to Sitka. It was

[18] *Bulletin*, San Francisco, February 12, 1868.

[19] *Call*, San Francisco, February 17, 1868.

[20] In the collection of the California Historical Society, whose *Notes*, March 1952, contain a reprint.

[21] Brochure in Scrapbook.

[22] Ibid., and advertisement following p. 59 of Hittell's guidebook.

[23] Prospectus, May 1872, for the second Yosemite series; in Scrapbook.

in connection with this trip, in August, that Muybridge was
employed to secure photographic documentation.

He apparently traveled north aboard the veteran steamer *Pacific*,
a side-wheeler of 1,100 tons which during the Gold Rush plied
the Nicaragua-California route and in the sixties served various
coastal ports from San Diego in the south to Port Townsend in
Washington Territory. On the Alaskan voyage, the *Pacific* went
first to British Columbia, where Muybridge took photographs
at Victoria, Esquimault, and Nanimo on Vancouver Island, noting
that

*The harbor of Esquimault, though a small area, is one of the
most beautiful in America. It is completely landlocked, and is the
rendezvous of the British vessels of war. Nanaimo, a few miles
to the south, is principally known for its extensive coal mines and
excellent shipping facilities.*[24]

The *Pacific* proceeded north, through the passes and channels
leading to Queen Charlotte Strait and across open sea to Hecate
Strait, in sight of mountains capped with perpetual snow and amid
an ever-changing succession of granite crags, waterfalls, fiords,
and coniferous forests. During a stop at Bella Bella, British Columbia,
Muybridge took photographs of the *Pacific* and other ships. His
"Wreck of the Steamer Suwanee" shows a 10-gun ship of the Pacific
Squadron that had gone aground in Shadwell Passage on July 9 of
that year. Among his subjects at Fort Tongass were Tlingit Indians.
At Fort Wrangell were photographed the totem poles that he
labeled "Indian Monumental Carvings."

The trip onward took the *Pacific* into an area of numerous
glaciers and through Sitka's "thousand islands" to the northern
terminus of the voyage at the wharf of the capital of Alaska, within
sight of Baranof's Castle and the green dome of the Russian
Orthodox cathedral. It was mid-August. Muybridge summarized
his impressions of the voyage thus far:

*Until the purchase of this territory, (the farthest west of our
country,) by the United States, at the instance of the far-seeing
statesman, William H. Seward, Alaska was scarcely ever heard of,
excepting by the fur merchant and geographer, and even now the
most erroneous ideas prevail, both with regard to its climate and
resources. Its climate, although damp, is warm, Sitka being not
nearly so cold in winter as Washington. The entire coast lines is a
succession of beautiful scenery, and the Indians are well advanced
in the industrial arts, some of them, such as the Tongass, being
polished and educated.*[25]

His photographs now documented the situation at Sitka — the
barracks, quarters, stockades, and blockhouses that the American
troops were engaged in building or repairing — and the historic
structures. Among his subjects were "Sitka, from the Japanese
Islands," "Sitka, from the North-west," "Sitka, from the Governor's
Garden," "Sitka, Harbor from the Governor's Garden," "Parade
Ground," "Lincoln Street," exterior and interior views of the
cathedral, "The Indian Village," several groups of "Indians," and a
"Group of Distinguished Chiefs."

As long as photographic conditions were favorable, Muybridge
gathered views, but the season was advanced and the sun was
often obscured by clouds or fog. After the return voyage he
submitted the results to General Halleck, who responded:

*I have to acknowledge the receipt of copies of your photographs
of forts and public buildings at Sitka and other military posts
taken for use of War Department and also views of scenery in
Alaska. These views besides being beautiful works of art give a
more correct idea of Alaska and its scenery and vegetation than
can be obtained from any written description of that country.*[26]

Halleck's report to Secretary of War Stanton and Muybridge's
photographs of Alaska, publicly circulated, helped vindicate the
purchase of the territory. Before long the knowledge of Alaska's
vast resources ended any doubt. Today, Seward's Folly has become
"Seward's Fortunate Folly."

Muybridge's photographs of Alaska evidently achieved great
popularity in their day. Four years after his trip the pictures
were still being sold, according to an advertisement:

PHOTOGRAPHS OF ALASKA

*Just previous to the late General Halleck's departure East, he
made a tour of inspection to Alaska Territory, and by instructions
of the Secretary of War, was accompanied by our celebrated
photographic artist Muybridge, who made a series of the most
picturesque and valuable photographs we have ever seen. The Hon.
Wm. H. Seward thought very highly of them and addressed Mr.
Muybridge a very complementary letter in acknowledgment of
his appreciation. They comprise about three dozen stereographic
views of Sitka, Fort Wrangle, Fort Tongass, etc., portraits of
Indians, illustrations of Indian life and flying views from shipboard;
giving a far better idea of the aspects of the country than a
volume of reading matter.*

*The price is three dollars coin per dozen and for this amount
we will forward a dozen or more, postage free to any part of the
world. There are also about a dozen larger sized views of the same
subject 7 x 9 inches of equal if not superior merit to the
stereographs; these we will forward free of postage upon receipt*

---

[24] *Catalogue,* pp. 40-41.
[25] Ibid., p. 39.

[26] October 13, 1868, in National Archives, Washington, D.C.

of $1.25, coin, each. — Orders for Pictures, as above, may be sent, care of the Publisher of the Herald, and will meet with prompt attention.[27]

Of particular interest is the reference to "flying views from shipboard." Muybridge took a number of photographs while the *Pacific* was in movement: "Bella Bella from Steamer Pacific," "Safety Cove, from Steamer Pacific," "Wreck of the Steamer Suwanee," and a small group entitled "Cone Mountain," in which the wake of the steamer is clearly recorded. These seem to portend his later preoccupation with rapid-motion photography.

Lighthouse of the Pacific Coast

Following the Alaska commission, Muybridge carried out additional projects for the War Department and also, notably, for the Treasury Department and the Lighthouse Board. The safeguarding of shipping off the long Pacific coast from Alaska to Lower California required the placing of buoys, fog signals, and lighthouses at many points. These aids to navigation were needed to protect the rapidly growing commerce of the West. Since the fifties the work had gone on, under the most arduous circumstances, atop sheer cliffs on lonely promontories, or on reefs and wave-swept islands far offshore.

Traveling aboard the U.S. revenue cutter *Shubrick*, the first lightship on the coast and the first steam tender in the entire service, Muybridge undertook to record the work of the lighthouse engineers. He wrote of this series:

Upon a coast line of so many hundreds of miles, California has but two harbors of any extent or accommodation, and Oregon is dependent upon the mouth of the Columbia for her maritime commerce. Washington Territory is more fortunate, and the magnificent expanse of water to which the general name Puget Sound is given affords, in its numerous beaches and excellent harbors, unequalled facilities for shipping the products of the immense forest upon its shores. The views . . . are principally of the light-houses and of scenery in their neighborhood.[28]

The *Catalogue* lists about 70 stereos that were marketed in the "Pacific Coast Series," together with 13 views available in the 7 x 9 inch size. Some prints of 17 x 21 inches are known also. Whether any photographs were taken exclusively for the government and withheld from public circulation has not been determined. The following titles indicate that Muybridge's coverage of Pacific Coast lighthouses and navigation aids reached

from the Straits of Juan de Fuca to San Diego: "Cape Flattery, Lighthouse on Tatoosh Island, First Order Fixed Light, 162 feet above Sea Level," "Cape Disappointment Lighthouse, (Mouth of Columbia River) First Order Fixed Light, 262 feet above sea level; and Fog Bell," "Cape Mendocino, evening: (Light-house obscured by fog); First Order Revolving Light, 423 feet above Sea Level," "Point Reyes, Steam Whistle Fog Signal and Coal Shoot," "Point Reyes, Lighthouse Keeper's Dwelling," "Point Reyes Light-house, First Order Scintillating Light, 296 feet above Sea Level."

Farallon Islands

Related to the "Pacific Coast Series" is the group of photographs listed in the *Catalogue* as "Farallone Islands":

About twenty-six miles west of the Golden Gate, (the Farallone Islands) present some of the most rugged, singular and interesting scenery upon the coast. Although of small extent, the rocky pinnacles, the water worn arches, and ever roaring waves dashing against the rocks, would alone be worthy of a tourist's visit. But the innumerable birds, the large numbers of sea lions, and the thousands of rabbits roaming about and subsisting upon — it is hard to say what — render the Farallones one of the most interesting places for a visit upon the coast.[29]

"South Farallone Island Light-house, First Order Revolving Light, 360 feet above Sea Level" is one of the views which links this series to the Lighthouse Board commission. But the poetic side of Muybridge's work reveals itself in other views of the Farallons: "The Ramparts, Funnel Rock, Hole in the Well and Pyramid, Fisherman's Bay," "The Murr Bridge, and rookeries of the Murr, (Uria California)," "The Sea Gull Club," and, in the larger series, "South Farallone Island, Tower Hill, Point Shubrick and South Cover, during a Fog." These last are among the most monumental of Muybridge's studies. They remind us that the painter Albert Bierstadt found the water-worn rocks, caves, and angular peaks of the Farallons a suitable subject for oil sketches at about the same time. His *Seal Rocks, Farallones* was painted in 1872.

Muybridge and Bierstadt seem to have been closely associated more than once, both in their work and in their subject matter. Bierstadt painted in the Yosemite Valley as early as 1863, and was there again in 1868, the year after Muybridge's first visit. In 1872 they worked together in the valley and may well have done so on the Farallons. Bierstadt encouraged Muybridge to take

[27]*Alaska Herald,* San Francisco, July 9, 1872; in Scrapbook.
[28]*Catalogue,* p. 34.
[29]Ibid., p. 37.

photographs which would be of use to painters. They seem to have shared in their work a "passion for the panoramic aspects of landscape — the great sweeps and dramas of the Düsseldorfian School in painting, the spectacular and heightened effects of nature."[30] This was the collective vision of an optimistic nineteenth-century America, made tangible in art.

Railroads: Central Pacific, Union Pacific, and California Pacific

The promise of the railroads in the West began to be fulfilled with the inauguration of passenger and freight service between San Francisco and Omaha in May 1869. The joining of the rails at Promontory Point in Utah climaxed years of struggle by the men who first projected such dreams and then gradually realized them. The world came to know how the summit of the Sierra Nevada had been conquered, when the first locomotive moved across California's state line, why forty miles of snow sheds were built and how many carpenters it took to build them, how the harried Chinese workers laid ten miles of track in a day for the Central Pacific while the Union Pacific's "Irish Terriers" laid only six, and how the surveying parties and construction gangs were in frequent scuffles with Indians. When the final spike was driven, the time was at hand when the West of prairie schooner and Concord coach would become "a flipped page of history."

Muybridge described the setting of his "Central Pacific Railroad" series in this way:

This road extends from San Francisco to Ogden, a distance of 881 miles, and crosses the Sierra Nevada mountains at an elevation of 7,042 feet above sea level. At Humbolt Palisades, on the banks of the Truckee, in the neighborhood of the Summit, Tricanyon Point and Cape Horn, views of surpassing grandeur abound; and in the immediate vicinity of the line, at Lake Tahoe, and Soda Springs are some of the finest mountain views in the world.[31]

Pictures that must have been compelling in their timeliness are "Snow Sheds," "Lake Donner, Sierra Nevada Mountains, Mount Stanford in the distance," "Trestle and crossing of the American River, near Sacramento, 5,145 feet long," and "Tunnel No. 1, the first bored on the C.P.R.R., looking East." In addition there are landscape views of the Sierra Nevada and the flatlands of Nevada and Utah.

Muybridge then described the eastern half of his series, the "Union Pacific Railroad":

The road extends from Omaha to Ogden, a distance of 1032 miles, and crosses the high plains [and then] the Rocky Mountains at an elevation of 8242 feet above sea level. For a long distance this road extends over elevated plateaus, affording few points of scenic interest; but in the neighborhood of Sherman, on the Black Hills, on the banks of the Weber, and in the Echo and Weber Canyons, many beautiful and interesting views may be obtained.[32]

What was lacking in scenic interest was made up for in the catalogue of place names, which must have carried their own romantic resonance to early travelers making the trip by rail: "Devil's Gate Bridge," "Index Rock, near Tunnel No. 3," "Sphynx Rock, and the Crossing of the Weber, near Devil's Slide, looking East," "Thousand Mile tree, 1000 miles West of Omaha, looking West," and "Witch's Rocks, Echo Canyon."

In the "California Pacific Railroad" series there are only two photographs of the railroad itself, taken at the crossing of the Sacramento River. The series could have been called "Calistoga Springs" instead. All the rest depict that area, developed by Sam Brannan, "California's first millionaire," who expected it to become the Saratoga of the West and constructed a forty-four-mile branch railroad of his own, from Vallejo to Calistoga, to serve it. Muybridge's photographs show Brannan's Hot Sulphur Springs Hotel and its grounds, a nearby petrified forest, and the surrounding mountain scenery.

Geyser Springs

A romantic pendant to the "California Pacific Railroad" series was made at Geyser Springs, twenty-eight miles north of Calistoga.

These great natural curiosities are situate in Sonoma County, about twelve hours from San Francisco by boat and rail, and a stage ride over one of the best and most beautiful mountain roads in the State. Apart from the novelty of the innumerable steam jets and boiling cauldrons of the great canyon, the Springs are celebrated for the medicinal qualities of the waters and baths, for the exhilarating atmosphere, the good hunting and fishing, and the loveliness of the scenery on the banks of Pluton Creek and the immediate vicinity.[33]

Besides the obligatory views of the "Geyser Springs Hotel," taken for the proprietor, and the group picture of that gentleman and his family, there are the more interesting atmospheric subjects. In "The Witches Cauldron — Macbeth, Act IV, Scene I" Muybridge has peopled the steaming landscape with three shrouded figures, hands clasped aloft, illustrating his literary reference.

[30] *Alta California*, San Francisco, April 7, 1872; in Scrapbook.
[31] *Catalogue*, p. 13.
[32] Ibid., p. 16.
[33] Ibid., p. 11.

Woodward's Gardens

In his guidebook to San Francisco of the 1870s, B. E. Lloyd took note of the great amusement park of the era, Woodward's Gardens. "Visitors . . . seldom fail to include in their rambles about the city, this beautiful resort. It is without rival on the Pacific Coast, and for diversity of attractions is not inferior to some of the celebrated parks in cities whose age in decades outnumber San Francisco's years."[34] The attractions, to which San Franciscans flocked of a Saturday or Sunday, included an art gallery and museum, a dance pavilion, refreshment rooms, a zoo, a course where Roman chariot races were performed, an aquarium, seal ponds, a bear pit, a deer park, and extensive gardens with "mosques, pagodas and rustic seats" amid lawns and sandy slopes where stuffed exotic birds and animals, thanks to the art of the taxidermist, seemed to disport themselves as if alive.

For a time in 1869 and 1870 Muybridge seems to have had a showroom at the entrance to Woodward's Gardens as well as one on Montgomery Street. In his series "Views in Woodward's Gardens," general vistas of the gardens, the lake, and the distant city, taken from the observatory on the grounds, define the topography of the popular resort and its amusements, while scenes of the art gallery (one with Muybridge posing as a bored gallery-goer who has fallen asleep while looking at the paintings), saloon, museum, and animal houses record the principal attractions. One group of photographers shows some of the sculptures in the gallery and gardens: *California* by Hiram Powers, *Bacchante* by Alexander Galt, and an *Indian Girl, Silence, Pandora,* and *Jove.* In another group, the animals and birds are amply represented: "Polar Bears," "Wild Boar," "Monkeys," "Hyena, Leopard and Tiger," "Ostrich and Young." In a charming sequence of tableaus, Muybridge photographed animals and a beautiful young woman — probably Flora Stone, whom he was soon to marry. In "Gentle Companions" the young woman poses fetchingly with a snarling stuffed Bengal tiger. In "Pet Friends" she is surrounded by deer, too complaisant to be real. In "Foxes" she peeks in upon a wicked group of little beasts about to fight over stolen food — Muybridge's humor is always a bit wry. Six photographs of "Japanese Performers" records the appearance at Woodward's Gardens of a group of musicians and acrobats, probably among the earliest to come to America after contacts with Japan were begun by Commodore Matthew C. Perry's visit. A final group, no less exotic, displays the Chinese giant, Chang Woo Gow, eight feet three inches tall, with his petite wife. All together, the "Woodward's Garden" series suggests that B. E. Lloyd caught precisely the tone of this popular resort: "The visitor, no matter how refined or eccentric his tastes, is sure to find many things that will please and instruct."[35]

During 1867 and 1868 Muybridge's production and distribution base was still Selleck's Cosmopolitan Gallery. Here he had his office, his facilities for printing, mounting, and labeling the views, and his salesroom and exhibition gallery. But by 1869, for what reason we do not know, he had shifted to premises at 121 Montgomery Street which he shared with two lively and well-known artists, the brothers Charles and Arthur Nahl. The Nahls, descendants of a long line of German court painters and art collectors, came to California during the Gold Rush, which provided subjects for their paintings. In addition they were commercial artists, engineers, and photographers. Charles secured the patronage of Judge E. B. Crocker, for whom he did a number of large paintings celebrating the life of the mines. Arthur was an expert photographic retoucher. Moreover, the Nahls were advocates of physical fitness. In 1863 they collaborated on a manual, *Instructions in Gymnastics,* illustrated with 53 of their own engravings. Muybridge shared many of their interests, and the three must have been very congenial. When the Nahls moved to new quarters at 12 Montgomery Street (where they advertised the "most extensive art and photographic gallaries on the Pacific Coast"), Muybridge went with them and remained there until 1873, when he became affiliated with Bradley and Rulofson's gallery, at 429 Montgomery Street.

Muybridge maintained various distribution outlets after 1868. One was the aforementioned booth at the entrance to Woodward's Gardens in 1869, where the "Flying Studio" could often be seen at the curb. In 1870 he had a showroom at 111 Montgomery Street, in the shop of Charles G. Ewing, an optician, maker of mathematical instruments, and seller of photographic views. Subsidiary outlets were available through agents such as Thomas Houseworth and Company, dealers in optical goods and stereoscopic views. Houseworth issued catalogues from 317 Montgomery Street and frequently commissioned photographers to secure views especially for him. Muybridge rarely produced pictures under such an arrangement, however, preferring to be his own publisher when he could do so.

The production and distribution of Muybridge's Pacific Coast stereographs eventually required a suitable staff and considerable working space. That the volume of his business increased

[34] *Lights and Shades in San Francisco,* San Francisco: A. L. Bancroft and Co., 1876, p. 325.

[35] Ibid., p. 329.

steadily from 1867 to 1872 is apparent from the character of his gallery affiliations and the variety of his distribution agencies. In the 1873 *Catalogue of Photographic Views*, published by Bradley and Rulofson, Muybridge presented himself to the public as a photographer "unrivalled in America" and described his "exquisite views . . . of the sublime and beautiful scenery of the Pacific States" as "marvellous examples of the perfection to which open air photography has attained."[36]

[36] *Catalogue*, p. 1.

14. The reverse of a stereo card showing Muybridge's affiliation with Nahl's Studio and his independent sales outlet at Woodward's Gardens, 1869-1872.

13. The reverse of a stereo card showing Muybridge's affiliation with the Selleck's Cosmopolitan Gallery of Photographic Art, 1867-1868.

15. The reverse of a stereo card showing Muybridge's old address at Nahl's Studio, which is overprinted in red with his new address at Bradley and Rulofson's, 1873-1874.

PORTFOLIO I
Views of the Far West: (1867–1873)

16. Muybridge's trade card for Bradley and Rulofson.
A montage of his series of photographic views to 1873.

17. Mt. Tamalpais from San Francisco.

18. View toward Alcatraz from San Francisco.

19. Savings and Loans Society, Clay Street, San Francisco. Shows Matt Grey's store and Muybridge's traveling van.

20. Montgomery Street, corner of Market Street, San Francisco. Fourth of July.

21. Ordinance yard at Alcatraz Island.

22. Yosemite tourists, 1867.

23. Cave at base of upper Yosemite Falls — man standing, 1867.

24. Summit of Pi-wy-ak, Yosemite Valley, 1867.

25. Loya, the Sentinel, reflected, 1867.

26. Group of Indians, Sitka, Alaska. (1867)

27. Point Bonita, fog siren house, distant view.

28. Point Reyes lighthouse, first order scintillating light, 296 feet above sea level.

29. South Farallon Island, Fisherman's Bay, The Ramparts, Funnel Rock, and Sugar Loaf.

30. South Farallon Island, the Murr Bridge 102 feet high, and rookeries of the Murr.

31. Geyser Springs. View up the canyon from Witch's Cauldron.

2. Geyser Springs. The Witch's Cauldron — Macbeth, Act IX, Scene 1.

33. Central Pacific Railroad. Snowsheds at Immigrant Gap.

34. Central Pacific Railroad. Fifth and last crossing of the Truckee, near Wadsworth, looking north.

35. Woodward's Gardens, San Francisco, showing statues. Muybridge pretends to be alseep in the art gallery.

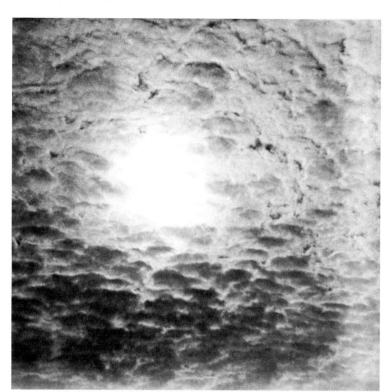

36 37

38 39

40. Menlo Park, a study of trees.

36-39. *Facing page*. Studies of clouds.

41. Fernside, Alameda County, 1873.

42. Mosswood, Alameda County, 1873.

43. Steamer *Golden City* on the California drydock, San Francisco.

44. Cone Mountain, Alaska,
The wake of the vessel is one of Muybridge's
early (1867) pictures of water in motion.

6. Flora Muybridge

Muybridge first met Flora Stone, the woman who was to become his wife, at the studio of the Nahl brothers, where she was employed as a photographic retoucher. Their friendship ripened after Flora left the studio to work at Ackerman's Dollar Store on Kearny Street. During this time she resided at 6 Montgomery Street, close to Muybridge's office.

The marriage presumably took place in 1872, though neither the date nor the place is exactly known. It followed upon Flora's divorce from an importer and manufacturer of saddlery, Lucius Stone, who was in business with his mother at Stone and Hayden's store in San Francisco. The husband's age and his "cruel mother" were matters of complaint in Flora's plea. A local paper was to report later on: "Her wedded life was not happy, and she procured a divorce and married Muybridge."[1] It was even hinted that Muybridge had urged Flora to get free of Lucius Stone. At any rate, she and Muybridge were eventually married, and despite their disparity in age — she was twenty-one, he forty-two — the union for a time seemed to be happy.

Flora had come to California as a girl of thirteen, leaving grandparents and a brother behind in Alabama. Her parents were dead. At first she lived with an aunt, Mrs. Downs, in Marysville. Here she had also an uncle, Captain Thomas J. Stump, who went

[1]*Examiner,* San Francisco, July 19, 1875.

45. Flora (Shallcross) Stone, ca. 1868.

46. Flora Muybridge, ca. 1872.

47. Flora Muybridge, during her pregnancy, with a symbolic bough of California pears, ca. 1874.

to Oregon to take charge of the *Colonel Wright* and, later, other steamers on the upper Columbia and Snake rivers.[2] Flora soon left Marysville under the protection of Captain W. D. Shallcross, who sponsored her education as his foster daughter at a prominent school for girls. At this time Flora was known also as Lily

Shallcross. Then she left her protector, without his consent, to marry Lucius Stone — a headstrong decision that she was to regret until her dying day.

As a young woman Flora was conceded by all who knew her to be exceptionally attractive — dainty, blonde, beautiful, seemingly intelligent, and well mannered. The public press was later to add qualifying terms. Muybridge, too, had much to recommend him. He was an active, attractive figure of a man, financially secure and respected in his profession. Although neither his temperament nor his work pemitted him to enjoy San Francisco's brisk social whirl, he was indulgent with Flora and permitted her to participate in it freely, particularly since his work kept him away from home for long periods.

The couple took up their residence near South Park, in an area which had once been "as elegant as a London square" but was no longer quite in style. Here they lived out two years of their marriage, happily enough at first. When it became apparent to Muybridge that their tastes and temperaments differed, he took it for granted that the difference in their ages was responsible.

Such a marriage must have caused some consternation in Kingston-on-Thames. Muybridge's industrious grandmother, Susannah Smith, would hardly have approved of either Flora or the circumstances. His mother, Susannah Muggeridge, if he took her into his confidence, must have been not a little concerned, though this elderly, lonesome woman had her own problems. She lived with her younger brother, Tom, near London, in his house full of clocks. Tom's "minor hobby was a desire to make all these clocks strike at exactly the same moment." In this environment, Susannah became very fearful of burglars. "She kept several of [Tom's] old hats hanging in the hall, after he had discarded them, in order that any man breaking into the house, might suppose from the number of hats, that it was inhabited by a great many men, and she always put upon the stairs in a place she thought would catch an intruder's eye, her small silver teapot. She thought when he saw the teapot he would take it, and after looking at the hats, would be content. . . . The big silver teapot was always carried upstairs into [Tom's] bedroom with the plate basket every night."[3] Her fears for herself, and the inherited silverware came to an end with her death, in 1874. She may have known that Flora had borne a child, but probably was spared the rumor that the child was not her son's.

[2] Stump's obituary is in the *Oregonian*, Portland, August 15, 1881.

[3] Anderson memoir.

7. Scenery of the Yosemite Valley and the Mariposa Grove (1872-1873)

In 1872, "H. H." (the future Helen Hunt Jackson, who won fame as the author of *Ramona* and *A Century of Dishonor*) traveled to California on the new transcontinental railroad, writing articles as she went. There were, she remarked, "two things to do in San Francisco (besides going to the Chinese theatre). One is to drive out of the city, and the other is to sail away from it."[1] A bit farther on in the account, she amended this judgment: "I said there were but three things to do in San Francisco. There are four. And the fourth is to go and see Mr. Muybridge's photographs."[2]

When she visited the studio, Muybridge had just finished preparing for publication a series of 30 stereographs and 8 prints of the 5½ x 8½ inch size, taken at the Buena Vista vineyard in Sonoma, which he titled "A Vintage in California." Helen Hunt's attention was drawn particularly to the large prints.

From the time photography was invented until the end of the nineteenth century, it was common for writers and critics to demand the qualities of paintings in photographs, and vice versa. So when Mrs. Hunt compared the skies in Muybridge's photographs to the skies painted by Turner, or called a photograph of workers breaking soil for a vineyard "as perfect a Millet as could be imagined," or compared another to the paintings of Teniers, she was offering the highest praise.

No man can so take a photograph of a landscape as to render and convey the whole truth of it, unless he is an artist by nature, and would know how to choose the point from which that landscape ought to be painted. Mr. Muybridge is an artist by nature. His photographs have composition. There are some of them of which it is difficult to believe that they are not taken from paintings, — such unity, such effect, such vitality do they possess, in comparison with the average photograph, which has been made, hap-hazard, to cover so many square feet and take in all that happened there.[3]

Before returning east, Helen Hunt made a side trip to the California mining country and the Yosemite Valley (which she preferred to call by its Indian name of Ah-wah-ne).[4] As she was climbing the trail out of the valley, her party met a long line of pack mules:

We drew aside to let them pass. They were loaded with a photographer's apparatus, lenses, plates, camera, carefully packed boxes of chemicals. Some of these parcels we had seen while in process of preparation in San Francisco. Their owner, Mr. Muybridge, has just established himself in the valley for the summer, for the purpose of taking a series of views, larger and more perfect than any heretofore attempted.[5]

At the studio, Muybridge had mentioned his intention of again photographing Yosemite. Helen Hunt now hailed the forthcoming work unequivocally: "This series of photographs will undoubtedly be the most magnificent ever taken in the world."[6] Muybridge presumably would not have quarreled with this estimate. In a prospectus sent out from the studio of the Nahl brothers in May 1872, he described his new project in similar terms:

At the suggestion of several artists and patrons of Art, I propose devoting the approaching season to the production of a series of large-size photographic negatives, illustrating the Yosemite and other grand picturesque portions of our coast.

I am encouraged in this undertaking from the generally expressed opinion, especially of our best Art Critics, that although many carefully executed large-size photographs of our scenery have already been published, yet the wonderful improvement in the science of photographic manipulation, and a judicious selection of points of view, with an aim at the highest artistic treatment the subject affords, will result in a more complete realization than has hitherto been accomplished of the vast grandeur and pictorial beauty for which our State and Coast have so world-wide a reputation. To those gentlemen who are acquainted with my works, or with me personally, it will be merely necessary for me to refer to the numerous smaller

it only to the waterfalls that still bear it, not to the valley. "H. H." wrote caustically: "Shall we ever forgive Dr. Brunnell [credited with discovery of the valley], who, not content with volunteer duty in killing off Indians in the great Merced River Valley, must needs name it the Yo-sem-i-te . . . It is easy to do and impossible to undo this species of mischief. No concerted action of 'the public,' no legislation of repentant authorities, will ever give back to the valley its own melodious name; but I think its true lovers will for ever call it Ah-wah-ne." Ibid., p. 87.

[1] *Bits of Travel at Home,* Boston: Robert Bros., 1878, p. 81; first published in the *Independent,* New York, August 29, 1872.

[2] Ibid., p. 85.

[3] Ibid., pp. 85-86.

[4] Yosemite is, of course, a name given by the Indians, but they applied

[5] *Independent,* New York, August 29, 1872.

[6] Ibid.

*photographs of my execution as an earnest of what may be
expected as the result of my anticipated labors, and to remark
that I have now an outfit of lenses and apparatus superior
to any other in the United States. . . .*

*The size of my proposed negatives will be 20 x 24 inches,
and the prints about 18 x 22, of which subscribers for each* **one
hundred dollars** *subscribed will be entitled to select FORTY
from the whole series, to be printed and mounted upon India
tinted boards, in every respect similar to my smaller ones.
It is scarcely necessary to say in consequence of the great expense
attending this production they will not be sold at this price
excepting to subscribers.*

*The most gratifying evidence I can offer of the favor with
which my proposition has been received, is to subjoin the names
of a few subscribers, well known for their taste, and their
appreciation of art studies.*

•   •   •   •   •   •   •   •   •   •

*Should you feel disposed to favor this enterprise by according
me the privilege of adding your name to the list of subscribers, I
shall feel obliged by your returning the accompanying form
with your name attached at your earliest convenience, as it is
essential I should make an early start in order to have the
photographs ready in the Spring of '73. Receive the assurance
that all my energies shall be directed towards rendering this
proposed series the most acceptable photographic publication
ever issued in the United States, with the object of attracting
attention to the magnificent scenery of our own State and Coast
in a manner worthy of the theme.*[7]

Besides the printed names of 64 subscribers, including the
officers and directors of the San Francisco Art Association,
Muybridge's personal copy of the prospectus carries in his handwriting the names of 100 or so additional subscribers — among
them the Union Club, the Pacific Mail Steamship Company, and
the Central Pacific and Union Pacific Railroads. The project
was handsomely endorsed, the subscription list "exceeding
twenty thousand dollars."

By the time the prospectus appeared, Muybridge had begun his
work in Yosemite Valley. Some of the pictures were made by
April and exhibited then in Sacramento. Most were taken during
the summer and fall of 1872, in six months of intense work
from June to November. The series started again at Moonlight
Rock.[8]

*Bridal-Veil Meadow Area — from Moonlight Rock to El Capitan
Meadow*
El Capitan Meadow Area — from El Capitan to Sentinel Rock
(expanded coverage, Merced River Views)

[7]Scrapbook.
[8]I adopt the Hoods' arrangement (see chap. 5, n. 15).

Sentinel Meadow Area — from Sentinel Rock to Yosemite Fall
Stoneman Meadow Area — from the Meadow to Mirror Lake
*Canyon of the Merced Area — from Happy Isles to the top of
Nevada Fall*
*Rim of the Valley Area and High Country — from Panorama Cliff
to Inspiration Point* (no photographs at Inspiration Point, but
first coverage of Four Mile Trail, Union Point, Cloud's Rest,
Mount Watkins, and top of Upper Yosemite Fall)
High Country Area (first coverage of Tuolumne Meadows, Cathe-
dral Pass, and Lake Tenaya)

These seven areas yielded 45 views, 17 x 21 inches; 36 views, 5½ x
8½ inches; and 379 stereos.

It is clear that Muybridge photographed much more heavily on
this second trip to the valley, concentrating for the first time on
the Little Yosemite area, expanding his coverage of the rim of the
valley, and moving on into the High Country for his most
pioneering foray.

In the five years since his first trip to Yosemite, Muybridge had
become a more consciously artistic photographer. Among his 1872
stereographs, along with the pictures of the crags, falls, peaks,
and vistas that every Yosemite photographer had to cover, he
included a series of 71 intimate landscapes that he titled individually
and collectively "Yosemite Studies," 16 views of landscapes as
reflections in the Merced River and Mirror Lake, 4 studies of
rainbows, and 5 "moonlight effects" contrived by means of deliberate
underexposure in daylight. These smaller landscapes are less dependent on dramatic, Dusseldorfian subject matter than his earlier views,
and more dreamy and painterly in feeling.

The stereos employing special effects are the ones on which he
lavished the most care; the poor quality of some others may suggest
that the work was turned over to his assistant and companion,
George Towne. (The two registered together as guests at Snow's
"Casa Nevada" hotel in Yosemite Valley on July 20, 1872.) Most
of Muybridge's attention, in any case, seems to have been given to
the production of the superb large-plate views. The 17 x 21 inch
photographs are extremely impressive — vastly different in effect
from the 5½ x 8½ inch ones of 1867. Softer, yet showing more
depth and detail, these landscape compositions stand as the peak of
Muybridge's Yosemite work.

On his way out of the valley, Muybridge stopped at the
Mariposa Grove of mammoth trees, where he took 25 stereos, 7
pictures in the 5½ x 8½ inch size, and one 17 x 21 inch study of
the "William H. Seward" tree. Another large photograph
apparently taken at this time shows Muybridge himself.[9] Sitting

[9]A print is in the Bancroft Library.

at the base of the "General Grant" tree, on a plate box bearing the name "Houseworth," is the exhausted and tattered man of forty-two years whose productive months in the practice of his craft under primitive conditions were soon to earn him a triumph.

Now the firm of Bradley and Rulofson courted him with the best production and distribution arrangements they could manage. They brought from the East a huge new apparatus for printing and mounting the large-plate pictures. The nearly 400 new stereos were issued on Bradley and Rulofson cards, replacing those of the earlier trip. Returns from the large prints and the stereos, both sold under the title of "Scenery of the Yosemite Valley," netted Muybridge well over the $20,000 presubscribed.

Although Muybridge announced his Yosemite trip from the Nahl's studio and published through Bradley and Rulofson, he may have gone to the valley in 1872 with a commission from yet another photographic publisher, Thomas Houseworth and Company. The photograph of Muybridge sitting by the "General Grant" tree on the Houseworth plate box was published by that firm rather than by Bradley and Rulofson. No photographer was credited. Since it is unlikely that Houseworth had another photographer in the Mariposa Grove when Muybridge was there who would have made a portrait of a photographer working for a rival gallery, we may assume that the picture was made by Muybridge and given to Houseworth in fulfillment of an earlier agreement that he would publish the Yosemite work.

When the "Scenery of the Yosemite Valley" was published by Bradley and Rulofson, a public fued broke out between the two galleries. Houseworth put in the display window and offered for sale a badly worn, poorly mounted print from the series, bearing the Bradley and Rulofson name. When the trick was discovered, Muybridge's new publishers promptly put notice in the press:

Messrs. Bradley and Rulofson are much obliged to Mr. Houseworth for giving their names a place in his window; but attaching them to an old, soiled print from a condemned negative of Muybridge's (neither print nor negative being made by them), shows to what a wretched straight the poor gentleman is driven in a fruitless effort to compete in business.[10]

Bradley and Rulofson had the leading photographic gallery and supply house, and were running some of the competitors out of business. Houseworth, nettled and feeling the pinch, was stung into replying:

Thomas Houseworth and Co. — To the public in general, and a reply to the card of Bradley and Rulofson — The Yosemite View exhibited by us in our window is one of a set of forty furnished to a subscriber by Bradley and Rulofson for the sum of $100 and bears their name as the publishers. The View is a fair sample of the lot which was sold to me at a heavy discount on the cost and is now in the same condition as when received by the original purchaser. We would further remark that we had tried to purchase from these gentlemen some of their views and they positively refused to sell us, for reasons which we leave others to judge.[11]

Hoping to keep the pot at boil for the amusement of its readers, the newspaper asked Muybridge for his comments, which were printed with the foregoing. His response was typically Olympian:

Aesop in one of his fables related that a miserable little ass, stung with envy at the proud position the lion occupied in the estimation of the forest residents, seized some shadowy pretext of following and braying after him with the object of annoying and insulting him. The lion turning his head and observing from what a despicable source the noise proceeded, silently pursued his way, intent upon his own business, without honoring the ass with the slightest motion. Silence and contempt, says Aesop, are the best acknowledgements for the insults of those whom we despise.

What personal or professional tensions really lay behind these exchanges we can only surmise. Two or three years later, the unfortunate Houseworth was in debt about $15,000 to various creditors, many of whom were photographers or photographic suppliers.

Bradley and Rulofson's portrait gallery had long been popular, with negatives on file of every person of note who had visited the area since 1849. Henry W. Bradley, a pioneer daguerreotypist from Virginia, founded the business, which was operated by William H. Rulofson, a New Brunswickian who traced his ancestry to George III and Hannah Lightfoot, the king's mysterious "first wife." Rulofson had come to California in 1850 with a daguerrian studio on wheels. There were now 36 employees, whose weekly payroll came to 600 dollars, gold, and the premises sported "the only elevator connected with a photographic gallery in the world."[12]

The 1873 *Catalogue of Photographic Views* publicly announced that Muybridge was considered a stellar addition to the staff:

[10] Scrapbook.

[11] Ibid.

[12] Robert Bartlett Haas, "William Herman Rulofson," *California Historical Society Quarterly*, XXXIV (1955), 289-300, and XXXV (1956), 47-58.

48. Eadweard J. Muybridge, ca. 1872.

BRADLEY & RULOFSON

*Have the largest and most complete Portrait Gallery upon the
Pacific Coast.*

*In every department we avail ourselves of the assistance of the
most accomplished artists and most skillful operatives. For many
years the work issued from our establishment has been unapproached
in this city and has enjoyed a most flattering comparison with that*

of the most celebrated galleries of the Eastern States and of Europe.

*We have recently effected arrangements for the publication of the
remarkable series of Photographic Views illustrating the Far West,
by*

MUYBRIDGE.

*To most persons in California the name of this artist is as
familiar as those of the majestic scenes he illustrates. The careful
execution and surpassing excellence of his work has occasioned his
being employed during several years by the U.S. Government in
the production of the numerous views upon this Coast, required by
the Treasury and War Departments.*

*For judicious selection of subject, artistic treatment, and skillful
manipulation, he is unrivalled in America, and the exquisite views
produced by him of the sublime and beautiful scenery of the
Pacific States, are marvellous examples of the perfection to which
open air photography has attained. . . .*

*The list of subscribers for his recent magnificent series of
Yosemite Photographs includes the names of every prominent artist
and nearly all the principal citizens and patrons of art in California.
The amount of the subscription list, exceeding twenty thousand
dollars, included one thousand dollars each from the Central and
Union Pacific Railroad Companies, and five hundred dollars from
the Pacific Mail Steamship Company. A sufficient evidence of the
estimation in which the works of this eminent artist are held,
without a reprint of any American or European "opinion," and a
result we think unprecedented in the history of Photographic
publication.*

*Muybridge will be constantly making additions to his superb and
comprehensive collection of negatives, which will be published by
us as soon after their receipt as possible.*

*Among his projected trips this season for a series of views, 20 x
24 inches in size, is one along the line of the Transcontinental
Railroad, and another to the Columbia River.*

June, 1873.   *429 Montgomery Street, S.F.*[13]

The San Francisco newspapers began to build up the renown of
Muybridge's Yosemite pictures. In its issue of April 7, 1873, while
some of them were on display in the Bradley and Rulofson gallery,
the *Alta California* devoted front-page space to a review:

*Eadweard J. Muybridge, photographic artist, has completed a
series of views of Yosemite and other points of interest, which will
attract attention in any gallery in the world. The artist has devoted
several months to the work of getting the negatives, sparing no
pains to get views from points calculated to produce the best
pictures; he has waited several days in a neighborhood to get the
proper conditions of atmosphere for some of his views; has cut
down trees by the score that interfered with the camera from the
best point of sight; has had himself lowered by ropes down*

[13] *Catalogue,* p. 1.

*precipices to establish his instruments in places where the full
beauty of the object to be photographed could be transferred to
the negative; has gone to points where his packers refused to
follow him, and has carried his apparatus himself rather than
forego the picture on which he had set his mind. The result is that
he has produced, by the use of Bradley & Rulofson's latest
apparatus in photographic printing, a series of eight hundred of
the most perfect photographs ever offered for public inspection —
some of them gems of art. The view of Temple Peak presents an
effect far beyond what had been thought possible in photography.
This should be taken as the subject for a great painting, and
probably will be by Mr. Bierstadt, who made several suggestions
to Mr. Muybridge, while in the Valley, and who is, in fact, a
patron and advisor. . . .*

*One pretty picture is called Sylvan Bar, a point on the river
where a distant view of Cathedral Rock suggests the motive for
the picture, but it is evident the artist has been charmed with the
bit of river winding round a sloping bank, and he has allowed
the graceful branches which fringe the stream and the majestic
trees in the foreground to have a liberal share in the treatment
of the picture.*

*To get the view of Yosemite Cliff, the artist clambered to a
point never before reached by artist or tourist, and made the
picture satisfactorily, though at considerable risk to his
personal safety.*

*These views will be issued to the subscribers during the week,
and those on the list may esteem themselves fortunate that*

*they have the opportunity to get such magnificent specimens
of the photographic art. They will adorn any gallery. If these
pictures are judiciously distributed they will have a great
effect in attracting tourists to this State, and we believe it is
the intention of the railroad companies to have some of
them put in the hotels of the principal cities of the United
States and in Europe.*

The Yosemite pictures of 1872 earned overseas fame for
Muybridge. At the Vienna Exhibition of 1873 they won the
International Gold Medal for Landscape. They were exhibited
also in Berlin, where they were seen by Dr. Hermann Wilhelm
Vogel, the leading figure in German photography and later
teacher of Alfred Steiglitz. Vogel's praise was reported in the
Philadelphia Photographer:

*To the visitors of the Vienna Exhibition these pictures were
no novelties, but in Berlin they were not generally known,
and the excellence and large size of the plates, the brilliancy
of tone, the happy selection of the objects, excited general
admiration.*

*Landscapes of this size are the exception here, and the
thought that Muybridge, with his mammoth camera for plates
of twenty-two inches, climbed mountains, fills many a one
with respect and admiration.*[14]

[14]"German Correspondence," February 1874.

8. Governor Stanford and the Controversy over Unsupported Transit (1872-1873)

Nobody now knows exactly how it happened, but the story has
become a California legend. The prime mover in the events
that were to produce the legend was Leland Stanford, governor of
the state for a biennial term in 1862-1863 and powerful president
of the Central Pacific Railroad.

Having suffered a physical breakdown after the completion of
the strenuous railroad-building project, Stanford took the advice of
his physician and tried to separate himself from business cares
for a while and spend more time in open-air activities. Never a man
to do anything halfway, he took up the driving of horses, first as
a diversion, and became so "passionately fond of the animals"
that he "would drop business at any time to talk of them. And
next to a horse he was said to love a horse trade."[1] From trading

he progressed to the systematic acquisition of fast animals, and
from there to the study, breeding, and development of horses,
which was to occupy him — first at Sacramento and later on a very
grand scale indeed at his Palo Alto Stock Farm — until his death
in 1893. Stanford's residence was in Sacramento until the fall of
1873.

An engrossing interest in how to train horses for speed led
Stanford eventually to the study of equine anatomy and to
systematic research in animal locomotion. In the early stages of
this interest, he and Mark Hopkins, treasurer of the Central Pacific
Railroad and a long-time horse fancier, undertook an experiment
at the Sacramento race track "where, after having the surface of
a stretch of the sandy track carefully smoothed, they speeded a
trotter over it and then accurately measured the depth of the
impressions made, respectively, by the animal's fore and hind feet.
By this original method they hoped to solve the problem whether

[1]George T. Clark, *Leland Stanford: War Governor of California, Railroad
Builder, and Founder of Stanford University,* Stanford University Press,
1931, p. 342; hereafter cited as Clark.

a speeding horse propelled himself by his hind quarters or pulled himself by his fore quarters."[2]

The issue does not seem very important today, perhaps, but in the 1870s horse racing was the most popular of all spectator sports. Staggering sums of money changed hands at the tracks, both in bets on favorites and in sales of promising animals to turf-struck aficionados. Western-bred horses were for the first time challenging the records made by European champions, as the lively memoirist Benjamin E. Lloyd, noted: "The grit and enterprise which distinguishes all other undertakings in California is also noticeable in the breeding of trotters and racers, which are rapidly bringing the Golden State into world-wide renown."[3] They were also beginning to win modest fortunes for local owners. Increasingly, wealthy turf-men and their friends were investing money in the breeding of "good goers."

Owners, trainers, and breeders all had their pet theories about developing winners. There was nothing scientific behind their beliefs, for the facts were few. The human eye was too slow to be depended upon for data about the various swift gaits of the horse. The few instruments that had been devised for studying the horse in motion were primitive and cumbersome, and almost as inconclusive as human observation in the data they yielded. The need for learning the facts about how animals really moved was pressing.

For some months in 1871 and 1872 an old argument was revived in California's "horsey crowd" as to whether a horse trotting at top speed ever had all four feet off the ground at once. This, and other issues about the locomotion of animals, provided the background for the series of events that was soon to involve Eadweard Muybridge in his pioneering use of the camera to extend observation beyond the former limits of human perception and read the secrets of rapid motion from the analysis of "instantaneous" photographs.

In the spring of 1872 Leland Stanford got caught up in the controversy about unsupported transit. A keen observer, he strongly believed that the trotting horse did have moments in the stride which were free of the ground. Concurring were two of Stanford's friends in San Francisco: J. Cairns Simpson, turf editor of the *California Spirit of the Times,* and Fred MacCrellish, owner and publisher of a prosperous newspaper, the *Alta California.* The contrary position was publicly taken by two wealthy sportsmen on the East Coast: Robert Bonner, owner of the New York *Ledger,* and George Wilkes, editor of the New

York *Spirit of the Times.* Aligned with them was a Californian, James W. Keene, president of the San Francisco stock exchange.

The controversy at first generated more heat than light. Sportsmen from coast to coast lined up for one side or the other according to their prejudices. Newspapermen hoped for colorful coverage and fanned the flames. Soon a wager was spoken of, and although the facts were never made clear, the legend grew that a stake of $25,000 would go to the side which could provide proof for its position.

Leland Stanford and Robert Bonner, both publicly known for their "uncompromising uprightness" where betting was concerned, probably stood well aside from the money matters involved in the wager. Bonner, owner of some of the finest horses in America, never raced them for money, but drove them for pleasure, holding the reins himself.[4] Stanford, like Bonner, was not a betting man, and made it a practice to return his earnings from racing to the track.[5] Each, however, was prepared to enjoy the controversy fully and to contribute ideas and practical means to prove his side of the argument.

The question of unsupported transit had been in the air some years before the sudden California interest, as had suggestions about methods to resolve it. One line of investigation was undertaken by E. J. Marey, the professor at the Collége de France who had been devoting himself to the scientific description of animal locomotion. Muybridge later termed him the "first to avail himself of scientific appliances to automatically register the characteristics of movements," and mentioned his use of "an ingenious apparatus, carried by the rider of an animal, which caused styles — actuated by pneumatic pressure — to leave a record on a revolving cylinder."[6] Marey's "graphic" charting of the pattern of footfalls identified several paces of the horse in which a moment of suspension occurs. A limitation of Marey's method in the early 1870s was that it yielded inconclusive data about the very fast paces, such as the rapid trot or gallop.

Another line of investigation had been rather suggested than fully applied. This was the utilization of the camera as a means of supplying proof, especially proof, as Stanford phrased it, that the "accepted theory of the relative positions of the feet of horses in rapid motion was erroneous."[7] The idea that the camera could be so employed had already been put forth in scientific

[2]Clark, p. 343.

[3]*Lights and Shades in San Francisco,* San Francisco: A. L. Bancroft and Co., 1876, p. 482.

[4]James D. McCabe, Jr., *Great Fortunes and How They Were Made,* Cincinnati and Chicago: E. Hannaford and Co., 1871, p. 416.

[5]Clark, p. 365.

[6]*Animals in Motion,* p. 19 (in Dover edition).

[7]In his preface to J. D. B. Stillman, *The Horse in Motion,* Boston: James R. Osgood and Co., 1882, p. iii; hereafter cited as *The Horse in Motion.*

literature. Sir John F. W. Herschel, in the London *Photographic News* of May 11, 1869, had written:

What I have to propose may appear a dream, but it has at least the merit of being a possible, and, perhaps, a realizable one — realizable, that is to say, by an adequate sacrifice of time, trouble, mechanism and outlay. It is the stereoscopic representation of scenes of action — the vivid and lifelike reproduction and handling down to the latest posterity of any transaction in real life — a battle, a debate, a public solemnity, a pugilistic conflict, a harvest home, a launch — anything, in short, where any manner of interest is enacted within a reasonably short time, which may be seen from a single point of view.

I take for granted nothing more than . . . the possibility of taking a photograph, by a snap-shot — of securing a picture in a tenth of a second of time; and . . . that a mechanism is possible . . . by which a prepared plate may be presented, focussed, impressed, displaced, numbered, secured in the dark, and replaced by another within two or three tenths of a second.

These plates could be presented on the Phenakistoscope. If in color, the illusion would be complete."

In this passage Herschel predicts the instantaneous analytical photograph, the serial photograph, the synthetic reconstitution of these in a device to portray motion, and the motion picture in color! How prophetic Herschel's plan was we can easily see a century later, but photographers were relatively slow to implement his proposals. For example, instant photographs in the 1860s were only "more or less" instantaneous. The shutter was a very new invention, and most photographers were still making their exposures by removing a lens cap and replacing it as quickly as they were able. Too often, rapid action was recorded only as a blur. The horse "Dexter" was photographed in motion in Philadelphia in 1867 by John L. Gihon. The photograph was sufficiently "instantaneous" to be utilized in a composite photograph showing bystanders and the horse moving against a painted background of the track, a hotel, and other scenery.[8] In 1870, Henry Renno Heyl, seeking to portray a waltzing couple, commissioned a Philadelphia photographer, Willard, to secure the shots. Willard did not attempt a series of "instantaneous" photographs, but rather posed the couple in various stages of the waltz for his purpose.[9] These photographs Heyl projected on a screen, creating the effect of motion. It is with some interest, then, that we read of experiments in 1871, again in Philadelphia, by Professor Fairman Rogers (himself a wealthy and enthusiastic horseman and amateur photographer) and Joseph Zentmayer to

design and build a shutter for the purpose of photographing horses when in rapid motion. In the following year Rogers reported success in the use of his method.[10]

It is no longer certain who suggested to Leland Stanford that photography might provide him with the data he needed to settle the controversy about unsupported transit. We do know that Muybridge considered it was Fred MacCrellish, whom he thanked in a letter for "asserting to Governor Stanford your confidence in my ability to make a photograph of 'Occident' while he was trotting at full speed. When he was approached to undertake the commission, Muybridge was "perfectly amazed at the boldness and originality of the proposition and wondered at first whether it could be accomplished."[11] But the nature of the problem was so attractive that he soon resolved to attempt its solution.

The setting for the experiment was to be the Union Park racecourse in Sacramento. The five-mile track was part of the twenty acres of ground where the state agricultural fairs were held annually. Stables with stalls for 400 horses were on the premises, and here Stanford kept his racing stock — notably "Occident," the first of his horses to gain renown. Stanford had begun to train the little-known gelding in 1870. By 1872 Occident was being hailed from both coasts as the fastest "green" horse on record.

Since Occident was to become the first "motion picture" performer in California, his pedigree is of some romantic interest.[12] It didn't amount to much. He was sired by "Doc," son of the old pacer, "Saint Clair." Occident's dam was a small bay mare of trotting gait, never trained, pedigree unknown, and not quite 15 hands high.

Occident was foaled in the Sacramento Valley in 1863. His first owner, Matthew Shaw, let him roam in a semi-wild state until he was five years old. Shaw then sold him to a Sacramento butcher who tried but failed in an attempt to break him. The butcher sold him to a duck hunter who drove him in a heavy cart, using a strong chain as a hitch, and often fired a shotgun between Occident's ears in a futile attempt to break his spirit. The duck hunter in disgust sold Occident to a man who was engaged to haul earth for the river levees. Occident was again made to do cruelly heavy work. Once more he was sold, this time to a German grocer who began to pet him and feed him properly. In two months Occident grew fat, sleek, and docile. This was the prelude to a dramatic success story.

Somehow Occident got into a scrub race and won it. This led

---

[8] Robert Taft, *Photography and the American Scene,* New York: Macmillan, 1938, pp. 408-9.

[9] *Philadelphia Photographer,* VIII (1871), 162-3.

[10] Ibid., June 1872.

[11] *Alta California,* August 3, 1877.

[12] Charles Marvin, *Training the Trotting Horse,* New York: Marvin Publishing Co., 1891, pp. 96-111.

a man named Eldred to buy him and train him in earnest. When he was transferred to the road, Occident showed such promise that he was brought to the attention of Stanford, who bought him for $4,000, gold. Trackmen thought the former governor was mad. But from the moment of this last fortunate change of ownership Occident made astounding progress. Developed according to Stanford's unique training theories, by 1871 he was locally celebrated and by 1872 his reputation was nationwide.

Upon acquiring Occident, Stanford addressed himself to the question of what there was about the horse that needed developing. In order to achieve a more scientific basis for training, he proposed to have the camera used to gather proof. To accomplish this, he sought out Eadweard Muybridge, the best photographer for the purpose on the West Coast, and put Occident, "The Wonder Horse," at his disposal as the photographic subject for the experiment. The story, as Muybridge was later to tell it, had a monumental simplicity:

In the spring of the year 1872, while the author was directing the photographic surveys of the United States Government on the Pacific Coast, there was revived in the city of San Francisco a controversy in regard to animal locomotion. . . .

[The] principal subject of dispute was the possibility of a horse, while trotting — even at the height of his speed — having all four of his feet, at any portion of his stride, simultaneously free from contact with the ground.

The attention of the author was directed to this controversy, and he immediately resolved to attempt its settlement.

The problem before him was, to obtain a sufficiently well-developed and contrasted image on a wet collodion plate, after an exposure of so brief a duration that a horse's foot, moving with a velocity of more than thirty yards in a second of time, should be photographed with its outlines practically sharp.

In those days the rapid dry process — by the use of which such an operation is now easily accomplished — had not been discovered. Every photographer was, in a great measure, his own chemist; he prepared his own dipping baths, made his own collodion, coated and developed his own plates, and frequently manufactured the chemicals necessary for his work. All this involved a vast amount of tedious and careful manipulation from which the present generation is, happily, relieved.

Having constructed some special exposing apparatus and bestowed more than usual care in the preparation of the materials he was accustomed to use for ordinary quick work, the author commenced his investigation on the racetrack at Sacramento, California, in May, 1872, where he in a few days made several negatives of a celebrated horse named Occident, while trotting, laterally, in front of his camera, at rates of speed varying from two minutes and twenty-five seconds to two minutes and eighteen seconds per mile.

The photographs resulting from this experiment were sufficiently sharp to give a recognizable silhouette portrait of the driver, and some of them exhibited the horse with all four of his feet clearly lifted, at the same time, above the surface of the ground.

So far as the immediate point of issue was concerned, the object of the experiment was accomplished, and the question settled for once and for all time in favour of those who argued for a period of unsupported transit.[13]

Although this statement is probably about as close as we will every come to knowing what really happened with the photographing of Occident in Sacramento, it was written by Muybridge a quarter century after the events he was describing and at a time in his life when he was concerned with establishing his pioneering position in motion-picture history.

Are there no contemporary accounts? The Sacramento *Union* for April 26 and *Record* for April 27, 1872, take note of Muybridge's presence in the capital city at just the time he first claimed to have photographed Occident for Stanford. But the Stanford commission is not mentioned, and Muybridge is described as "soliciting subscriptions from those who desire to secure the series of views" of the Yosemite Valley which he was proposing to complete during the summer and fall. We have only Muybridge's word for it that he photographed the horse in 1872, but the date was widely publicized in 1877 and was not contested by those who still knew the facts.

In 1873, however, the San Francisco *Alta California*, MacCrellish's paper of April 7 carries an absolutely clear account of a successful attempt by Muybridge to photograph Occident:

QUICK WORK

Governor Stanford's fondness for his trotter is well known. He wished him to win the race in the contest with the Queen of the Turf, because the triumph would redound to the credit and fame of California, nor has his faith been shaken by the defeats experienced in those trials, and he is confident that time will put the brown beauty where he belongs — at the head of the list of trotters. The Governor is a judge of the points of a horse, too, and he appreciates the beauty of movement of "Occident" as highly as the speed he developed in his trials; and appreciating this beauty of movement, he wanted his friends abroad to participate with him in the contemplation of the trotter "in action," but did not exactly see how he was to accomplish it until a friend suggested that Mr. E. J. Muybridge be employed to photograph the animal while trotting. No sooner said than done. Mr. Muybridge was sent for and commissioned to execute the task, though the artist said he believed it to be impossible; still he would make the effort. All

[13]*Animals in Motion*, p. 13.

the sheets in the neighborhood of the stable were procured to make a white ground to reflect the object, and "Occident" was after a while trained to go over the white cloth without flinching; then came the question how could an impression be transfixed of a body moving at the rate of thirty-eight feet to the second. The first experiment of opening and closing the camera on the first day left no result; the second day, with increased velocity in opening and closing, a shadow was caught. On the third day, Mr. Muybridge, having studied the matter thoroughly, contrived to have two boards slip past each other by touching a spring and in so doing to leave an eighth of an inch opening for the five-hundredth part of a second, as the horse passed, and by an arrangement of double lenses, crossed, secured a negative that shows "Occident" in full motion — a perfect likeness of the celebrated horse. The space of time was so small that the spokes of the sulky were caught as if they were not in motion. This is considered a great triumph as a curiosity in photography — a horse's picture taken while going thirty-eight feet in a second!

Neither the date, nor the month, nor even the year of the photographing is stated in this account. One might as easily read it, at first glance, as referring to an 1872 picture as to one taken in 1873, were the event not reported as current by the newspaper. What established 1873 as the year of the picture described by the *Alta California*, rather than in 1872, is the reference to Stanford's desire for Occident to "win the race in the contest with the Queen of the Turf," and to Occident's defeat "in those trials." The race in which Occident challenged "Goldsmith Maid" — the Queen of the Turf — was run in October 1872. It was Occident's first race. He led to the quarter, and he led to the half, but he lost.[14] The photograph referred to in the article, therefore, was not only taken after April 1872 but before September 1873, when Occident justified Stanford's "fondness for the trotter" by equaling the Maid's record of a mile in 2 minutes, 16¾ seconds, to become the fastest trotting gelding on record.

Muybridge justified Stanford's belief in his work by providing a

[14] Clark states (p. 343): "The next year [October 1872] Occident was beaten by Goldsmith Maid, the queen of the turf, [but] in the year following, 1873, in an exhibition race at the State Fair, Occident did a mile in the best time ever made by a trotter in California, 2:16 ¾, and equalled the trotting record as it then stood."

"perfect likeness of the celebrated horse" taken "while going thirty-eight feet in a second." In the light of his subsequent work for Stanford, in 1877 and after, Muybridge never claimed more quality for either the 1872 or the 1873 pictures than that they were "little better than silhouettes,"[15] and that "the object of the experiment was accomplished.[16]

So far, no one today has discovered either the 1872 or the 1873 photographs of Occident. But it is possible that the Currier and Ives print of "The California Wonder OCCIDENT, owned by Gov. L. Stanford," entered for copyright in 1873, was intended to make both the pictures and the results of the experiment public. As translated to the lithographic stone by the "equestrian artist," J. Cameron, Occident proudly shows himself in harness at a private trial of speed, with all four feet free of the ground.

[15] In his *Descriptive Zoöpraxography* (see chap. 25, n. 7, below), p. 5
[16] *Animals in Motion*, p. 13.

49. Currier and Ives, *The California Wonder, Occident, 1873;* may have embodied the results of Muybridge's 1872 photographs.

9. Modoc Interlude (1872-1873)

After Muybridge left Sacramento in April 1873, he returned to San Francisco, but not for long. The course of events was to lead him northward, to the California-Oregon border, where he was to develop a new and dramatic aspect of his profession, war photography.

The Modoc War has been called the Indian's "final, desperate resistance to the impact of the white man's culture on the ancient Indian folkways."[1] The main action took place in the Modoc's traditional hunting stronghold in the Lava Beds, near Tule Lake in northern California. In 1864 the Modocs had reluctantly moved, under a treaty that was never satisfactory to them, to the reservation of the Klamath Indians in Oregon. A small band of Modocs, under a leader known as Captain Jack, at first refused to go and then seemed to accede to the terms of the treaty for a brief period. In 1870, Captain Jack and his followers quietly left the reservation and returned to the old tribal grounds, requesting that a reservation be given them on Lost River. This request was not granted by the Indian Office. By 1872 there were armed conflicts between the Indians and the white ranchers who were settling on the hunting grounds, the Interior Department and the War Department were at odds over policy, and the basic opposition between Modoc ethics and the "white man's law" had mounted until open war was inevitable.

When the new superintendent of Indian affairs for Oregon, T. B. Odeneal, telegraphed to the Interior Department for instructions, he was told to get all the Modocs back to the Klamath reservation, "peacefully if you can, but forcibly if you must." Peaceful persuasion proving impossible, Odeneal applied to the army commander at Fort Klamath for a force of men sufficient for the task. The Modoc War began on November 28, 1872, when Captain James A. Jackson, who had for some time found the Indians "very insolent," rode out with 35 soldiers to cooperate with the Indian Office in seeing to the execution of the order. After a running battle of three hours with a handful of Captain Jack's men, Captain Jackson led his troops off in confusion, giving the Modocs a clear victory. Indeed, the Indians had "so bewildered the enlisted men opposite them that the private soldiers became almost worthless as fighters," and had "confounded

the strategy of officers who had taken part in victorious campaigns in Virginia, Georgia and Tennessee."[2] Gathering up their arms, horses, and families, the Indians withdrew to the Lava Beds.

At this point, Oregon dispatched several companies of volunteers, and California sent a troop of riflemen who "wanted to see the fuss" up close. Early in 1873, Colonel Frank Wheaton, with a force of 400 men, sought to engage the Modocs. On the morning of January 17, Captain Jack and his men, concealed at vantage points in an area full of jagged rocks, ledges, and caves, met the troops with barrage after barrage of deadly fire. Though not a Modoc was seen, thirty-five of Wheaton's men were killed and numerous others were wounded. Wheaton ordered his troops to withdraw. For a second time in three months the newspapers of the nation reported an Indian victory and military mismanagement on the side of the whites.

Dispatches from the front now made household names of the chief figures in the conflict. On the one side were General William Tecumseh Sherman, issuing orders from the army headquarters in Washington; Major General John M. Schofield, of the Military Division of the Pacific, in San Francisco; General Edward R. S. Canby, in command of the Department of the Columbia; and Colonel Wheaton in the arena of battle. On the other side were Captain Jack, Young Schonchin, Steamboat Frank, Bogus Charlie, Ellen's Man George, Hooker Jim, Barnacho, and Sloluck.

The war moved to its next phase when General E. L. Applegate of the Oregon Militia urged the Interior Department to appoint a peace commission, on the grounds the "big talk" was cheaper than "big war." This proposal was accepted and a four-member commission was sent to General Canby's headquarters. This was in February 1873. The place was Hot Creek, twenty-five miles west of the Lava Beds. After several days, during which the commissioners were unable to make any contact with the Modocs, Elisha Steele, of Yreka, California, was sent for. Steele was an interpreter and lawyer whom the Indians had learned to respect. He managed to visit the Indians in the Lava Beds and offered them an amnesty for all offenses on the condition of their immediate removal to Angel Island in San Francisco Bay and their eventual removal to some distant reservation, to be selected by themselves.

Although Steele was convinced that the Modocs had accepted these terms, it presently became apparent that they had not and

---

[1] Keith A. Murray, *The Modocs and Their War,* Norman: University of Oklahoma Press, 1959, p. 4. The following account is based mainly on Murray's study.

[2] Ibid., p. 6.

that he had misunderstood their intentions. Early in April, Canby moved his camp to the edge of the Lava Beds, and Captain Jack responded by agreeing to a "big talk," but tensions and suspicions of bad faith on both sides made the ensuing meeting of April 7 unproductive. Army headquarters in Washington then ordered Canby to move against the Modocs as he saw fit. He now had a thousand men in readiness against 150 Indians.

On Good Friday, April 11, the peace commission and a Modoc delegation met under a flag of truce. All present were to be unarmed, but two of the commissioners secretly carried weapons, as did some of the Modocs, who also had two of their men hidden nearby among with rocks with a cache of arms. The real hell of the Modoc War now began.

Of a sudden the Indians split the air with war whoops. Captain Jack drew a revolver from his coat and instantly put a bullet through General Canby, who was present as counselor to the commission. At this cue the Modocs opened a fusillade. Ellen's Man George put a second bullet through Canby and slit his throat; he and Barnacho then stripped him of his uniform. One commissioner was shot and killed by Sloluck; the others managed to escape. By the time soldiers could reach the scene, the Modocs had disappeared into the Lava Beds, where uncertainty of the terrain made it imprudent to follow them. Army headquarters was notified by telegram, and word came from General Sherman that the Modoc's punishment must be severe.

Colonel Gillem took over and prepared for "war to the bitter end." In four days of running battle, sixteen of Gillem's men were killed and fourteen wounded. Thirteen more then lost their lives in an ambush. Other strategies were clearly called for. Colonel and Brevet Major Jefferson C. Davis, a veteran of both the Mexican War and the Civil War, was sent in to replace Canby. By then, despondency was pervading the whole command because of the repeated failure of civil and military authorities to deal with the Modocs on any terms.

The terrain of the Lava Beds, to which the Modocs had retired, was so little known, if at all, that already General Schofield in San Francisco had ordered a reconnaissance and authorized Captain Garrett A. Lydecker, of the Corps of Engineers, to proceed there for that purpose. Oliver Applegate, the secretary of the peace commission, recalled long afterward how Eadweard Muybridge had come with Lydecker's party:

Muybridge represented the old San Francisco firm of Bradley and Rulofson, commercial photographers, by whom he was employed to obtain pictures of the Modoc War. This firm produced many valuable and excellent photographs of scenic *features of the Pacific coast, and also what in modern times would be termed "news pictures" of current events of the period in which they were in business.*[3]

Although Muybridge was not able to record any of the fighting, he made stereoscopic pictures of the men and the locations during the last stages of the conflict: the officers of the campaign, the Indian scouts, wounded soldiers being carried in after an engagement, the caves in which the Modocs had hidden, the stone on which General Canby was sitting when he was shot by Captain Jack, and panoramas of the Lava Beds and the army encampment on the shores of Tule Lake, as well as the strictly topographical views Lydecker needed. His pictures, taken under arduous circumstances, served their primary function in Washington. In a report to the Chief of Engineers, Lydecker stated:

GENERAL: I have the honor to transmit herewith photographic copies of the two sketches, made to accompany preliminary report to the commanding general of the division, on my reconnaissance of the lava beds. . . .
Besides these, I have forwarded copies of the stereoscopic views taken under my direction, by Mr. E. J. Muybridge. I trust an examination of these will convey a clear idea of the exceedingly difficult country in which our forces have been compelled to operate against the Modoc Indians.[4]

At this time war photography was still a novel enterprise. In 1855, Roger Fenton had made 360 memorable photographs during four months spent covering the Crimean War. Matthew Brady had sunk his fortune into creating a massive historical documentation of the American Civil War through photography. Alexander Gardner and George N. Barnard had published impressive photographic albums of the Civil War. Now Muybridge aspired to join their ranks. Although the Modoc War was a small local conflict, the stubborn resistance of the Indians and the assassinations under a flag of truce aroused great national interest in the "sanguinary Modocs" and their suppression. In his photographs Muybridge was securing topical pictures of immediate newsworthy interest. *Harper's Weekly*, which had been publishing a series on the war since April, scored a journalistic coup when the account in its issue of June 21 was illustrated with engravings from "photographs by Muybridge, furnished by the courtesy of Bradley & Rulofson, San Francisco."

Muybridge staged some dramatic tableaus. For example, "A

[3] Letter to Almo Scott Watson, November 2, 1937, in collection of the California Historical Society.
[4] Letter to Brigadier General A. A. Humphries, May 28, 1873, in Exec. Doc. 122, House, 43d Cong., 1st sess.

Modoc Brave on the War Path" — reproduced in *Harper's Weekly* as "Modoc Brave Lying in Wait for a Shot" — shows an Indian crouched behind a volcanic outcropping, rifle extended, apparently ready to ambush the enemy. This brave was not, however, a Modoc. He was a Tenino Indian scout fighting for the United States Army.

Louis Heller, a studio portraitist from nearby Fort Jones, also ventured into the final stage of the war and photographed some of the same persons as Muybridge, but his stiff portraits could just as well have been taken in his studio. Muybridge, on the other hand, always took care to relate his subjects to their environment and their role in the war. Even in a simple portrait such as "Donald McKay, the celebrated Warm Spring Indian Scout," McKay holds, cradled in his lap, his rifle — the sign of his profession. Copied in the press as woodcut engravings, Muybridge's dramatic images brought the distant events of the campaign close for Eastern readers, and his Modoc pictures became widely known. It would be another thirty years before newspapers and magazines would be able to reproduce photographs directly.

Soon after the winding-up of the war, Bradley and Rulofson circulated a trade card with a montage of Muybridge's photographs on one side and this description on the other:

BRADLEY & RULOFSON

Have the pleasure to announce the publication of a New Series of Stereoscopic Views illustrating the

MODOC WAR

These views were made for the U.S. War Department to accompany the report of Captain Lydecker's topographical survey of the Lava Beds; by

and are characterized by the same judicious selection of subject, artistic treatment and skillful manipulation that mark all the productions of this celebrated artist.[5]

The *denouement* of the Modoc War followed Davis' arrival and the relief of Gillem from command. Severe troop training began. When Davis finally sent his men after the Modocs it was with a new discipline and with orders to pursue them and give them no rest. Soon the Indians were in retreat. On May 22 an exhausted band of seventy-five surrendered. Captain Jack and a small group of followers fled to a hiding place on Willow Creek, near the headwaters of Lost River. For nearly a week they were hunted down. The last to surrender was Captain Jack. The war was over "when a band of beaten and spiritless prisoners were forced aboard a Central Pacific Railroad train bound for exile on a tiny reservation in Oklahoma."[6]

Muybridge went on north from the Lava Beds and spent the early summer months preparing "Pacific Northwest Scenes", a stereoscopic series which included views of the Columbia River, The Dalles, the Cascade Range, and a seven-part panorama of Portland, Oregon. These were published by Bradley and Rulofson upon his return to professional and family life in San Francisco.

[5] In Bancroft Library.
[6] Murray, *The Modocs and Their War,* p. 4.

50. *Above,* "Modoc Squaws," a wood engraving made from Muybridge's photograph to illustrate Harper's coverage of the Modoc War. The photograph was simplified and reversed in the process of reproduction.

51. Modoc women, Indian agent, a Modoc War stereo by Muybridge, 1873.

PORTFOLIO II
Views of the Far West: (1872–1873)

52. The Stanford Sacramento home, entrance.

53   54

55   56

57. The conservatory of the Doyle home, Menlo Park. With four subjects almost camouflaged by the décor.

The Stanford Sacramento home. 53. Jane Stanford, Mary Lathrop and Leland Stanford, Jr., in the billiard room. 54. Jane Stanford and her family on the enclosed porch. 55. Facade. 56. The double parlor in the old part of the house (now a chapel).

58

59

0. Yosemite Valley: Pi-Wi-Ack (Shower of Stars), 1872, "Vernal Fall." A view of the Valley. (Muybridge touched out
the tree at left center. The tips of the missing branches may be seen in front of the rock dome).

cing page.

8. *Top,* Three photographs that may have been taken by Muybridge during his 1872/1873 experiments at Sacramento.

9. *Left,* Ancient Glacier channel at Lake Tenaya, Yosemite, 1872. A view of the high country.

61. Falls of the Yosemite from glacier rock, 1872. A view of the rim of the Valley.

62. Valley of the Yosemite, from Union Point, 1872. A view from the rim of the Valley.

63. Cathedral Rocks, 1872. A view of the valley.

54. *Buena Vista vineyard.* Loading grapes for the press house.

65. *Top, Buena Vista vineyard. Top,* disgorging the sediment and recorcking sparkling wines.

66. *Left,* The cooper shop.

67. *Directly above,* Bottling wine.

PART THREE:
A Startling Tragedy

10. Harry Larkyns (1873-1874)

It was in the Bradley and Rulofson gallery that Flora Muybridge introduced her husband to Major Larkyns, the new dramatic critic for the San Francisco *Post.* Interested in the arts, Larkyns soon was asking the opinion of Eadweard Muybridge on aesthetic matters, which helped him prepare his notices for the newspaper. In return he offered theater passes and occasionally invited the couple to accompany him. Eadweard was at first standoffish, not caring to be under obligation or form a closer connection.[1] In time, however, the affable major became a frequent visitor in the Muybridge home.

Thanks to his pleasing manners and address, Harry Larkyns was a great favorite wherever he went, especially with the ladies:

He was every inch a Bohemian and debonair man of the world. He spoke divers tongues, all equally well as he did English. He had been everywhere and seen everything. He had roamed the world and been a soldier of fortune, writer, poet, musician. . . . He could box like Jem Mace, and fence like Agramonte. . . . He could hit more bottle necks with a pistol at twenty paces than anyone else, and he never sent his right of left fist into a bully's face but that the bully was carried away. . . . Larkyns was a scientist, chemist, and metallurgist. . . . No one could mention anything he could not do better than anybody else, and when it came to cooking a delicacy in a chafing dish, Delmonico was simply not in it. A sniff and a shrug [from him] would put any brand of wine out of commission with the epicures. . . . Larkyns was over six feet tall, straight as a lance, and had the gift of spreading a ripple of sunshine wherever he went. His wit and clever stories and general affability won him a legion of friends.[2]

A greater contrast can hardly be imagined than that between the dedicated Muybridge and the happy-go-lucky major, as Flora discovered. She was swept off her feet by the newcomer and enchanted by his history.

Larkyns let it be known that he was connected in England with a family of wealth and respectability.[3] He posed as a man of irreproachable character, the son of a rich Scotsman by whose death he came into a good deal of money, and claimed to have received his education on the Continent, with a bit of adventurous living thrown in.[4] Back in London, so he said, he entered business by investing in the Lyceum Theater, thereby outraging his family. Only his sister continued to recognize him. When the theatrical venture ended in financial ruin, relatives bought him an army commission and happily shipped him off to his regiment in India. "Arrived there, he soon wearied of the routine, sold out his service, and started for Central Asia. . . . He fell into the good graces of a heathen potentate, administered his government for him, and finally freed him from all further care by making himself Rajah." Larkyns claimed to have succeeded to both the palace and the harem, and for a time to have led a life of barbaric magnificence. By his account, he succeeded also to the royal treasury and after six years of solitary splendor decamped with it and a trunkful of jewels, which he carried off to London.

His family was less critical of him now, but he quarreled with them and went to the Continent again, to amuse himself by

---

[1] Interview given by Muybridge to George W. Smith, in the *Chronicle,* San Francisco, December 21, 1874.

[2] *Examiner,* San Francisco, October 19, 1874.

[3] My efforts to determine Larkyns' true identity and locate the family connections in England have been in vain.

[4] Here and for several paragraphs I draw upon and quote from the *Free Press,* Calistoga, Calif., November 21, 1874.

living luxuriously while plotting destruction for the crowned heads of Europe. "He carried a musket under Garibaldi, and is said to have belonged to Mazzini's Secret League. The spies of Europe knew him. He grew accustomed to being escorted across the frontier. . . . He declared that he never meant to do any king harm, and indeed his schemes always failed." A second period of beggary coincided with the outbreak of the Franco-Prussian War, whereupon he joined the French army. He was promoted to the rank of major for services on General Bourbaki's staff, wounded at Metz, and taken prisoner by the Germans at Sedan.

This was the legend that Larkyns told of himself. In the early part of 1871 he came to the United States. At this point the facts of his life become verifiable. He appeared briefly in Salt Lake City, where he took money from a traveling companion in exchange for fictitious drafts. Proceeding to Virginia City, in Nevada, he promptly charmed that community, which was rich then from the ore of the Comstock Lode.

Harry Larkyns was a man whom all early Comstockers will remember. . . . He fitted in with an Opera Company and during the theatrical engagement had such a good time that he chose to remain. . . . One day Larkyns had a chance to play the organ in the Bishop's church. . . . It was an improvisation, but it kept the crowd glued to their seats at the time [the] music was expected to cause the audience to leave. [5]

Drifting away from the lode, Larkyns wandered as far as Honolulu. On his return, he landed in jail in San Francisco. The fictitious drafts had caught up with him. Only his former companion's failure to prosecute set him free. "As a day laborer, as a stevedore, as a clerk, as a translator, as a critic, and as a correspondent, he worked to gain money and regain reputation." [6]

Larkyns settled down for a time as dramatic critic for the *Post*, but his propensity for trouble dogged him:

He found a poor devil, one night, shivering and hungry in the streets, and took the fellow to his room. The fellow's name was Coppinger, and Larkyns allowed him to write the dramatic criticisms and divided salary and rooms with him. One day the Post *got an anonymous letter saying that Larkyns was not doing the dramatic work he was pretending to do. Asked if he did his own work as*

[5] *Examiner,* October 19, 1874.
[6] *Free Press,* November 21, 1874.

dramatic critic, Larkyns promptly answered, "No" and was discharged. Coppinger, who had written the note, secured the place.

From that time on, whenever Coppinger met Larkyns, Larkyns would take him by the nose and the lower jaw, and spreading open his mouth with a grip of iron, would spit down Coppinger's throat! He was arrested for this and tried. When the jury heard the story of Coppinger's baseness, they acquitted Larkyns amid the cheers of the spectators. The newsboys of San Francisco had hired old Colonel Dudley to conduct Larkyns' defense, and the vituperation which Dudley poured out over Coppinger was long remembered in the annals of the old Police Court. . . . It became the custom for no newspaper man to associate with Coppinger and he continued to be the most despised man in San Francisco. [7]

For a while Larkyns worked in the "literary industries" of Hubert Howe Bancroft, who amassed an enormous library of historical materials and employed a corps of helpers in the task of research and writing that went into his 39-volume history of western North America. In the chapter of his autobiography devoted to his assistants, Bancroft mentions "Harry Larkin" as "an English adventurer of good abilities, many accomplishments, and an adventurous career." [8]

Larkyns was welcome in the Muybridges' circle for a while, too. He quickly saw that Flora and her husband had tastes which were not in harmony, although Muybridge, engrossed in business and indifferent to social amusements, always seemed willing for Flora to seek diversion independently. Without Muybridge's knowledge, and frequently in his absence from home, Larkyns began to see Flora regularly and to draw her into the web of his own dashing but confused life.

There were some who afterward were to judge Muybridge harshly for the freedom he permitted his wife, but they remained silent during this time. Muybridge was blind to the fact that Flora was infatuated. Her affair with the major had already blossomed before Muybridge went off to the Modoc War, and even before she introduced him to Muybridge at the gallery. During the summer and fall of 1873, whenever her husband was away from the city, Flora continued to meet secretly with Larkyns.

In the fall, when he was about to leave for an extended photographic trip along the line of the transcontinental railroad, Muybridge learned that his wife was to have a child.

[7] *Examiner,* October 19, 1874.
[8] *Literary Industries,* San Francisco: The History Co., 1891, p. 273.

11. Floredo Helios Muybridge (1874)

Eadweard Muybridge was not in San Francisco when the child, Floredo Helios Muybridge, was born on April 13, 1874. He had arranged for an excellent nurse to be with Flora. This was Mrs. Susan C. Smith, whose daughter Sarah Louisa was an employee at Bradley and Rulofson's and was one of Flora's closest friends. The choice at first seemed a blessing. It later led to disturbing complications.[1] Mrs. Smith became a go-between, carrying messages from Flora to inform Larkyns when Muybridge was away from home.

The lovers were careless, and before long Muybridge surprised them in each other's arms. He forbade Larkyns ever to come to the house again. Shortly thereafter he happened upon Mrs. Smith and Larkyns in conversation on a street corner and saw them exchange letters. When he got home, he challenged the nurse to tell him why she had been talking to Larkyns. Flora came into the room immediately, deathly pale, and looked warningly at Mrs. Smith. When he could get no answer, Muybridge said, "You know more than you are willing to tell me. How can the woman I love treat me so cruelly?"

Larkyns stayed out of the way. He took a job as manager of John Wilson's circus for a few months. By chance a letter that he wrote to Flora came into Muybridge's hands: "Why doesn't the old man get out of town and leave us alone? At the place on Montgomery Street they think you are my wife."

Muybridge then hunted down Larkyns in the offices of the *Post* and in a terrific verbal row cautioned him never to try to see Flora again or communicate with her. If he ever found that Larkyns had done so, Muybridge said, he would kill him without regret.

Larkyns got out of town. He gave up his job at the circus and went to Calistoga to work for William D. Stewart as a surveyor at the Yellow Jacket mine, high on the slopes of Mount St. Helena, making maps of the mining areas in Napa, Lake, and Sonoma counties.

Muybridge, full of suspicion and anger, packed Flora and the baby off to spend the summer at The Dalles, Oregon, with her uncle, Captain Stump, and his family. She left quickly, taking no more luggage than was necessary for a short visit, and told no one

[1] My account is from the testimony of Mrs. Smith and other witnesses at Muybridge's trial as reported in various contemporary newspapers.

It is to be noted that no clippings or other records of the trial and the events leading up to it were preserved by Muybridge in the Scrapbook.

but Mrs. Smith where she was going or how long she would stay. Muybridge, in his haste, put Flora and Floredo on a steamer that was carrying John Wilson's minstrels to an engagement in Portland, and then feared that he had sent her off on the same ship with Larkyns, but this proved not to be the case.

For his part, Larkyns was hard at work at the Yellow Jacket mine. When he learned that Flora had sailed for Portland on the ship with the minstrel troupe, he thought that she had run off with Wilson, and suffered pangs of jealousy. He inserted a desperate message in the Personal columns of the morning and evening Portland newspapers: "Flora and Georgie, If you have a heart you will write to H. Have you forgotten that April night when we were both so pale?" Then he wrote to Mrs. Smith, begging for some word of Flora and the baby. Meanwhile Flora had written to Sarah Smith, asking that her address at The Dalles be given to Larkyns. Then began a direct correspondence in which she reassured Larkyns that he had no cause for jealousy.

By the fall of 1874, Mrs. Smith had decided to press Muybridge for payment of a bill for $100 that she had presented for her services at the time of Flora's confinement. This Muybridge refused to pay, on the grounds that he had already given Flora money for the purpose and considered the bill to have been paid. Mrs. Smith then initiated court proceedings and Muybridge paid the bill. Later Mrs. Smith declared:

In order to prove my assertions I was compelled to produce a letter from her [Flora] to me acknowledging her indebtedness. From some expressions which occurred in the letter, and Larkyns' name being mentioned in it, Muybridge appeared agitated and said it was strange that his wife should mention Larkyns' name so familiarly. After the trial, Muybridge asked me if I had any more letters from his wife. I said, "Yes." He asked me if I would give them to him, and I said, "Yes." That was October 14th, 1874.

The next morning she met Muybridge outside the lawyer's office. He was pacing up and down, looking wild and excited. He wanted to know if she had proof of his wife's guilt. When she replied "I don't know," he said: "Mrs. Smith, if you don't tell me the truth I shall consider you a bad woman."

After some conversation they went upstairs. Mrs. Smith gave some letters to the lawyer and left. As she closed the door, she heard a scream and a fall. The contents of the "guilty letters," as they came to be called, were later printed in the newspapers.

(Harry Larkyns to Mrs. Smith)

Calistoga, Wednesday

Dear Mrs. Smith

You'll be surprised to hear from me so soon after I left the city, but I have been so uneasy and worried about that poor girl that I cannot rest, and it is a relief to talk or write about her. I think you have a sufficiently friendly feeling towards me to grant me a favor, rest assured I will find means to do you a good turn before long. I want you and your girls to be perfectly frank, open and honest with me. If you hear anything of that little lady, no matter what, tell me right out. She may return to the city and beg you not to let me know, but do pray not listen to her. Do not be afraid that I shall get angry with her, I will never say a harsh word to her, and even if things turn out as badly as possible and I find that she has been deceiving me all along, I can only be very grieved and sorry, but I will never be angry with her. I ascertained today that all the minstrels will return today from Portland on the next Steamer, which will arrive on Tuesday next. I **cannot** *and* **will not** *believe anything so bad as that rumor, but I almost believe she will come back, or she would have sent for her clothes. I have written to the morning and evening papers in Portland today, and advertised in the personals. . . . She will understand this. I have also put a personal in the* **Chronicle.** *Mrs. Smith I assure you I am sick and ill with anxiety and doubt, the whole thing is so incomprehensible and I am so helpless. I fear my business will not let me go to Portland and I see no other way of hearing of her. If an angel had come and told me she was false to* **me,** *I would not have believed it. I cannot attend to my work, I cannot sleep, and the longer matters stay like this the more I suffer, besides even if she does write now, I shall not know what to believe. I cannot help thinking of that speech of hers to you the day before she left, when she begged you not to think ill of her, whatever you might hear, it almost looks as if she had already settled some plan in her head that she knew you would disapprove of. And yet Mrs. Smith after all that has come and gone,* **could** *she be so utterly untrue to me, so horribly false? It seems impossible, and yet I rack my brain to try and find some excuse, and cannot do it. If she had nothing to conceal why has she not written? If I go to Portland I must give up my situation, but I think unless we hear I shall go. I shall be in the city about Thursday next, tell the girls to look out for the next steamer and find out if Flo comes down. Mrs. Smith again I beg you to be open and candid and conceal nothing from me. With many thanks for all the kindness you have shown Flo. Yours very Truly,*

Harry Larkyns

(Flora Muybridge to Sarah Smith)

The Dalles, July 11, 1874

DEAR SARAH:

Yours of the 3rd has just come to hand. I had begun to think you had all forgotten me, I write again to your Mother. I received such a letter from H. L. saying that he heard I had not gone

any further than Portland. I was so provoked that I wrote him a letter and sent it to the Geysers and which, if he receives it will not make him feel very happy. He ought to know me better than to accuse me of such a thing but I may forgive him. Don't forget to tell him if he wrote to me at **Portland** *to send and get the letter as it might be* **advertised** *and sent for by someone else. . . . About coming to San F you will see me back before you know it, I do not like this place at all, they have a great deal of Company and try to make me go out, but I care for no one here and never shall, I have invitations every day to go to parties and picnics, but have been to only one picnic since I came. . . . I wish I had a nice little home with you know who and your mother and all of you near me. I would be so happy to get away from California from all my pretend friends for instance Mrs. Gross. . . . She or anyone else may talk about Harry all they please. I am not ashamed to say I love him better than anyone else upon this earth, and no one can change my mind, unless with his own lips he tells me that he does not care for me any more — I don't want Harry to come up here, much as I would like to see him, for this is a small place and people cannot hold their tongues.*

Mrs. Muybridge

Destroy my letters after reading them, for you might lose one and it might get picked up.

Flo[2]

Muybridge's ordeal was just about to begin. Sensing there was more that Mrs. Smith could tell him, he went to her home on Saturday noon, October 17. He had barely slept the night before. He said, "Mrs. Smith, are you busy? I want to see you." She asked him inside, and his attention was immediately drawn to a photograph of Floredo on the center table. "Who is it?" he said with a start.

"He is your baby," answered Mrs. Smith.

"I have never seen this picture before. Where did you get it and where was it taken?"

"Your wife sent it to me from Oregon. It was taken at Rulofson's."

Muybridge turned the picture over and began to tremble. "My God," he cried, "what is this on the back of this picture in my wife's handwriting — 'Little Harry'?" He came at Mrs. Smith with his hands upraised as if to strike her.

Out of fear that he would kill her or himself, she told him all that she knew. She told him how Larkyns and Flora had come for her the night the baby was to be born. As they drove back to

[2] The letters were introduced in evidence at the trial on February 4, 1875. Copies in Muybridge's handwriting are still in the archives at the county courthouse in Napa. They were quoted almost verbatim in the San Francisco *Chronicle,* February 6. I have followed the text of Muybridge's copies, retaining syntax and punctuation which the newspaper emended.

the Muybridge home in the carriage, Larkyns held Flora in his arms, calling her his baby.

Susan Smith had first suspected their real relationship when Flora said that she was worried lest the baby should have sandy hair like Larkyns. Floredo was born with light hair, and when Larkyns returned to the house, after a day or two, Flora asked the nurse to bring the baby for him to see.

"Who does the baby look like?" Flora asked him.

Larkyns replied, "You ought to know, Flo." Leaving, he said to Mrs. Smith, "I want you to take good care of that baby. . . . I have two babies now."

On another of his visits she heard Flora say to him, "Harry, we will remember the thirteenth of July. We have something to show for it now."

There was a final blow. Mrs. Smith told Muybridge: "After Larkyns was appointed manager of the circus, he and Mrs. Muybridge wanted to travel together and leave the child with me. Larkyns spoke of taking Mrs. Muybridge to England with him as his wife."

She later recounted that Muybridge reacted to her story like one dumbfounded. He fell on the floor in a fit. Mrs. Smith thought that he was going to die. Finally he got to the door and, turning as though he had awakened from a trance, cried: "Flora, Flora, my heart is broken. I would have given my heart's best blood for you."

Muybridge went next to Bradley and Rulofson's gallery. On the way, at about one o'clock that afternoon, he ran into Harry Edwards, a popular actor-manager. They talked of business, and Edwards had the impression that Muybridge was in good spirits. But he was wild-eyed when Rulofson met him at the entrance to the gallery elevator. Knowing that he disliked the elevator and never used it, and noticing his distraught expression,

Rulofson tried to delay him and find out what was the matter.

"You will find out soon enough," Muybridge said, and moved about so nervously that Rulofson, apprehensive of his attracting the customers' attention, got him into a private office and closed the door.

Muybridge continued, "Do not ask me to name my dishonor. Promise me, Rulofson, that in the event of my death you will faithfully give my wife all that belongs to me." Rulofson thought Muybridge was going to do away with himself and tried to reason with him. Thereupon Muybridge thrust the "guilty letters" into his hands, asking that they be kept until his return or be burned if he should die. He assured Rulofson that the letters contained absolute proof that Flora had dishonored him.

With this, Muybridge went to his own office, put his business affairs in order, loaded a pistol, and by two-thirty was leaving the gallery to go to Calistoga and find Harry Larkyns.

Rulofson tried to delay him long enough to make him miss the ferry to Vallejo, which would leave at four o'clock and make connection with a train to Calistoga. "Many good women are wrongly slandered," Rulofson began.

"One of us will be shot," replied Muybridge, showing him the pistol.

"For God's sake, don't kill him!" Rulofson entreated, trying to hold back Muybridge, who broke away and ran the several blocks to the ferry wharf.

An old friend, J. P. Wentworth, stood on the upper deck of the ferryboat and saw Muybridge rush aboard just as it was about to leave the slip. When Wentworth passed him in the cabin, Muybridge turned away to avoid a meeting.

The boat docked at Vallejo two hours later. Here Muybridge transferred to the cars of the California Pacific Railroad. He reached Calistoga by seven-thirty.

12. Murder (1874)

It was nearly dark when Eadweard Muybridge left the train. He went straight to a livery stable and asked for a wagon and team and a driver. The stableman objected that the night was very dark and the roads muddy, and suggested that the trip be delayed until morning. Muybridge told him that he had business with Harry Larkyns which would not wait, so the stableman sent for a boy, George Wolfe, to drive him to the superintendent's residence at the

Yellow Jacket mine, near Knight's Valley, about seven and a half miles past Calistoga.[1]

A team was rigged up, and the two set off in the darkness. Muybridge offered the boy five dollars if he made the trip safely

[1] As in chap. 11, here and on through chap. 16 I have drawn on testimony, including reported conversations, given by witnesses at Muybridge's trial and printed in contemporary newspapers.

and in good time. George stated afterward that his passenger appeared perfectly calm throughout the trip, chatting about the rich farming area through which they were passing, its scenery and its history. Muybridge evidently began to worry whether his gun was in good order, for he brought the conversation around to highway robbery. George had never heard of holdups in this area. Muybridge then said he was armed and asked whether the horses would be frightened if he tried his pistol. George thought not, and Muybridge fired one shot.

They turned off the main road for the final, winding climb of a thousand feet up the steep side of Mount St. Helena. Near the top was the house of the mine superintendent, William Stewart, positioned like an eagle's nest and close by the Yellow Jacket and Ida Clayton mines, which were each producing a bar of silver a day at the time.

The house was ablaze with lamps. A party was in progress, and the voices of men and women floated out into the night. Muybridge directed George Wolfe to remain in the wagon, went to the porch, and knocked at the door. Benjamin Prickett, the mine foreman, answered. Muybridge asked for Larkyns. Prickett invited him in, but Muybridge said that his business with Larkyns would only take a minute. He wished to see him, briefly, outside.

Harry Larkyns was at the moment engaged in a game of cribbage. He excused himself and appeared at the door, standing in the light that shone from behind him. "Who is it?" he asked. "It is so dark I can't see you."

"Good evening, Major," said the visitor. "My name is Muybridge. Here is the answer to the message you sent my wife."

Muybridge fired out of the darkness at Larkyns, who fell at the

68. The superintendent's residence, Yellow Jacket mine, where Harry Larkyns was murdered by Eadweard Muybridge on October 17, 1874.

base of a huge oak tree at the entrance to the house, struck below the heart. Witnesses later claimed that Larkyns, reeling back into the house, had run through the kitchen and sitting room, and then out the door, to fall by the tree. But Dr. Reid, who was summoned that night, declared that Larkyns must have died instantly from the wound.

After firing, Muybridge entered the house. He surrendered himself immediately. Then, turning to the ladies in the room, he said, "I am sorry this little trouble occurred in your presence."

Some of the witnesses, however, stated that these were the last words of Harry Larkyns.

13. Sinner's Funeral (1874)

The remains of Harry Larkyns were brought to Calistoga on Sunday morning and conveyed to San Francisco that afternoon. Newspaper accounts of the murder appeared on Monday morning, and an elaborate funeral followed.

Meanwhile Muybridge was taken to Calistoga in the wagon that he had hired to bring him to the Yellow Jacket. He sat on the back seat, between two men, with his feet securely tied. The guards seemed surprised that he made no attempt to escape. Talkative and exhilarated, he freely told the men the history behind the occurrence they had witnessed. He said that he had deliberately planned to shoot Larkyns and was now prepared to suffer the

consequences of his act. He had either expected to be shot or lynched at the mine, so he was relieved to be safely brought to Calistoga. The constable there found him "remarkably cool" and gentlemanly in every way.

On Monday, Muybridge was brought before Justice Palmer of Calistoga. After waiving examination, he was bound over to the grand jury and detained in jail at Napa, the county seat. Wirt Pendegast of Napa and Cameron King of San Francisco were retained as counsel. They made application for his release on bail, but this was denied, and Muybridge began a lonely three months in the county jail.

The truth of the legends that grew up around Harry Larkyns, both before his death and afterward, may never be known. He had a powerful group of allies, and his friends in the press watched out for his reputation to the end. One of the grimmer legends has to do with "Cuspidor Coppinger" again. He was supposed to have been drinking in a San Francisco saloon when news reached him that Larkyns had been murdered and his body returned to the city for burial. The story goes thus:

A glass of beer stood before him. Pushing it from him he called for a glass of something stronger, at the same time saying, "There is, indeed, a special Providence in the killing of that man. I drink to the special Providence." This speech was so brutal, that the men who stood about placed their glasses on the bar and moved away. But the infamy was to go further. This individual who had trembled before the deceased while he lived, went out and walked hastily to the rooms where Larkyns lay in his coffin. He gazed long and maliciously at the features of the dead, and then turned and walked out, rubbing his hands and grinning like a human jackal. Outside the door he spoke in a voice loud enough for all about to hear him, "I'd walk twenty miles the stormiest night that ever was seen to gaze on that sight!"[1]

On Monday, before Muybridge's side of the story could have been made known, the funeral services "over the body of the late Major Harry Larkyns" took place at the Church of the Advent, where the ceremonies were conducted according to the solemn rites of the Protestant Episcopal church. The Reverend Henry D. Lathrop officiated.

Between four and five hundred San Franciscans attended, as from every extreme of life came friends, or the curious, to pay tribute to Harry Larkyns. The floral display, the newspapers reported, was the greatest ever seen in the city. George Russell, baritone, vocalist at Macguire's Opera House, sang "Flee as a Bird to Your Mountain, Thou Who Art Weary of Sin." Tears flowed freely, as if everyone had lost a member of his own family.

The actor Harry Edwards played a central role in the services. He delivered the memorial address:

Friends: — I little thought when, less than three weeks ago, I clasped hands with him and bade him God-speed upon the work he had just undertaken, that I should so soon have been called upon to stand beside the dead body of Harry Larkyns and pay this last sad tribute to his memory. And I know that in a moment like the present I may claim and receive the sympathy of those around me, for here are gathered those who loved him well, and to whom my poor words can convey but little meaning. Still it is

[1] *Examiner,* San Francisco, October 20, 1874, "The Depth of Infamy."

good to be here. It is good for us to linger for a moment about his remains, and from the grave which soon will cover them to pluck a blade of memory, greener than the grass; to weave it into a chaplet of sorrow lighter than the air; to waft it upon the current of our sympathy over land and sea to the home of his birth, and laying it with the tenderness of our pity at the feet of the mourning ones who loved and cherished him, say, in all the grand fraternal feeling of sorrow: "Though you were absent he was not alone, for man's grief and woman's tears attended him to the last, and he sleeps in peace, for gentle and loving hands have laid him in his grave." Of him who now lies cold and still before us what shall we say? We who knew him best, knew well the struggle of his life, the torments he endured, the wearying conflict of his one poor heart against a world of selfish, pitiless pride; a pride so pitiless that a single tone of manly friendship or a word of womanly sympathy came to him like an echo of the voices which he heard in childhood, — voices which he longed again to hear, but which he resolved never more to listen to until the thorny path which misfortune had placed before him had been cleared by the energy of his own endeavor, and he could stand proudly before those loved ones of an earlier time and say: "I bring you back the honor you bestowed upon me, unstained as when it left your hands, and claim, in common justice to my nature, a full oblivion of the past." He was a gentleman in the truest sense of the word. Upon his lips the breath of slander never lived, the cruelty of corrupting tongues never found a home; vulgarity of every kind was a perfect stranger to his soul, and in the retrospect of his own sorrows he knew how to find excuses for the follies of his fellow-men, and to cover with the mantle of chairty those errors which the world too often blackens with the name of crime. A soldier by profession, distinguished upon the battle-field, the grandest and most heroic struggles of his life were the hand-to-hand conflicts which he waged against those who reviled him here and who were far beneath him in every point of manliness and truth and honor. And now that he is dead, let those detractors know, that no mother's tender hand ever smoothed his head, no father's gentle voice ever offered him counsel. Those natural protectors and advisers were snatched from him at so early an age that his memory of them was but a faded recollection. Deprived of their care and protection he had to fight the battle of his life alone. How nobly he struggled, how grandly he toiled, we, who knew his sacrificing heroism can testify, and the number of those who loved and honored him, and who are to-day gathered in the depth of sorrow around his poor remains, will be the best evidence of the affection he inspired, and of the regrets at his unhappy death which are now breathed about his tomb.

And now, gentle and loving friend and brother, farewell! The blessing of eternal rest has fallen upon your soul! Is it too much to hope that in your home of peaceful calm, your spirit now hears the words of the friend who loved you well, and still more the unspoken sorrow of those who stand around your bier, and that their love and regard may testify to you how bitter is their grief at their untimely loss, and how deep the affection with which they will cherish your memory in the years which are yet to come?

Edwards must have known Larkyns well, and many of the painful circumstances which surrounded his early life, as well as his life in California. Eight years later, in his book of memoirs, he printed the funeral oration and added a paragraph which humanizes Larkyns in a way no newspaper account of the time did:

The melancholy circumstances surrounding the death of Major Larkyns, which took place in October, 1874, are so fresh in the recollection as to need no further mention here. But the present opportunity is taken advantage of to allude to his great abilities, and to regret that the influences about him were such as to fetter their fullest action, and to prevent him from adorning more distinctly the walk of life in which he moved. Poverty always hung like a gaunt spectre about his footsteps, and the generous fountains of his nature were dried up by her touch. He walked among men as if they knew him not, and it was only the few who were admitted to a close intimacy with him who felt the warmth of that heart which showed its secrets but so rarely. He was an admirable linguist, familiar with the literature of most continental nations, — a brilliant writer, to whom no theme appeared to come amiss, — a musician of culture, — an artist of refined and polished taste, — and, as a conversationalist rarely excelled. Beyond all these, he was a warm and true friend, and where his sympathies were aroused, his generosity led him often far beyond the bounds of prudence. Many a story of his kindness to those in want is well known to his associates, and the recollection of his unselfish character is with them a sacred memory. He was followed to the grave by many who knew and loved him, and whose appreciation of his worth was evident by the depth of their sorrow. [2]

Larkyns' remains were taken to the Masonic Cemetery. "The body will not be interred," the Calistoga *Free Press* reported, "until the relatives have been heard from." If the relatives were in London, Larkyns may have been a long time above ground. In the half-dozen newspaper obituaries, the outlines of his romantic background were sketched. Accounts before the trial of Muybridge tended to emphasize Larkyns' "blameless character" and "tragic end."

According to the San Francisco *Examiner* of October 19, a friend went to Larkyns' room after the funeral to gather up and burn Flora's love letters. They were consigned to the flames at a time when the newspapers were offering big money for them. What the friend supplied, instead, was a poem which he said was found among Larkyns' effects:

WHO CAN TELL

How do we know what hearts have vilest sin,
How do we know?
Many like sepulchers are foul within
Whose outward garb is spotless as the snow.

[2] *A Mingled Yarn*, New York: Putnam, 1883, pp. 152-154.

And many may be pure we think not so.
How near to God the souls of men have been,
What mercy secret penitence may win,
How do we know?

How can we tell who have sinned more than we,
How can we tell?
We think our brother walked but guiltily
Judging him in self-righteousness, ah, well,
Perhaps had we been driven thru the hell
Of his temptation, we might be
Less upright in our daily walk, than he.
How can we tell?

Dare we condemn the ills that others do,
Dare we condemn?
Their strength is small: their trials are not few,
Their tide of wrong is difficult to stem,
And if to us, more clearly than to them
Is given knowledge of the good and true,
More do they need our help and pity, too,
Dare we condemn?

God help us all, and lead us day by day,
God help us all.
We cannot walk alone the perfect way;
Evil allures us, tempts us, and we fall;
We are but human, and our power is small.
Not one of us may boast and not a day
Rolls o'er our head, but each have need to pray
God help us all!

Larkyns was supposed to have written this "outpouring of a penitent sinner's heart." Seven years later a sharp reader of the local *Argonaut* would have found the same poem, slightly amended, run as an anonymous contribution. [3] This time it was called "Judge Not." Of such stuff were sinners' funerals made in San Francisco.

[3] Issue of March 5, 1881.

69. The Napa County courthouse and jail where Muybridge was imprisoned 1874-1875.

14. Napa Jail (1874~1875)

Muybridge was indicted by a grand jury on December 8, 1874, for "feloniously, willfully, unlawfully, and of his malice aforethought" killing and murdering Harry Larkyns. The defendant pleaded not guilty, and his counsel entered a plea of insanity. The trial was set for February of the coming year.

A week after the indictment, Flora Muybridge, who had returned from Oregon, filed a complaint in the district court at San Francisco for a divorce from Eadweard Muybridge on the grounds of extreme cruelty. She asked alimony of a hundred dollars a month, and estimated her husband's financial worth at five to ten thousand dollars. The judge dismissed the complaint and denied the plea for alimony.[1]

During the same week Muybridge gave his first interview to the press. He had told the Napa jailer that he did not want to see reporters, but when George Smith of the San Francisco *Chronicle*, "being in Napa," happened to present himself at the jail, Muybridge immediately changed his mind and granted a long interview.

Muybridge met Smith in the corridor of the jail with an air of cheerfulness and good health, although he looked somewhat paler than usual. His full gray beard was unkempt and his hair was almost white. Smith thought he looked ten years more than his age. Muybrdige's eyes did not impress Smith as those of a killer. He was so plainly dressed that the reporter characterized him as a "quiet, good-natured old farmer."

The prisoner conversed freely about the homicide and its causes, "only making occasional stipulations regarding the publication of certain statements" which he thought might anticipate his defense at the trial. He began with his stay in the jail. He said "I am quite comfortably situated here. I have one of the best cells in the prison; have it comfortably furnished, and have books, papers and writing material in plenty to divert myself with. My meals are sent to me from a hotel, and I have everything I want to eat." He expressed his appreciation for the consideration the sheriff and the jailer had shown him.

Smith then asked Muybridge whether his friends had visited him since the murder. Muybridge replied, "Many of them have, and I have received a great many letters from others — piles of them — expressing sympathy with me. Some have been from people I do not know. I have received many offers of assistance, in several

[1] *Call*, San Francisco, January 9, 1875; *Daily Register*, Napa, Calif., January 16.

cases from influential and wealthy men in San Francisco with whom I had previously no personal acquaintance. One of them was here yesterday, and offered to go upon my bail bond for all he was worth and to procure others to bail me for $100,000 if I would make the application." His counsel had advised him to forego bail to avoid disclosing evidence before the trial. Satisfied that he had not lost one friend by his action against Larkyns, but rather gained some, he was willing to wait.

He now begged Smith to set to right some of the misstatements regarding himself that had appeared in accounts of the murder: "For instance, it was stated that I was in the employ of Bradley and Rulofson. I was attached to their establishment but was conducting my branch of the business on my own account." Smith expressed the interest of himself and his employer, Charles De Young, in printing the truth about Muybridge, and obtained the following interview:

REPORTER: How and when did you form the Major's acquaintance?
MUYBRIDGE: In the early part of 1873 he came into the gallery when I was at work. Mr. Rulofson and Mr. Max Burkhardt, who were employed in the gallery, had known him for some time previous to that. He wanted to get some of my views for some purpose he had in mind, I do not now remember what. My wife, who sometimes worked in the gallery a little, touching up pictures, was present, and she introduced him to me. I had frequently heard her speak of Major Larkyns before but did not know that she was much acquainted with him — but it seems they were better acquainted than I expected they were. She afterward told me that she was introduced to him at the house of [a] produce dealer who resides at South Park, with whom I am acquainted. After his introduction to me he frequently came up to the gallery, and I often gave him points in regard to art matters which he was then writing about for the Post. *He was under such obligations to me frequently, and as a return he was always trying to get me to take passes to the theatre, of which he said he had plenty. I didn't want to accept them from him. In fact, I am not much of a man to take favors from anybody. I seldom go to the theatre, and when I do I am always willing to pay for it. Besides, I did not fancy the Major's style of man, and did not feel like placing myself under obligation to him.*

But he insisted so often and so strongly that one day I accepted passes from him, and in the evening myself and wife went with him to the California Theatre. After the play he and I had a drink of whiskey together and he accompanied us home. I did not invite him to come and see me, for the reason I have given you; but he came to my house once on some matter of business. I never invited him to come as a friend, and I had no idea that he

*ever came in my absence. I did not know or suspect that he was
visiting my wife or even went anywhere with her. But one night,
while Neilson was playing her engagement here, my wife was out
when I got home, and did not come in until late. I asked her
where she had been, and she said, "To the theatre with Major
Larkyns." I then said earnestly, "Now, look here, Flo, I don't
want you to be going out with any man at night without my
knowledge or consent. It is not proper, and will bring you into
scandal if you persist in it. Now, do you never go out with him in
that way again." She promised me solemnly and faithfully that
she would not.*

*The next morning I went to see Larkyns about it. I met him on
Montgomery Street just coming down from his rooms, and he
said quite gaily, "Good morning, Mr. Muybridge." I said, "I hear
that you were at the theatre with my wife last night." "Yes," said
he, "but I didn't think there was any harm in that." I said, "You
know very well that, as a married woman, it is not proper to
her to be running about at night with you or with any other man
but me, and I want you to let her alone. Do you never take her
out in that way again. You know my right to speak in this
matter. You know my right in the premises as a married man. So
do I, and I shall defend them. If you transgress them after this
morning I shall hold you to the consequences, and I suppose you
know what that means in California." "Oh yes," said he, "and
if there is any objection on your part to her going out with me, I
will take her out no more."*

*Then we parted, and I supposed that they had kept their
promise to me. I had no idea that my wife had ever went with
him again or that there was anything wrong between them until
I got those letters from the nurse on the morning of the day on
which the shooting was done. I never had entertained any
suspicion that my wife was guilty of infidelity to me with him
or any other man until that time. But the letters from her to
him and from him to her left me no room for doubt. I was thrown
completely off my balance. The revelation was like a stroke of
lightning to me. I objected to the plea of insanity when it was
made because I thought a man to be crazy must not know what
he was doing, and I knew what I was doing. I was beside myself
with rage and indignation, and resolved to avenge my dishonor.
I said to Rulofson on that morning — and my words have been
mistaken in that respect by him — "One of us will be shot." I
did not say as he states, "One of us must die," but he said, "For
God's sake don't kill him," and I answered, "One of us will be
shot." I took the first boat for Vallejo resolved to seek him at
Calistoga and punish him for the injury he had done me. I had
no idea that I should come back from Calistoga alive. I thought
that I should find him armed, as I supposed that such men would
always be prepared for the consequences of their wrongdoings.
I expected that a fight would ensue, and that I should probably
be shot by him even if I killed him. My pistol had not been
discharged for months before.*

*I found out where he was staying and went to the door of
the house, knocked and asked to see him. As soon as he came to
the door I said to him, "My name is Muybridge; I have received
a message about my wife —" Before I could say more he started
to retreat into the house although I had made no demonstration
against him. I saw that he would be gone in a moment and that
I must act on the instant or he would escape me; so I fired on
him. I did not intend to shoot him at once, but thought to parley
with him and hear what he had to say in excuse or extenuation,
but he turned and ran like a guilty craven when I pronounced
my name and said I had heard about my wife, and I had to shoot
him so or let him go unpunished. The only thing I am sorry
for in connection with the affair is that he died so quickly. I
would have wished that he could have lived long enough at least
to acknowledge the wrong he had done me, that his punishment
was deserved and that my act was a justifiable defense of my
marital rights.*

REPORTER: *You said you had no suspicion of your wife's
infidelity before you saw these letters on the day of the shooting,
and yet it is generally understood that you sent her to Oregon
to get her away from Larkyns. How is that?*

MUYBRIDGE: *Nothing of the kind. I will tell you why my
wife went to Oregon. I had been negotiating several months with
the Pacific Mail Steamship Company for a trip down the coast
on one of their steamers to photograph the coast. I had my
arrangements completed and expected to go in a short time, but
the agent of the company delayed from time to time, and I did
not get away as I expected to. My wife had no relatives in the
city, and I did not like to leave her alone with her baby while I
was gone on a trip from which I should probably not return in less
than five or six months. So I told her I would send her up to
Oregon to be with her uncle who was living in Portland, and gave
her money to pay her expenses there while I was away if she would
go. She consented, and I gave her the money.*

REPORTER: *Previous to your acquaintance with Larkyns
had you and your wife lived happily together?*

MUYBRIDGE: *Yes, we never had any trouble to speak of. We
sometimes had little disputes about money matters, but they were
not serious. I was always a man of very simple tastes and few
wants, and I did not spend much money. What I had left after
paying my little expenses I gave to her, and yet she was always
wanting more. I could never see that she bought anything with it
to speak of, or imagine what she did with it. We sometimes had
little spats about the money, but nothing serious — nothing more
than married people have every day and forget the next. I told her
that I would allow her $50 per month while she was in Oregon;
that sum was sufficient to support her and the baby comfortably,
and if she wanted more she could easily earn as much as that by
her wax-work, at which she was very proficient, and by touching
up photographs which she did pretty well. She took the money and
sailed in June and remained there until she heard of the shooting
of Larkyns. I had no intimation or suspicion that there was
anything wrong between her and Larkyns until I received the
letters from the nurse. But since the shooting I have been told
many things to which, in my confidence in my wife, I was
previously blind. Friends whom I should have expected to inform
me when they saw how I was being deceived have since this affair*

told me all. Among other things I have ascertained on undoubted authority that the money which I used to give her and which I could never see what she did with, she gave to Larkyns. That explains what used to puzzle me — how he managed to live in such style as he did on the salary he got from the **Post.** *He sometimes sent her theatre passes with which she told me she used to go to matinees with Mrs. Selleck and Mrs. Armstrong and her daughters. I have since ascertained that on occasions she went to fulfill assignations with Larkyns. I was away from home a great deal, and being unsuspicious when at home, it was an easy matter for them to deceive me.*

REPORTER: *Have you seen your wife since the shooting.*

MUYBRIDGE: *No, and I do not expect or desire her to come and see me. I have heard that she is in the city, but we are now, of course, completely estranged, and I do not desire to see her again. Having deceived me so cruelly, I can never have any confidence in her. I am prepared to expect anything from her, even to her taking part with the prosecution at my trial. But I am not afraid of anything they can bring against me. I have lived here over twenty years, and am well known. They may ransack my record as much as they please, and I defy them to bring anything against me.*

REPORTER: *Your wife was divorced before you married her?*

MUYBRIDGE: *Yes.*

REPORTER: *It is intimated that you were the means of her estrangement from her husband, that you instigated and assisted her to get a divorce for the purpose of marrying her; that you knew her character before you married her, and that her alienation from you by Larkyns was of a piece with your conduct when she was Mr. Stone's wife.*

MUYBRIDGE: *All of which is untrue. I never had any agency in getting her divorce. I never counseled her to get it, and did not assist her in any way. She was working in Nahl's gallery where I was engaged at the time, and I was acquainted with her in this way, but not intimately. We were married a few months after she got her divorce. She told me that the trouble between her and Stone was inequality of age — she is now but twenty-three — incompatability of temper and cruel treatment of her by him and his mother. I never before or since this affair knew or heard anything against her chastity. I loved the woman with all my heart and soul, and the revelation of her infidelity was a cruel, prostrating blow to me, shattering my idol and blighting the bright affection of my life. I have no fear of the result of my trial. I feel that I was justified in what I did, and that all right-minded people will justify my action. I am ready and anxious to be tried tomorrow, if possible. There will be no appeal for delay in my case, I assure you.*[2]

[2] Issue of December 21, 1874.

For the most part Muybridge was pleased with Smith's treatment of the interview. On a few points he felt compelled to explain himself further in a confidential letter posted to Smith from the Napa jail on the same day that the article appeared:

I am obliged for your elaborate and upon the whole **correct** *report of our interview, I had no idea you intended making it so voluminous, or I should not have requested the favor of your making no* **notes.** *The consequence of your writing it altogether from memory are two or three errors,* **one** *of which only is perhaps important. With regard to your report of what "I expected from my wife at my trial." It should be "*I am told to be prepared to expect anything of her." *Etc. This you will see is a very important correction, and unless so represented may unnecessarily* **exasperate,** *when I have every wish to* **conciliate.** *For my wife's present position I have the most sincere pity. I have never thought other than that she was the unwilling victim of her seducer's perfidy.*

*With regard to my interview with Larkyns. I ordered him not only never to go out with my wife, but "*never to speak to her or recognize his acquaintance with her under any circumstances or wherever he saw her." *These were my words.*

My wife gave me the same promise. He *pledged his word not to do so on his "*honor as a **gentleman."**

With regard to my "regret" — I said that "I had **expressed** *no other regret" Etc.*

What regret I may feel, my heart alone knows.

If you will be kind enough to make these corrections — which would naturally occur in your omitting to jot the items down at the time — I shall feel much indebted to you. I will ask you **not** *to mention that I had corrected them myself, for reasons you will appreciate at once.*

Be kind enough to tender my grateful thanks to Mr. De Young for the interest he has manifested in my case, and in the impartiality and justice with which he views it. For this he will however probably reply he wants no thanks for his duty to the public. They are his all the same.[3]

Smith's article was generally considered to have influenced public opinion in Muybridge's favor. What happened at the trial itself was another matter.

[3] Addressed to "Mr. Smith, Reporter, 'Chronicle' Office, San Francisco"; original in courthouse at Napa. Published in the *Chronicle,* January 21, 1875.

Muybridge's trial for the murder of Larkyns was held during the first week of February 1875. The press was amply represented in the courtroom: James Hutchings of the Sacramento *Union*, Larkyns's old friend Sam Davis of the San Francisco *Post* and *Chronicle*, and H. C. McLean of the *Call* and *Bulletin;* the *Examiner* and the Napa *Daily Register* also had men on the spot. A shorthand reporter for the district court took down the proceedings and was paid $150 for his work.

The legal talent was impressive. The prosecuting attorney, Dennis Spencer, had asked for assistance, knowing his own limitations. The county supervisors reluctantly granted an appropriation because of the importance of the case, and the court appointed Judge Thomas P. Stoney as assistant counsel. Muybridge was defended by Cameron King and Wirt Pendegast, with Pendegast's partner F. E. Johnston added. The presiding judge was William T. Wallace, chief justice of the Supreme Court of California.

William Wirt Pendegast was a notably gifted lawyer, still young. At twenty-six he had been elected to the California State Senate, where he was an acknowledged leader and at the time of the trial was serving his fourth term. "His oratory was splendid. His person was handsome. . . . His vigorous intellect, comprehensive grasp of mind, quickness of apprehension and promptness in dispatching business, added to great urbanity of manner, gave him a commanding influence."[1]

Most of the morning of Wednesday, February 3, was taken up with impaneling the jury. Then Stoney, in an opening statement to the jury, made an eloquent summary of the evidence to be presented. He wished to demonstrate that Muybridge was guilty of murder in the first degree, or guilty of nothing. He read the statute defining murder, from which definition he deduced the prisoner to be "just as guilty as possible," adding that self-defense could not be claimed as a means of excusing Muybridge.

Four witnesses were called to support this line of argument. Dr. Reid recounted how he had been called to the Yellow Jacket mine on the night of October 17 to attend a wounded man, whom he found dead. In his opinion, Larkyns could not have lived more than twenty seconds after he was shot. Next, the stableman gave testimony that he had supplied Muybridge with a wagon, team, and driver that night and had directed him to the home of William

Stewart near the mine. Prickett testified that he had called Larkyns to the door at Muybridge's request. He did not see the fatal shot. Another witness offered substantially the same story. The court was then adjourned until the next morning, when three more witnesses for the prosecution appeared.

A miner told how he had overheard the exchange of words between Larkyns and Muybridge, and how after the murder he had helped carry the body inside. Another described how Muybridge had entered the house. This miner had disarmed him and been one of the guards on the return trip to Calistoga. Young George Wolfe reported his conversation with Muybridge on the way to the mine and the request about firing the pistol.

Cameron King made the opening statement for the defense. He outlined the evidence that he intended to present to vindicate his client. The defense did not deny the killing, but proposed to establish it as justifiable homicide and to plead insanity on the part of the defendant. King dwelt upon the wrongs Larkyns had done, the agony he had caused Muybridge, and the "mental aberration which had of late years appeared" in his client, claiming the blow in the head that Muybridge received in the 1860 stagecoach wreck as the basic cause.

Then began the hearing of the witnesses for the defense. Susan Smith, according to the Napa *Register*, "gave her testimony readily and unconfusedly, and seemed to have about as clear a view of the situation as the attorneys themselves. . . . She talked with vigor and at times rose with the excitement of her story and delivered it with considerable dramatic effect." She elaborated on Muybridge's reaction to her revelation about the love affair; he was struck *dumb* with grief; he staggered; he gasped; he threw himself upon the sofa; tears started from his eyes, perspiration from his skin; he cried, "Flora, if you did not love me, you might at least have respected me too much to put that man in my shoes."

Here the marriage license of Muybridge and Flora was shown.[2] Photographs of Flora and of "Little Harry" were introduced. The "guilty letters" were read aloud.

Louisa Smith, continuing the story in the same vein as her mother, testified that Muybridge had been kind and affectionate with Flora, had given her plenty of money, and was indulgent. She told as well of his "eccentric habits" and peculiarities, of his nervousness and excitability.

William Herman Rulofson was next called. He was San Francisco's

---

[1] From remarks of Judge Stoney at the memorial service for Pendegast held by the Napa County Bar Association in March 1876; in papers of Janet Pendegast Leigh, daughter of Wirt Pendegast, now in my possession.

[2] The actual date of the marriage has not been discovered.

society photographer, popular, affluent, and genial, but something of a showman. He said he did not think Muybridge perfectly sane. He claimed that before 1860 Muybridge was pleasant, gentlemanly, and a good businessman. After the accident he was careless of money, receipting bills for his clients when they protested the charges. Rulofson also thought no sane man would stand on the brink of a precipice in the Yosemite Valley, to be photographed 3,400 feet above the valley floor, as Muybridge had done. He could not understand why Muybridge would refuse to take a picture which did not happen to suit his artistic tastes, no matter how much money he was offered to do it. Rulofson said it would take two years to tell all the reasons he had for believing in Muybridge's insanity.

Muybridge never forgave this performance. Although Rulofson had no doubt been advised by Muybridge's lawyers to strengthen the case for "insanity," something in his tone cut too close. After the trial Muybridge changed his gallery affiliation at once and never returned to Bradley and Rulofson's.

John Wentworth, editor and publisher of *Resources of California*, testified that he had known Muybridge intimately for eighteen years. He told of the great impatience Muybridge showed in ordinary business transactions when coolness would have been necessary to success. Silas Selleck, who had known Muybridge for a quarter century, called him "eccentric and wavering." He stated that Muybridge on returning from Europe in 1867 with new photographic supplies refused to sell him any but told him to make free use of them as if they were his own. Joseph Eastland, with whom Muybridge had served on the board of the Mercantile Library, admitted to noticing a "change" in Muybridge's behavior after the coach accident, but added that he had never known him to do violence to any person although he was often justifiably excited.

The trial passed into its third day, February 5, and Muybridge himself was finally put on the stand. He related the story of his injuries on his trip east in 1860. It was true that he had been sorely hurt and that whereas his health had always been excellent before the accident, he was now subject to frequent headaches. He said nothing more, and he was not cross-examined.[3] Wirt Pendergast then stated to the court that the testimony for the defense was complete.

The carefully presented case for Muybridge's sanity was now made subject to rebuttal. Dr. C. H. Shurtleff of the Stockton

[3] The *Chronicle,* February 6, reported that "upon his request, which was in accord with the secret policy of his lawyers," Muybridge was "not asked anything about his wife and the circumstances of the killing of Larkyns."

70. Detail of a Yosemite view by Muybridge, which shows him "on the brink of a precipice" where "no sane man would venture . . . ," as William Herman Rulofson stated, during his testimony as a witness, in an attempt to establish the plea of insanity which Muybridge subsequently rejected.

Insane Asylum was called to give expert testimony. While Shurtleff
was acquainting himself with the case, and before his statement
was introduced, the evidence of five or six other witnesses was
taken about Muybridge's state of mind before and after the killing.
Harry Edwards, the actor who delivered the eulogy for Larkyns,
stated that he had met Muybridge on the afternoon of the killing,
passed the time of day with him, and noticed nothing unusual
in his appearance or conduct. George Wolfe was called again; he
had seen "nothing unusual" in Muybridge's manner. The guard
testified that Muybridge was "exceedingly cool, collected,
and deliberate" after the murder: "In the barroom at Calistoga Mr.
Stewart asked us all to have a drink — Muybridge among the rest.
I noticed his hand as he raised the bottle to pour out his drink,
as a matter of curiosity, and it was unusually steady. When I took
his pistol from him at the time of the shooting, I noticed the
same thing." A Calistoga constable testified that Muybridge was
delivered into his custody when he was brought from the scene
of the homicide: "He was very cool — much cooler than I should
be if I had just killed a man, or than I think most any other
man would be." Two others were called by the prosecution to
show that Muybridge clearly knew what he was doing at the time
of the shooting and therefore could not be judged insane. Rulofson,
however, described flashes of temperament in which Muybridge
would "give way to bursts of grief; then become, by turns,
suddenly greatly excited and cool, immovable as stone." The
sheriff told of Muybridge's great excitement and anger when he

"learned that the District Attorney had been down to San
Francisco interviewing his wife to get testimony against him,"
and how he had said that he would denounce the district attorney
in court for it.

All this testimony only added to the anticipation of the doctor's
appearance in court. Stoney put to Shurtleff the question, "What
would you say as to the prisoner's mental condition at the time
of the act?"

To this Shurtleff replied, "There is nothing that would convince
me of his insanity. I have read the interview with him published in
the *Chronicle*. It shows me that the killing was premeditated, and I
see no indication of insanity. I think from that that he understood
the nature of the act, its unlawfulness and the consequences, but
he felt justified in committing it. . . . I am of the opinion that at
the time of the killing he was a sane man." This testimony, despite
a spirited rebuttal by King, blasted the plan of the defense to
press the plea of insanity.

Muybridge's fate hung in a delicate balance. Today the very
symptoms detailed by the state's witnesses — immobility, sudden
contrasts of excitement and no excitement, "coolness" — might
be taken as evidence of temporary insanity. In 1875, to be calm,
cool, and collected was to be a healthy man.

Thus when the testimony in the case was closed, and prosecution
and defense had summoned all their powers of oratory for their
last appeals to the jury, the question became simply, "Was the
homicide justifiable or not?"

16. Verdict (1875)

On the afternoon of February 5, Stoney began the argument for
the prosecution. He spoke for more than an hour, with great
clearness and force of reasoning. Well aware that juries do not like
to convict a man who has been wronged and who then avenges
himself, Stoney took the position that the defendant was guilty
of murder in the first degree unless he could make the defense of
insanity. Stoney discussed Muybridge's state of mind at great
length, contending that he was sane at the time of the murder. If
so, the murder was premeditated and, therefore, murder in the
first degree. If the jury did not find the act of murder the act of
an insane man, then the jury's duty would be to find Muybridge
guilty, as charged in the indictment.

The climax of the trial was reached during the long evening
session. In the opening statement for the defense, King delcared:
"There are six witnesses for one against. . . . If Dr. Shurtleff had

heard the testimony . . . rather than merely [heard] it read, his
opinion of the defendant's sanity would have been different. . . .
If you do not believe that all of those six witnesses perjured
themselves, you must acquit the prisoner."

He then took up the main issue. Was Muybridge's act justified?
"Was not the information Muybridge received on the morning
of the homicide sufficient to impel him to insanity and the rash
act of homicide?" King argued that although the word "insanity"
does not occur in the Bible, its passions are nevertheless
provided for: " 'The man that committeth adultery with another
man's wife, even he that committeth adultery shall surely be
put to death. So shalt thou put away evil from Israel.' Though
this be not the law of California, I believe it is the sane moral
guide."

After citing Biblical authority, King shifted to a personal appeal:

"It has been said I have worked long and arduously on this case. I feel a deep interest in it. The prisoner is my friend. I love him as such. He has a noble, honest heart; his life's work is done, and he seeks now only an honorable grave in which to lie down to blissful forgetfulness for all his troubles. . . . If you love virtue, good women, home and fireside, acquit him, and teach the libertine that in this state, at least, the purity and sanctity of the domestic hearth will be preserved inviolate."

All this was but the warm-up for the extravagant forensic effort expected of Wirt Pendegast. He spoke for two uninterrupted hours. He began by agreeing with Stoney that the prisoner at the bar was either guilty of murder in the first degree or guilty of nothing. "He deserves absolute freedom, or he deserves death. Between the two ye are the judges." He agreed that Muybridge took the life of Harry Larkyns and took it in "no self defense." Yet there was another side to be considered — the character of the defendant: "He loved his wife; recognized the difference in their tastes and habits, and granted her every privilege which a loving and devoted husband could grant a loved wife. Then what a great shock to discover that his wife had fallen — had betrayed him — and undone the happiness of his life."

Pendegast began to move into the great line of his argument: "Has, in the face of all this, the prosecution read cold law to you and [said] there is 'no law' for vengeance for such wrongs? There was no law because there was no need for it. . . . It was provided by a higher one. Neither is there a law to compel a mother to give her nourishment to a child, though it perish for want of it. Such cases are covered by the higher law of God and Nature. Even Stoney was moved. Later he described Pendegast's unforgettable power at this moment: "In one memorable case, fresh in our minds, in this courtroom, with the evidence overwhelmingly establishing the guilt of his client, and with the law confronting him on every side, he exhorted from the jury a verdict . . . not by perverting the facts, nor by distorting the law, but by raising the minds of the twelve men whom he addressed, *above* the influence of the law and the facts."[1]

Pendegast brushed aside the issue of insanity and continued: "It is the weakness of the law that there is no adequate punishment for the seducer." He read from the statute to show what justifiable homicide is: "The statute gives a man in much less case a right to kill, why not in this when so infinitely greater wrong was done?" The atmosphere in the courtroom was electric. Muybridge was violently convulsed throughout the speech.

His head trembled as he held his hands before his eyes and sobbed with grief.

Pendegast's peroration was an eloquent appeal to the feelings of his audience:

I cannot ask you to send this man forth to family and home — he has none. Across the arch of his fireplace where once was written the words "Home, Wife, Child, Content and Peace," there now appears as a substitute for all, in black letters, placed there by the destroyer, the single, awful word DESOLATION. But I do ask you to send him forth free — let him take up the thread of his broken life, and resume that profession upon which his genius has shed so much lustre — the profession which is now his only love. . . . Do this, but this, and from every peaceful household, and from every quiet home within the state there will come to your verdict the echo of a solemn and a deep Amen![2]

As Pendegast closed his address, the building shook with applause.

At half-past nine Dennis Spencer, the district attorney closed for the prosecution. Brief and to the point, he appealed to the jury to do its duty. Judge Wallace then read his instructions to the jury. They were lengthy and carefully reasoned. The jury went out at a quarter to ten. At eleven-fifteen, when it had not returned, the court was adjourned untill morning. Crowds waited outside the courthouse through the morning of February 6. When it was understood that a verdict had been reached, after thirteen hours of deliberations, Muybridge was brought from his cell to hear it.

The clerk called the names of the jurymen and asked, "Gentlemen of the jury, have you agreed on a verdict?"

"We have," replied the foreman. He passed the clerk a slip of paper. The clerk unfolded it amid a deathly silence, perused it, passed it on to the judge, and asked, "Gentlemen of the jury, is this your verdict?" The foreman replied that it was.

"Record the verdict," directed Judge Wallace. The pen of the clerk flew nervously over the paper before him. All eyes were fastened on his work. Suddenly the pen stopped moving. Rising, the clerk read from his book. "Gentlemen of the jury, listen to your verdict as it stands recorded. 'The People of the State of California versus Eadweard J. Muybridge.' We the jury find the defendant — not guilty!"

Muybridge sank forward in his chair and Pendegast caught him in his arms to prevent his falling on the floor. Then Muybridge wept convulsively, but neither in joy nor pain. He was "prepared for anything," he said, "except for what he most desired." Pendegast begged Muybridge to control himself and to thank the

[1] See chap. 15, n. 1.

[2] *Daily Register*, Napa, February 6, 1875.

jury. He rose and tried to speak, but sank back and was carried from the courtroom to a couch in the judge's chambers. A doctor was sent for, but before he arrived Muybridge had recovered his composure.

Judge Wallace, overcome, had left the courtroom. He had to be recalled to the bench to discharge the jury and conclude the proceedings. Upon motion of Pendegast, Muybridge was discharged from custody. He was cheered wildly as he left the courthouse, a free man. The editor of the Napa *Register* put the final words: "The seducer is an outlaw, and an injured husband may be the avenger of his own wrongs — even to the taking of human life." The brilliant defense of Mr. Pendegast, he concluded, was such an effort as is seldom heard in a lifetime.

After the conclusion of the case it was determined how the jurymen had deliberated. The first ballot showed five for conviction and seven for acquittal. One had taken off his coat and, making a pillow of it, "told his fellow jurymen when they came to adopt a certain view of the case, to awaken him, swearing, in effect, to stay there until Resurrection day rather than to acquiesce to any other view." The rest discussed currency, taxation, fees, and "other relevant questions." The sheriff was the only one awake during the latter part of the night.

At breakfast one juryman remarked that he was willing to stay three days rather than change his mind. Another ballot was taken, with the same result as the first. "The difference between them was on the question of insanity. Few, if any, of them, believed Muybridge insane . . . and the majority contended that they cared nothing about his sanity or insanity; that, sane or insane, Muybridge was justified in killing Larkyns for having seduced his wife, and they, if placed in the same or similar circumstances, would have done as he did." Upon this they all agreed. Their only quarrel was now with the form of the verdict, not guilty, or not guilty by reason of insanity. "A ballot was taken, and to the surprise of every one of them, although five minutes before they had no expectation of ever agreeing, they all fell into line, and on counting the ballots it was found they had agreed on a verdict."[3]

Muybridge was vindicated. He returned to San Francisco with his friends to find they had been so sure of victory that a banquet had been arranged for that evening in his honor.

[3] Ibid., February 8.

71. The verdict of the jury, from the trial minutes, February 6, 1875.

PART FOUR:
Recovery and Return

17. Central America and the Isthmus of Panama (1875-1876)

During the long, depressing weeks of custody in the Napa jail, Muybridge formed a plan for an extended photographic tour in Central America and across the Isthmus of Panama. Upon his release, friends encouraged the plan as a way to resolve his domestic situation. Flora had tried once more for a divorce and failed again.[1] Now Muybridge turned his back on both her and the child.

Arrangements for the trip appear to have been made rather quickly with the Pacific Mail Steamship Company — his sponsors, as Muybridge called them. On February 19, 1875, he sailed on one of the company's ships from their wharf at the foot of First and Brannan streets. A leisurely course took the ship to Cape San Lucas, at the tip of Lower California, and to Mazatlán, Manzanillo, Acapulco, and other ports on the Mexican west coast. The climate became increasingly warm, and the landscape rich, lush, and flamboyantly tropical. By March, the coast of Central America was passed and Panama was reached. Between March and November, Muybridge secured superb photographic views there and in the towns of Colón and Chagres on the Atlantic side, and in Guatemala and El Salvador.

The Isthmian rail route, much used by travelers to and from California in Gold Rush days and afterward, had now largely been replaced by the transcontinental railroad. The Panama Railroad Company had its most prosperous year in 1868, but by 1872 its income from passenger and freight charges alike had fallen off alarmingly. Thus the Pacific Mail Steamship Company, with its business greatly reduced also, was eager to stimulate Central and South American commerce, and to interest capitalists and tourists in visiting the countries of the area.[2]

Panama, a once proud city, had sunk to a state of apathy. "It had no foreign commerce and very little trade. A few members of some of the leading families of Spanish ancestry were sent abroad to be educated; but for the most part, poverty or indifference or both kept the inhabitants captive within their picturesque old walls."[3] As Muybridge began his photographic work, the Panama *Star* explained his mission: "It is gratifying to know that he comes now to illustrate by view all the curious places that a traveller by Railroad and Pacific Mail Company's ships can see or be within reach of in a journey from New York to San Francisco via the Isthmus. We have no doubt Mr. Muybridge will find around Panama many views worthy of his peculiar photographic talent."[4]

Beginning in Colón (or as it was often called at the time, Aspinwall, after W. H. Aspinwall, one of the three early promoters of the railway across the isthmus), Muybridge photographed the

[1] *Call,* San Francisco, January 9, 1875. In the small town of Mariposa, near Yosemite Valley, the *Gazette* in April reported that Muybridge had "gone to Central America to photograph the scenery," and had "eluded the attachment of his divorced wife, who had decided upon a summary proceeding to get alimony" (information from Mary V. Hood).

[2] Tracy Robinson, *Panama, 1861-1907,* New York: Trow Press, 1907, p. 53.
[3] Ibid., pp. 1-2.
[4] Issue of March 10, 1875; in Scrapbook.

new "Lighthouse," the "P.M.S.S. Co.'s Wharf," the town as seen from the Lighthouse, the "Statue of Columbus given by the Empress Eugenie" (in its original setting in the railraod yard), the "Monument to Aspinwall, Chauncey and Stephens," and several views of the roads along the beach showing palm trees and aspects of the inhabitants' everyday life.[5] Chagres produced views of "The City Front" and "The Principal Street," showing native dwellings of the most primitive sort, and a very pictorial study, "Entrance to Fort."

Panama City provided far richer fare. Muybridge took the obligatory waterfront scenes and a series of about a dozen views entitled "A walk around the walls," showing the "Palace of the President," "Cabildo," "Grand Hotel," "Grand Central Hotel," and "Pacific Mail Steamship office." Everyday life was recorded in such views as "Native Hut," "Laundry," and "Water Carrier," and magnificent architecture in "Cathedral" and in the ruined churches of the Spanish Colonial period: "Church of La Merced," "Church of San Francisco," "Church of San Felipe," "Church of Santa Ana," and "Church of San Jose." Scenes of Old Panama appear in "Church of Los Monjas," "Water Tower," and "Bridge on Porto Bello Road."

The *Star* again mentioned Muybridge's work, two months later:

Mr. Muybridge the celebrated photographic artist from San Francisco, who has been here for some time back, and has made a large collection of negatives of all the buildings, old castles, and picturesque spots to be found in this part of the Isthmus between Aspinwall and Panama, will take his departure today in the steamship Honduras for Guatemala. One must see the splendid results of Mr. Muybridge's special talent in such matters to appreciate the value of such pictures and the pleasure to be expected from such models of photographic landscapes when they are printed and given to the public. We can therefore congratulate all Central Americans that in Mr. Muybridge they have an artist who will do for their interesting section of America what has never been so well done for it before, either by pen or pencil, in making it become known. . . . We heartily recommend [him] to our friends and to all lovers of Art, official or private, in any part of Central America to which he may be able to carry his photographic apparatus, his talents, and his commendable social as well as artistic qualities.[6]

[5] All the quoted titles are those printed on the stereograph cards or written on Muybridge's album labels.

In a brochure (in Scrapbook), the entire series is designated "Central America and Isthmus of Panama Illustrated by Muybridge, 618 and 620 Clay St., San Francisco, California. Published by Henry Ehrman, Panama." The San Francisco address is that of the photographic supply house of Henry W. Bradley, run independently of Bradley and Rulofson's gallery. Ehrman was the agent of Wells, Fargo and Co., in Panama from 1873 to 1898. See chap. 1, n. 2.

[6] May 1, 1875; in Scrapbook.

Muybridge was in Guatemala for about six months. During that time he took about 400 photographs of the country and the activities of its people. His most extensive coverage was of Guatemala City, beginning with a kind of panorama, "Guatemala from the South" and "Guatemala from the Cerro del Carmen." There are numerous handsome views of the city center: "Cathedral," "National Theatre," "Prison," "Laundry of Calvario," "Castle of San Jose," "National Bank," "Public Market," and "Church of San Francisco," among others. A few rural scenes of great beauty include "Baranca of Ynsiensi" and "Ancient Sacrificial Stone."

Quezaltenango yielded "Cabildo, Cathedral, and Volcan," numerous photographs of the crater of the volcano, and "Church of the Calvario," the volcanic "Baths of Amolongo," and "Bridge across the Ocosito River" at Retalhuleu. Mazatenango produced river views and an untitled village street scene. Antigua is represented by a dozen views, including "Palace of the Viceroy," "Church of El Carmen," "The Cabildo," and a panorama.

Las Nubes produced two curious views of the "Matapala Tree." In the vicinity of Las Nubes and San Isidro Muybridge photographed stages in the production of coffee: "Harvesting at San Isidro," "Bringing in the day's crop at San Isidro," "Drying the berries on the Patio at Las Nubes," and "Loading carts for the port at Las Nubes." The Las Nubes scenes were photographed at the hacienda of William Nelson, commercial agent of the Pacific Mail Steamship Company at Panama City, who "began at an early day to make investments on his own account in Guatemala, which made him rich."[7]

Before leaving Guatemala, Muybridge prepared a two-page circular in Spanish describing his work and listing the Central American views that were available for purchase. He was now "Sr. D. Eduardo Santiago Muybridge." He also offered for sale his "vistas" of San Francisco, the Geysers, Yosemite Valley, the Big Trees, and the railroads.[8] Some further views were obtained in El Salvador — "La Union, from the wharf," "Cathedral," and "Army of Salvador" — before he returned to Panama for a final stay.

Here he hoped to market his Central American work for a substantial profit and to prepare special albums of views for the Pacific Mail Steamship Company. Again the *Star* carried a notice of his work:

Mr. E. S. Muybridge, well known in Panama, where he was daily seen a few months ago in the streets and about the walls of the city, with his apparatus for taking photographic landscapes

[7] Robinson, *Panama, 1861-1907*, p. 64.

[8] In Scrapbook.

and views, has returned to this place. Since he left us Mr. Muybridge has made the tour of the Republic of Guatemala, during which time he has taken 400 pictures of all that is to be seen remarkable in that country. The most interesting of Mr. Muybridge's labors in this way is perhaps, a series of 20 views illustrative of the cultivation of coffee in all its stages from the time the forest is cleared away to receive the seed, all along until the crop is ready to be embarked.

Mr. Muybridge has also with him some 80 specimen pictures of views taken in and about Panama, with all its public buildings and curious ruins. His views of Old Panama, which are superior to any taken before, were obtained at the expense of clearing away the trees and brushwood that concealed ruins of the highest interest. . . . Mr. M. will be here for some days previous to his departure for San Francisco. Those who take an interest in the fine arts and at the same time wish to obtain a series of views which will in fact constitute a pictorial history of Panama as seen in 1875, can see the specimen pictures, and order the number they desire, which will be sent from San Francisco, where they will be printed, under the superintendence of Mr. Muybridge, which is itself a guarantee that they will be the finest specimens of the kind that can be produced by photography.[9]

The *Star* then commented on his continuing efforts and made announcement of his approaching departure:

Mr. Muybridge, the celebrated photographic artist from California, is still very busy with his characteristic activity in search of the picturesque and the beautiful. He has secured a splendid view of the Plaza with its Cathedral, the Grand Hotel,

[9]November 1, 1875; in Scrapbook.

&c. These, with the fine collection he already possesses of views of new and old Panama, cannot fail to give to people abroad a better and more favorable idea of the city and the Isthmus than is generally accepted. In this respect every citizen who aids Mr. Muybridge in his mission, either by orders for pictures or otherwise, does a benefit to the country. Having exhausted Panama Mr. Muybridge will proceed to Taboga, to add to his collection the many striking and picturesque scenes with which that Island abounds, and especially in connection with the buildings which yet remain on the Morro, the site of the works of the Pacific Steam Navigation Company before they were removed to their present locale at Callao. On the morning of the 5th instant, Mr. Muybridge took a magnificent picture of the National troops and their officers in the Cathedral Plaza.[10]

One can only speculate what happened to Muybridge inwardly during his sojourn in Central America. Apparently, at this remove from the atmosphere of blame and conflict arising from the murder of Larkyns and the disintegration of his own marriage, he was able to regulate his life again and return to the demonstration of his abilities as a pictorial photographer. His mastery over novel subjects — the tropical leaves and blossoms, the dusky, half-nude bodies and calm poise of native workers, the highland villages and volcanoes, the Mayan and Spanish ruins, and commercial life of the Central American republics — suggests that he was freed from the disharmonies that he brought with him from San Francisco, and that he returned with confidence and clear plans for the future.

[10]Undated; in Scrapbook.

18. Panorama of San Francisco (1876-1877)

Muybridge was to be confronted with a series of disquieting events in the months following his return to San Francisco early in 1876. For one thing, Flora had died in sad circumstances while he was still in Central America. The *Alta California* reported on April 19, 1875:

POOR FLORA IS COLD

Flora Muybridge, she whose name attracted so much attention a few months since in connection with the shooting of Harry Larkyns by her husband in Napa County, died yesterday morning at St. Mary's hospital. She had lingered there alone for a couple of weeks, suffering from paralysis, when death released her of a life which must have been a regret.

The *Examiner* of the same date carried further details:

The unfortunate woman had no relatives here except her infant, but had an uncle in Oregon, and a brother in Alabama. Her

husband, from whom she is separated after the killing of Larkyns, is in South America photographing the scenery of that country. Her baby is with a French family [in the Mission district of San Francisco], who have kindly cared for it during the illness of its mother, and will, it is believed, adopt it. Her friends and acquaintances in this city are making efforts to procure the means of giving her remains a burial befitting the station she formerly occupied in life.

A doctor had signed the death certificate: "Flora Muybridge, died July 18, 1875, white, 24 years old." From a friend of Captain Shallcross, Muybridge learned that Flora's last words as she lay in the hospital were, "I am sorry."[1]

[1]Information from the Muybridge file, Pioneer Room, California State Library, Sacramento. Flora was buried in the Odd Fellows Cemetery, San Francisco, but at some later time her remains were transferred to Greenlawn Memorial Park, at Colma in the suburbs.

Muybridge sought out the French family that cared for the child during Flora's illness, and reimbursed them. Floredo, he found, had been placed since then in a Catholic orphanage. Being a Protestant himself, Muybridge transferred the boy on September 16, 1876, to the Protestant orphan asylum in San Francisco. Believing that he was not the father, he nevertheless treated Floredo as his own child, publicly giving his name to him and visiting him regularly during the next few years. Thus Muybridge seems to have come to terms with his conscience and sense of justice in the matter of his unhappy marriage.

Another event to which he had to accommodate himself was connected with the steamship company. In a brochure announcing the publication in San Francisco of his Central American photographs, Muybridge stated that the pictures were "executed by instruction from the Pacific Mail Steamship Company." He went on to thank the Guatemalan government for its interest, which enabled him to "obtain many picturesque views which, under other circumstances, would have been impossible." He further stated that he had brought back 260 photographs "at least equal to those" which, exhibited at Vienna, had won for him "the Grand Prize Medal for Landscape Work, in competition with the most eminent artists of all nations." These were large photographs, about 6 x 8 inches. He offered portfolios of 120 prints for $100 gold, explaining that "through the liberal enterprise of the Pacific Mail Steamship Company" he was enabled to publish the series at "less than would have been possible" if the work had been undertaken on his own.[2]

The Central American stereos were published and offered for sale from the Clay Street address of Henry W. Bradley, with whom Muybridge continued his friendship, and presumably were the bread-and-butter item of Muybridge's production for the year.

Some prints of the large photographs, presumably taken for the steamship company, were mounted and superbly bound in presentation albums. No more beautiful examples of Muybridge's work exist, and it is apparent that his personal attention was lavished meticulously on their production. The albums, titled *The Pacific Coast of Central America and Mexico; The Isthmus of Panama; Guatemala; and the Cultivation and Shipment of Coffee. Illustrated by Muybridge, San Francisco, 1876,* were intended to repay kindnesses extended over the past two years.

The first was given to Mrs. Wirt Pendegast. The brilliant lawyer died on February 29, 1876, leaving a widow and young children. Muybridge learned from Mrs. Pendegast how Leland Stanford, with a number of prominent men, had started for the

funeral in Stanford's private railroad car and encountered heavy rainstorms that caused a landslide along the track. Stanford went forward to the locomotive and offered the engineer a substantial sum of money if he could reach the destination in time. But the party arrived too late, and Stanford said, "I would have given two thousand dollars if I could have looked on the face of Wirt Pendegast again."[3] Muybridge had lost the noble champion of his freedom with the death of Pendegast who had refused to take any pay for his legal services. As an expression of gratitude and sympathy, Muybridge presented to the widow the album he would have given to her husband. Mrs. Pendegast expressed her appreciation and Muybridge answered her thus:

My Dear Madam,

Your kind note afforded me much happiness in its perusal, although I feel I am entirely undeserving of the thanks you so kindly proffer me.

It is I who should and do thank you for permitting me to offer you so slight an acknowledgement of my lasting appreciation of the noble and disinterested generosity shown me by your late husband, when I, bowed down with grief, and crushed with broken pride, so sadly needed the support and friendship I received from him. To my dying day I shall ever cherish his memory as that of the best and dearest friend I ever had.

Accept, Madam, the assurance of my highest esteem, and believe me to be

Yours Faithfully,
E. J. Muybridge[4]

The second album was presented by Muybridge to his other lawyer, F. E. Johnston. The third was presented to Mrs. Leland Stanford, no doubt in appreciation for her husband's behind-the-scenes help in the trial. It was lost when the Stanford mansion in San Francisco was destroyed in the earthquake and fire of 1906. The fourth went to Frank Shay, who for many years was Stanford's private secretary.[5]

Muybridge sent the last copy of the album to the president of the Pacific Mail Steamship Company.[6] He believed that the company had made his Central American trip possible and now might make it profitable. With the album he presented a bill, but the company refused outright to pay it or order additional

[2] Brochure, in Scrapbook (see chap. 17, n. 5, above).

[3] Janet Pendegast Leigh to Haas, April 20, 1956.

[4] This first album is preserved in the Pioneer Room, California State Library. The library also has Muybridge's letter, dated May 25, 1876. Both were given by Janet Pendegast Leigh.

[5] Shay presented his copy in 1915 to Stanford University, which has also the Johnston copy.

[6] The copy in the Museum of Modern Art, New York, presumably is this one.

pictures. When Muybridge threatened a suit, the "proof was too conclusive that there was no contract."[7]

It is fortunate that the albums were given away, for every one of the Central American negatives was destroyed by a fire in 1878. "As a consequence there exist today but [the] four bound volumes of these rarest of rare Central American photographs. Historically, they are priceless."[8]

Amid these bleak events that followed his homecoming, Muybridge was making efforts to reestablish himself. He announced his availability for commissions as follows:

The experience I have acquired as Chief Photographer, during many years, for the U.S. Government, in the illustration of this coast has been most comprehensive; and my equipment of lenses and apparatus being the most perfect and complete in the United States for the execution of every class of Open Air Photography, with plates from 20 x 24 inches in size to the smallest card, I am prepared to undertake commissions for the illustration of Railroads, Engineering Works, Private Residences, and every description of Landscape and Marine Work and the Copying of Pictures, Drawings, etc.

Muybridge
618 & 620 Clay Street[9]

As a result, he photographed in 1878, with wonderful effect, both the exterior and the interior of the Stanfords' vast new, bay-window-studded home on Nob Hill. A dozen photographic proofs bearing Muybridge's penciled notes to his assistants survive to show his concern for quality: "All these proofs are too dark." "Printed too dark — Muybridge."[10] Mrs. Stanford's personal album of these pictures, meticulously prepared and elaborate in conception, reconfirmed his position as master photographer with San Francisco's elite.

The album contains 41 views, 5½ x 9 inches, and records, as Anita Ventura Mozley writes, the Stanfords'

increasingly realized taste in decorative and fine art, a taste that was later to be expressed in the building of Stanford University, especially in its Museum and Memorial Church. There is the rotunda, with its amber glass skylight, from which mosaics of Asia, America, Africa and Europe peer down from their semicircles to the second floor hall; the Pompeiian Room; the large circular mosaic of the signs of the zodiac in the entrance hall, with the marble statues of **Morning** *and* **Evening** *beyond; and, particularly, there is*

the "Picture Gallery," with one of the Stanfords' recent purchases, a large landscape by William Keith, **Upper Kern River** (1876), on prominent display.[11]

Muybridge also reopened the matter of further experiments in the photographic analysis of motion with Leland Stanford while executing his commission at the Nob Hill house. He claimed that his work with "new chemicals and apparatus" while on shipboard now made it possible for him to anticipate taking pictures at 1/1,000 of a second. Stanford was ripe for a new series of studies, for his horses were beginning to show the value of their training according to his intuitive hunches, and he was now interested in elaborating a truly scientific theory for the proper breeding and training of fast animals. The experiments were meanwhile "desultorily continued," according to Muybridge,[12] and it seems likely that one of his photographs was the model for another Currier & Ives lithograph of Occident, entered for copyright in 1876 with the legend:

OCCIDENT. (Formerly "Wonder,") brown gelding, by pacing stallion St. Clair, dam's pedigree unknown. Owned by Ex Gov. Leland Stanford of California.
RECORD 2:16¾. Sept. 17th, 1873.

Since Currier & Ives prints certainly circulated more widely than would have been possible for any photograph, Stanford may have been pleased to keep Occident before the public in this popular medium. Muybridge, whether or not he supplied the model for the lithographer, was about to find his way back to the field of photographic specialization on which the fame of his mature career has come to rest.

But by far the most monumental accomplishment by Muybridge in the years following his return from Central America was the "Panorama of San Francisco from California Street Hill," a de luxe depiction of the city and its surroundings, and a tour de force of photographic skill.

The panorama as an art form was not new — European panoramists exhibited in New York as early as 1795. By 1815

[7] Notation on verso of title page of the Shay copy, written in 1920 by H. C. Peterson, then curator of the Stanford Museum.
[8] Ibid.
[9] Advertisement, in Scrapbook.
[10] In the Stanford University Museum of Art.

[11] In *Eadweard Muybridge: The Stanford Years, 1872-1882,* Stanford: Department of Art, Stanford University, 1972, p. 66; hereafter cited as *Muybridge: The Stanford Years.* This book, issued as a catalogue to the Muybridge exhibition at the Stanford University Museum of Art in late 1972, contains commentaries by Anita Ventura Mozley, Robert Bartlett Haas, and Françoise Forster-Hahn.
The album is preserved in the university archives, where are also 65 of the 6 x 10 inch negatives from which prints selected for the album were made.
[12] *The Science of Animal Locomotion (Zoöpraxography),* Philadelphia: University of Pennsylvania, 1893, p. 3.

the American painter John Vanderlyn was showing the 3,000 square feet of his "Panorama of Versailles" in New York. Panoramists continued to amaze the American public well through the 1850s, while engraved and lithographed "views" carried the tradition into popular art, as did magazine illustration. In the latter half of the century, painters such as Albert Bierstadt, Thomas Moran, and Frederick E. Church won renown with landscapes of staggering dimensions both in the amount of canvas covered and in the subject matter. Such work always was "latently theatrical."

The discovery of photography resulted naturally in panoramic efforts in the new medium. Daguerre himself was associated with scene painters, dioramists, and panoramists before he began his photographic work. In 1842, Antoine Claudet, using a specially built camera, took a large number of views of London from the top of the Duke of York's column in Pall Mall. From these daguerreotypes, an artist made a huge engraving, 36 x 50 inches, which was given to faithful readers of the *Illustrated London News* as a bonus. In 1858, Francis Frith exhibited a panorama of Cairo eight feet long, printed from seven negatives. In 1867, a 35-foot panorama of the Krupp Steel Works was made from 15 prints.

Muybridge's next essay, in a form of photography characterized by bravado, carried on the tradition. Panoramic photographs had been made in California since the 1850s. An extensive "Panorama of San Francisco, 1863, from Russian Hill," by C. B. Clifford, was well known on the coast when Muybridge began his panoramic work with stereographic cameras.

Muybridge had been interested in taking panoramic views from the beginning of his photographic career. A number of his less ambitious San Francisco panoramas from the late 1860s and early 1870s are found in the collection of the Bancroft Library, and a simple north, east, south and west series from the roof of a three-story building is in the Collection of the Wells Fargo History Room, San Francisco. He even made panoramic views during the Modoc War, of the Army camp on the shores of Tule Lake, "from the Signal Station." His Panama photographs included an eleven-panel panorama of Guatemala [City], "taken from Carmen Hill." [13]

In 1877 and 1878 Muybridge produced two masterpieces of early large-plate photography and added his name to the list of craftsmen who had taken the panorama form seriously.

Nob Hill was heavy now with the houses of millionaires, and very notably those of the railroad barons who became residents of

[13]*Muybridge: The Stanford Years,* pp. 59-62.

San Francisco after the offices of the Central Pacific were moved from Sacramento in 1873. Mark Hopkins, for example, had rather reluctantly paid $40,000 for the block bounded by California, Powell, Pine, and Mason streets. Half of this, sold to Leland Stanford, became the site of the mansion that Muybridge was commissioned to photograph in 1877. Next door, and higher on the block, Hopkins allowed his wife to busy herself with the building of one of the most riotous wooden fantasies ever to rear its head in San Francisco. The tower of the incredible Hopkins house, 400 feet above the waters of the bay, offered a commanding vantage point, and here Muybridge obtained his panoramas.

In early January of 1877 he set up a camera using 8 x 10 inch plates and photographed the full sweep of the city to produce a panorama in eleven perfectly matched panels, extending to 7½ feet in length. In September he announced its publication from George D. Morse's gallery:

A PANORAMIC CITY
The photograph of San Francisco, recently made by putting together a succession of views which, taken from a commanding central point, make a complete circuit of the horizon suggests to us that among the many wonderful features of our city, the panoramic character of its topography is not the least deserving of attention, although it has been overlooked, at least by people generally, until Mr. Muybridge discovered and utilized the artistic value.

Let us imagine a small ant wishing to get a comprehensive view of a painted Japanese dinner-plate. He would succeed if he could get a thimble upright in the middle of the plate, then climb to the top of the thimble and look by turn in every direction. The ant, in that hypothesis, occupies a position similar to that of the man in San Francisco which represents the saucer, and the palatial dwelling of Mark Hopkins, on California Street Hill, is the thimble. The rim of the saucer is furnished by various ridges and spurs of the Coast Range, varying in height from 300 to 3800 feet. Starting near the west we see Point Bonita, the northern pillar of the Golden Gate, whence there is a gradual rise to the summit of Tamalpais, 15 miles off and 2603 feet above the sea; and beyond that, 40 miles away, we see the ridges between Petaluma and Sonoma, between Sonoma and Napa, between Napa and Vaca Valley, and from 15 to 40 miles distant the ridge between the plain along the eastern shore of San Francisco Bay and San Ramon Valley, and above its summit, 30 miles off, appears Mt. Diablo, the culminating peak 3856 feet high of a more distant ridge; to the southward, eight miles away, is Mt. San Bruno, about 1300 feet high; to the south westward, three miles off, are the Mission Peaks, 900 feet high, and nearly west is Lone Mountain, 300 feet high. Besides these prominent figures visible on the line of the apparent horizon, are a multitude of others less notable below the horizon, including a large part of San Francisco Bay and its entrance, Angel, Alcatraz,

*Goat and Mission Islands, the Alameda Plain, with its towns, inlets
and wharves, the coves, long bridges, wharves, and shipping of
the harbor; Telegraph Hill, 300 feet high, a mile distant to the
northeast; Rincon Hill, 120 feet high, a mile off to the southeast;
Portrero Hill, South San Francisco Hill, and the Bernal Heights to
the southward, and the Mission Ridge to the southwestward,
all rise up in amphitheatric fashion, so as to permit this house to
see and be seen. While the further sides of these hills and ridges
are not without their occupants, it may safely be said that the
homes of more than a quarter of a million people within
this saucer-like panorama, 50 miles long and 15 wide, are distinctly*
*visible from the corner of California and Mason streets, 281 feet
above ordinary high tide.* . . . [14]

The *Panorama of San Francisco from California Street Hill, by
Muybridge* was entered for copyright in 1877 and was distributed
from Morse's "immense establishment," of "no less than thirteen
rooms," where Muybridge enjoyed the most congenial environment
for work that he had yet found in San Francisco. The first

[14] Prospectus for the small edition, published at Morse's Gallery, 417
Montgomery Street, San Francisco, September 1877; in Scrapbook.

1. (Looking West). The Denman School House, numerous private
residences of our wealthy citizens; the Mission Hills in the distance.

2. (Looking West). Lone Mountain, the
cemeteries, and the western
part of California St. . . .

panorama was advertised as "nearly 8 feet long, mounted on cloth, folded into eleven sections and bound in a cloth cover nine inches wide by twelve inches high, accompanied with a key and index of 220 references." The price was ten dollars. An unmounted edition, "properly secured upon a roller," could be sent" to any part of the world, free of postage, upon receipt of Eight Dollars."[15]

In November, working with a mammoth camera using 18 x 22

[15] Ibid.

inch plates, Muybridge photographed the city from the same vantage point and produced a panorama of thirteen panels each 20½ x 16 inches, extending to more than 17 feet in length. In this second panorama are visible two landmarks that had not appeared in the first: the newly completed California Street cable car line, and the celebrated "spite fence" that a Nob Hill mogul had built meanwhile around the modest home of a poor owner in order to obstruct the latter's view and force him to sell the property.

3. (Looking West). In the foreground the residences of D. D. Colton, Charles Crocker, and other prominent citizens . . . (note spite fence).

It is not known how many copies of this edition of the *Panorama of San Francisco from California Street Hill* were prepared or sold by Muybridge, but it was not to be his last version of the work. Early in 1878, the fire at Morse's that destroyed the glass plate negatives of Muybridge's Central American views also consumed the negatives of the two 1877 panoramas. In April of 1878, therefore, Muybridge photographed the city again with his large-plate camera from the tower of the Hopkins residence.

Muybridge started at about 11 a.m., and, probably with the help of an assistant, made each section in a matter of fifteen minutes. The seventh panel from the left was taken last; it is a second shot of a section that was not successful on the first try. He used a 40 in., near telephoto, lens, which determined the number of 20 in.-wide glass negatives needed to make the complete circle. He had chosen the day for the execution of the panorama carefully; the shadows are sharp, and the atmosphere [is] clear.[16]

[16] *Muybridge: The Stanford Years*, p. 62

alifornia Street Hill and a glimpse of the Golden Gate. . . .
an Hill; Mt. Tamalpais, Sausalito and Richardson Bay in istance. . .

5. (Looking North) Meigg's Wharf; Alcatraz Island; Angel Island . . .

Copies inscribed "With compliments of The Artist — 1878" were presented to Mrs. Leland Stanford and Mrs. Mark Hopkins.[17]

The panoramas, besides being of extraordinary artistic quality, are primary sources of pictorial information about San Francisco as it was before the earthquake and fire of 1906 destroyed so many of its early landmarks. They are, also, the culmination of Muybridge's landscape work in California.

[17]Mrs. Stanford's copy is in the Stanford University Library; Mrs. Hopkins's copy is in the San Francisco Public Library.

6. . . . . Red Rock on the route of the Sacramento River boats; and Contra Costa Hills . . . St. Francis Church . . . Telegraph Hill.

7. . . . Commercial Hotel . . . The eastern shore of San Francisco Bay.

8. . . . The foreground to the left is known as "Chinatown," beyond
are the City Hall; Post Office; Custom House; Appriaser's Store;
U. S. Courts; St. Mary's Cathedral; the San Rafael, Oakland and S.F.
& N.P.R.R. Ferries; Goat Island and the long wharf of the C.P.R.R.,
at Oakland; Mount Diablo is visible in the distance. . . .

9. (Looking East) . . . the principal Banks, Insurance Offices, and large mercantile houses; Merchants and Stock Exchanges. . . .

10. (Looking East) . . . In the central portion are the Occidental, Cosmopolitan, Russ and Lick Hotels, Masonic and Odd Fellows' Halls, California Theatre, Club Houses and Literary and Art Societies. . . . Grand, Palace and Nuclens Hotels. . . .

11. (Looking South) . . . Jewish Synagogue, Trinity (Church), Union Square . . . Lon Bridge over Mission Bay. . . .

12. (Looking South) . . . The Baldwin, U.S. Mint, the Portreros; and Dry Dock in the distance . . . Calvary Church. . . .

13. (Looking South) . . . First Congregational Church, Mechanics Exhibition Pavilion, New City Hall, the Mission; and San Miguel Hills in the distance . . . completes the circle.

19. Occident Photographed at a 2:27 Gait (1877)

In the 1872, 1873, and 1876 photographs of Occident, Muybridge carried forward his research in the analysis of motion with increasingly practical results. During the same time, photographers elsewhere were concerning themselves with similar schemes. Some reports of their ideas and efforts appeared in print and may have been known to him. For example, Fairman Rogers in 1872 claimed success in photographing horses in rapid motion.[1] These pictures have never reached the public. In the same year, O. G. Rejlander suggested ways in which photography might be used for the study of animal locomotion.[2] No pictures were taken by him according to his suggestions, but in 1873 an extraordinary series of documentary photographs of transient expression was produced by Rejlander to illustrate Darwin's book *The Expression of the Emotions in Man and Animals.* Also in 1873, the first edition of Marey's *La Machine Animal* appeared, followed by an English translation in 1874. This work spurred Leland Stanford on to new photographic experiments with Eadweard Muybridge. In 1874 the French astronomer P. J. C. Janssen obtained successive images of the passage of the planet Venus across the sun, using a "révolver astronomique" to take 48 photographs in succession on a single sensitized plate at intervals of 70 seconds. Thus the first half of the decade was a time of much creative dreaming and some modest accomplishment. "Instantaneous" photographs had become a reality, but the idea of taking such photographs in rapid sequence, or of reconstituting them to achieve the effect of portraying the original motions, was only "in the air."

In 1877, Muybridge was again called to Sacramento by Leland Stanford to make a series of photographs of Occident. Long out of the way was the concern with defending unsupported transit. Now Stanford was interested in obtaining photographs from which he could build a general theory of locomotion. In order to do this, he posed many new questions for photographic exploration. Does the foot of the fast trotter strike the ground at its furthest projection? Does the heel come in contact with the ground first? Are the forelegs perfectly straight when the shoe touches? What are the precise differences in the movements of

different horses? Of different animals? What are the defects in action that prevent an otherwise promising trotter from going fast?

Muybridge told a newspaper reporter that on his Central American trip he "had occasion to make a series of experiments in photographing scenes offshore from the deck of a rolling vessel. These experiments resulted in the construction of an apparatus and the preparation of chemicals so as to permit the photographing in outline of a rapidly moving body."[3] This method he had tried at Sacramento in 1876, and he had perfected it for the latest try.

The last of the Sacramento pictures was taken in July 1877. Occident was again the subject. In 1874 he had won his first race, beating "Judge Fullerton" on the Bay City track in San Francisco and achieving the fastest time ever made on the Pacific Coast. Occident's successes on the track had triggered Stanford's acquisition of a string of fleet-footed horses. Stanford also began to buy tracts of land on the San Francisco Peninsula, where his "Palo Alto Stock Farm" would soon become a famous horse breeding and training establishment.

The 1877 Sacramento photograph was the most successful in the series of experiments made by Muybridge between 1872 and 1877. Circulated among newspapermen in August, it caused a proper furore:

"OCCIDENT" PHOTOGRAPHED AT FULL SPEED

Mr. Muybridge made us a copy of an instantaneous photograph of "Occident" taken when he was trotting at a speed of 36 feet per second, or a mile in 2 minutes and 27 seconds. The negative was exposed to the light less than one-thousandth part of a second, so brief a time that the horse did not move a quarter of an inch. The photographer had made many experiments to secure the highest sensitiveness and the briefest possible exposure, and the result was a novelty in photographic art, and a delineation of speed which the eye cannot catch. At 2:27 the spokes of a sulky are invisible to the eye, as they spin around so fast that, taken separately, they are not distinguishable. The photograph shows each plainly, without blur. The negative was retouched before the photograph was printed but we are assured that the outlines are unchanged; and we can well believe this, for much of the work has a character that could scarcely be secured by hand. Mr. Muybridge intends to take a series of pictures, showing

[1] *Philadelphia Photographer,* June.

[2] "On Photographing Horses," in *British Journal Photographic Almanack, 1872/3,* London, p. 115.

[3] *Bulletin,* San Francisco, August 3, 1877.

the step of "Occident" at all the stages, and in this manner, for the first time, the precise differences in the motions of different horses can be clearly represented — a matter of much interest to horsemen, for trotters vary in their action, one having his foreleg straight when it touches the ground, another crooked, and so on.[4]

Muybridge had sent the photograph to the publisher Fred McCrellish with the following letter:

San Francisco, August 2nd, 1877

. . . I herewith enclose you a photograph made from a negative, which I believe to have been more rapidly executed than any ever made hitherto.

The exposure was made while "Occident" was trotting past me at the rate of 2:27, accurately timed, or 36 feet in a second, about 40 feet distant, the exposure of the negative being less than one thousandth part of a second. The length of exposure can be pretty accurately determined by the fact that the whip in the driver's hand did not move the distance of its diameter. The picture has been retouched, as is customary at this time with all first-class photographic work, for the purpose of giving a better effect to the details. In every other respect, the photograph is exactly as it was made in the camera.[5]

San Francisco papers reported the event under headings such as "A Feat in Photography," "A Triumph of Photographic Art," "Occident Photographed at a gait of 2:27," and "Progress in Photography — an Astonishing Result."

Two periodicals, *Resources of California* and the *California Spirit of the Times*, offered their readers a reproduction of the photograph in the form of a wood engraving. J. Cairns Simpson, of the latter, praised the photograph unreservedly: "It is the most important thing in the education of the trotting horse that has ever appeared, and will be of greater benefit in perfecting the profession of the art of training the trotting horse, than all that has yet been written."[6] Another paper commented that the position of Occident in the photograph "bears out Stanford's theory that the forelegs are perfectly straight when the shoe touches the ground."[7] Praise for the picture was being expressed in London the next month.[8]

Muybridge entered the photograph of Occident for copyright on August 11, but it was never marketed.

Although Mr. Muybridge has liberally distributed the photograph among his friends, he has persistently declined filling numerous and repeated orders, both here and from the East for the purchase of them. To all such applications he has replied in his usual courteous and decisive manner, that the photograph was not made for the purpose of selling, and he must therefore decline.[9]

This difficulty in acquiring the picture led to the belief by some of the newspaper fraternity that the photograph was "got up," or was merely a humbug. Ringleaders in the attack — for an attack it was — were former cronies of Harry Larkyns on the *Post*:

Let us look at this triumph of an art seemingly in its infancy: The driver, Mr. Tennant — I presume it is Mr. Tennant, though I do not enjoy the gentleman's acquaintance — is not driving a horse; he is sitting for his photograph. He is stiff, un-natural; he does not encourage his horse; he would lean forward were he driving at the rate of 36 feet per second; he would be alive with movement and the 'hie yar' would, as it were, ring in our ears. His position is that of a man in whom, whether Occident went a mile in 2:40 minutes or a mile in 240 minutes, is a matter of like indifference. . . . Decidely, Mr. Tennant, you were not driving Occident at the rate of 36 feet per second when you sat for that photo. You have been retouched by Koch [John Koch, photographic retoucher in Morse's studio], and he has not improved on the camera.

The writer went on in this vein for two columns, complaining that the coat sleeve of Mr. Tennant was not properly wrinkled at the elbow, that the off-wheel must be "higher up in the plane of perspective than the near one," and that the hind off leg of Occident should be higher up in the plane of perspective. "Either that camera did lie," he asserted, "or Stanford has got the most extraordinary horse in the world."[10]

This new controversy did not bother Muybridge very much. To the curious who came to his studio to see the picture and condemn or praise it, he responded objectively by showing a sworn statement from the driver, James Tennant, as to the gait the horse had been traveling; and to those who held that the picture of Occident had been "doctored" by Koch to conceal the true facts, Muybridge unhesitatingly showed the negative itself.[11]

When the "Panorama of San Francisco from California Street Hill" was published in November, with a key for identifying the city's principal landmarks, Muybridge treated this insert as a kind of trade card. On the back one read the following:

---

[4] *Alta California,* San Francisco, August 3, 1877.

[5] Ibid.

[6] *California Spirit of the Times,* San Francisco, August 11, 1877.

[7] *Call,* San Francisco, August 4, 1877.

[8] *Once a Week,* September 15.

[9] *Resources of California,* San Francisco, October 1877.

[10] September 1877 (day uncertain); in Scrapbook.

[11] *Resources of California,* October 1877.

MUYBRIDGE
Landscape, Marine, Architectural and Engineering
PHOTOGRAPHER
Official Photographer   *Grand Prize Medalist*
of the   *of the*
U.S. GOVERNMENT   VIENNA EXHIBITION 1873
Reproductions of Paintings, Drawings and Art Manufactures

PHOTOGRAPHIC ILLUSTRATIONS
*Of Alaska, California, Mexico, Central America
and the Isthmus of Panama
Horses photographed while running
or trotting at full speed.*

Morse's Gallery   *417 Montgomery Street*[12]

"Horses photographed while running or trotting at full speed," now added to Muybridge's previous professional claims, indicates that he at last felt able to demonstrate publicly his success in the area of motion photography, which he had begun on a private basis, and for Stanford only, in 1872. Recognition was forthcoming when, in November 1877, the jurors of the Twelfth Industrial Exhibition in San Francisco awarded him a medal for his instantaneous photographs of Occident.[13]

Time has added perspective to Muybridge's claims. Although no negative or print of the 1872 or 1873 photographs of Occident has come to light, assurance that the photographs did exist, in some form, is supported by (1) Muybridge's public statements, made in writing and never seriously controverted in his lifetime, (2) Stanford's statements attesting the existence of a satisfactory early picture, and (3) McCrellish's editorial assertions of 1873, which seem to have provoked no further controversy with persons involved in the "bet." To these may be added, tentatively, (4) the Currier & Ives lithograph of 1873, which represents Occident free of the ground and suggests that the artist, Cameron, may have been following a photographic source.[14]

An even more interesting problem has to do with the photographs of 1876 and 1877. No negative or print of these has come to light, either. Muybridge in 1877 copyrighted a card entitled "The Horse in Motion" and described as an "Automatic Electro-Photograph" in which the "details have been retouched." It shows Occident trotting "at a 2.30 gait over the Sacramento track, in July, 1877."[15] Fortunately the Stanford Museum

of Art retains an apparently almost totally hand-painted gouache by Koch which apparently was in turn photographed by Muybridge as "The Horse in Motion." Only the face of the driver, carefully pasted to the surface of the painting, is a photographic print. X-ray studies do not show a photographic base for the rest. One is at first inclined to believe that Muybridge has been caught out in a gigantic hoax.[16] Considering the state of development of instantaneous photography generally during the 1870s, however, it is no wonder that neither Stanford nor Muybridge was aiming for the production of a commercially distributable photographic print of rapid motion. Stanford's initial interest lay in proof of unsupported transit, and in the processes leading to that proof. The product was for him the proof, not the photograph or its quality.

If, for example, Muybridge's 1872 and 1873 photographs had been shown to Stanford not as paper prints but as lantern slides, the screened images could easily have been traced on paper as a model for the Currier & Ives lithographic print of 1873. The deliberate delineation of Occident free of the ground would suggest that Muybridge's chancy photographs had somehow told this scientific story and that the Currier & Ives artist was entrusted with putting that story into a popular, more easily reproducible form. The same could hold for the 1876 lithograph, for which Muybridge's 1876 photograph may have served as a "correction."

The feasibility of this hypothesis is apparent from a double equine portrait discovered in 1972 at the Stanford museum — a drawing and a painting by Thomas K. Van Zandt, of Albany, New York, both dated 1876. The drawing could well have been traced from a lantern slide projection of the Muybridge photograph of the horse in motion, or from a drawing that Van Zandt made from the photograph. At any rate, the existence of the drawing and the completed painting taken from the same image suggests that the drawing was submitted to Stanford for approval of the delineation before the painting was undertaken. If this should be the case, the fact that the 1877 "Horse in Motion" was not printed directly from a retouched Muybridge negative can be understood: It would have been intentionally printed from the negative of a gouache drawing projected for the purpose by Muybridge.

Graphic processes in the 1870s gave great latitude to the artist, and retouching was thought of as not only an elegant embellishment for photography, but as a positive improvement over the "accidents" of the camera and its cumbersome wet-plate

---

[12] With copy of panorama in Stanford University Library.

[13] Clipping in Scrapbook.

[14] The 1876 Currier and Ives print appears to have been based on a Muybridge photograph taken after 1873.

[15] The card was sold through Morse's gallery. The speed of 2:30 differs from the 2:40 reported in the press.

[16] See the discussion in *Muybridge: The Stanford Years*, pp. 19, 63.

processes. Such latitude marked the work and the claims of photographers: "composite" photography, retouching, "moonlight effects," and manipulative tricks of all kinds were not unusual. Photographs were described as instantaneous that would not be so called today. For example, John L. Gihon, of Philadelphia, had claimed in 1867 to have produced an instantaneous photograph of the famous racehorse "Dexter" in motion. "A number of photographs of individuals were taken as 'bystanders' and prints of the horse and bystanders cut out and pasted on a prepared painting which showed the track, a hotel, and buildings. The whole thing was then rephotographed and prints made."[17] Dexter had not been photographed in movement at all; instead, judicious cutting and pasting had thrust his legs and neck forward to give the appearance of motion that one finds in a merry-go-round horse. That Muybridge was a more tasteful heir to this tradition we can be grateful. That in his work the artist and the photographer should have joined hands would not have surprised anyone in his day, and should not surprise us.

[17] Robert Taft, *Photography and the American Scene,* New York: Macmillan, 1938, p. 358 and n. 370.

Absolute proof that Muybridge produced successful instantaneous photographs of motion between 1872 and 1877 will depend on discovery of the negatives, or of the lantern slides made from these negatives which I suggest here. The hundreds of uncatalogued Muybridge lantern slides in the basement of the Science Museum in London offer a promising area for research.[18]

To the contemporary accounts in the case can be added the recollections of an eyewitness of the proceedings at Sacramento in 1877. Albert Tietjen was there in Stanford's employ. Writing about 1930, he had this to say:

About 25 or 30 years ago I read an article in the Sunset Magazine by H. C. Peterson, at that time curator of the Stanford Museum. . . . He had the snapshots of the horse Occident taken by Mr. Muybridge. He said the pictures were taken in 1871. I wrote Mr.

[18] I was permitted to study these in 1964. The high cost, at that time, of making positive prints from the hundreds of lantern slides in storage precluded further work. A number of prints from the collection have since appeared, sketchily and in part wrongly identified, and often cropped, in Kevin MacDonnell's *Eadweard Muybridge,* Boston: Little, Brown, 1972. Thorough study of the collection will probably reveal much new information about Muybridge. The museum's collection of optical, photographic, and cinematographic instruments includes a model of Muybridge's Zoöpraxiscope.

Peterson telling him the pictures were taken in 1877. He came to see me and was pleased to get all the data that I gave him. I told him of Mr. Tennant's brother and I stretching the sheeting on the fence about 8 feet high. After Mr. Muybridge took the snapshots he showed us the negatives. James Tennant drove the horse Occident. Now the snapshots have disappeared. Mr. L. Peck, the editor of the Standard Magazine, wrote to Palo Alto to get those pictures. They sent him the snapshots of a horse [Abe Edgington] taken in 1878. I don't know what became of the Occident picture.[19]

A further point about the 1877 picture: the words "Automatic Electro-Photograph," printed on the copyrighted card of that year, attest that Muybridge was already using an electrical device, set off automatically by the wheels of the sulky, to trigger his shutter. Men in the Central Pacific Railroad "car shops" at Oakland helped in the development of this device, for which credit has been given to John D. Isaacs.[20] Of him, Albert Tietjen stated: "Now you mentioned John D. Isaacs in your letter. I do not know anyone by that name."

[19]Tietjen letter, n.d.; Haas collection (formerly in collection of Janet Pendegast Leigh).
[20]See chaps. 33, 34.

73. *Top,* a drawing by T. K. Van Zandt which may have been traced from a Muybridge lanternslide made from an 1876 photograph and presented to Stanford for approval of the horse's posture before the printing was undertaken. This may well have been the source for the 1876 Currier and Ives print, "Occident."

74. *Middle,* a finished painting by T. K. Van Zandt from the Stanford collection based on the drawing. The existence of both the drawing and the painting suggests that Stanford wanted to be sure the posture of the horse corresponded to the "findings" of a photographic print which was not in itself sufficiently clear to be circulated as finished work.

75. *Bottom,* A painting of Occident by John Koch, based on the July 1, 1877 "automatic electro-photograph" by Muybridge. Koch's painting was photocopied by Muybridge since he considered it a more valid or acceptable form for presenting his findings than the unretouched photograph.

PORTFOLIO III
Views of Central America, Mexico, San Francisco, and Sacramento 1875–1878

76. Frontispiece to Muybridge's Central America Album.

77. Road to Portobello, Old Panama.

78. Laundry at Quetzeltenango, Guatemala.

79. Las Nubes, a coffee plantation in Guatemala.

80. Lake Atitlan, Guatemala. Clouds printed from a second negative.

81. Coffee plantation, Las Nubes.

82. Hacienda Serigiers, Guatemala.

83. Public Laundry, City of Guatemala.

84. The Pompeiian room.

85. Mrs. Stanford's conservatory.

The Stanford Residence, San Francisco.

86. The dining room.

87. The gallery.

88. The rotunda balcony.

89. The entrance hall.

PART FIVE:
Creative Expansion

20. Palo Alto Farm and the Series Photographs (1878-1879)

The mansion on Nob Hill could not give much scope to Leland Stanford's enthusiasm for fast horses. According to his biographer, it was "in the natural order of things that Stanford should wish to proceed a step farther and establish a breeding farm where by careful selection he might be able to produce animals that would conform to his ideals. [Thus] he began in 1876 the acquisition of the various parcels of land ultimately comprised in the Palo Alto Farm." He first bought "Mayfield Grange," a delightful country residence thirty miles south of San Francisco, on the peninsula, with 650 acres in the parcel. Other properties were added until the extent of the farm was more than 8,000 acres. The name was taken from the ancient, solitary redwood called El Palo Alto by Spanish explorers who camped beside it in 1769. Stanford, who "thought in generous terms," lost no time in collecting animals to stock his breeding farm and preparing buildings and grounds for their accommodation.[1]

Eadweard Muybridge had made numerous photographs of the Stanford residences in Sacramento and San Francisco. Now he was called upon for views of Mayfield Grange, a handsome dwelling in the Italian villa style, and the newly constructed corrals, paddocks, shops, stables, and barns. Occident and other treasured horses were brought to the farm by 1878.

During the summer of that year, San Francisco newspapers began to report a Stanford-Muybridge collaboration, bolder than any yet undertaken, at Palo Alto Farm. The *Alta California* said: "Mr. Muybridge intends to take a series of photographs showing the step of Occident at all its stages,"[2] and the *Bulletin:* "It is Mr. Stanford's desire to have a series of photographs taken of the horse while in rapid motion to illustrate the position of the animal's feet, as he entertains a theory concerning the subject very different to the popular idea."[3]

The 1872 picture had already demonstrated to Stanford's satisfaction that there was a point in the horse's stride when all four feet were free of the ground. The 1877 picture had further demonstrated that the foreleg of a trotting horse is perfectly straight when the shoe strikes the ground. These were isolated findings. A full-scale study of the horse in motion was now projected. The new scheme called for a practical elaboration of Rejlander's idea of 1872/3, which envisioned the use of a battery of cameras. In the resulting pictures, Rejlander conjectured, "the forelegs may be clear in one if the hind ones are blurred; in another the case might be reversed. . . . By combining all, a true drawing might be made to please a Landseer or a Rosa Bonheur."[4]

Twelve magnificent Scoville cameras were ordered from

[1] Clark, pp. 344-350. The present city of Palo Alto did not come into being until later, when the university was established on the farm.

[2] August 3, 1878.

[3] August 3, 1878.

[4] O. G. Rejlander, "On Photographing Horses," in *British Journal Photographic Almanack, 1872/3,* London, p. 115.

New York, and their double lenses for taking stereoscopic pictures were ordered from Dallmeyer of London. Swift-action shutters were constructed by "Arthur Brown of the C.P.R.R. Company. Mr. Tiffany, of the San Francisco Telegraph Supply Company manufactured the electrical apparatus" which was to fire the cameras.[5]

At the farm, a suitable camera shed was constructed along the south side of the mile training track. This low, whitewashed structure, some 50 feet in length, was designed to house the battery of twelve cameras (later increased to twenty-four). Each camera was fitted by Muybridge with a double shutter arranged, as he put it, "one above [and] the other below the opening through which the light was admitted to the lens, and held by india-rubber springs, constructed in the form of a ring, with a lifting power of one hundred pounds, and secured by latches, to be liberated at the completion of a magnetic current."[6]

By June the picture taking was in progress. In order to forestall a charge that the new pictures were "got up," as some had said of the 1877 photograph of Occident, Stanford invited several groups of interested sportsmen and newspaper reporters to view the proceedings.

The reporter for the *Pacific Rural Press* wrote that a series of twelve pictures was "taken in less than half a second, while the horse was traveling in front of the cameras at forty feet per second."[7] Powdered lime had been sprinkled on the track to give a light-reflecting surface. The twelve cameras, placed 21 inches apart, were aimed across the track to a wooden fence 15 feet high and somewhat longer than the shed. The fence was hung with sheeting marked off "by vertical lines into spaces of twenty-one inches, each space being consecutively numbered." Against this background the horses showed distinctly. Each picture's place in the series was indicated by the numbers on the backdrop, which were photographed along with the equine subjects.[8]

As the reported told it, the trotter "Abe Edgington" was first brought out before the viewing party by Charles Marvin, Stanford's master trainer. Wires were stretched across the track, in line with each camera. When the metal rims of the sulky wheels passed over the wires, successive contacts were made and the shutters of the cameras were electrically released. After Abe Edgington had been warmed up a little over the track, and the apparatus made ready, Muybridge signaled for the show to begin.

The horse, driven by Marvin, was put past the cameras at 2:20 speed:

He came down the track in splendid style, with a good, square motion and firm trot. As soon as the wheel struck wire No. 1, Camera No. 1 was closed by the means described, and the first picture taken; when it struck No. 2, the second camera had the second picture, and so on until 12 pictures were taken 21 inches apart. . . . The sound of the slides closing was like a continuous roll, so quickly was the feat accomplished.

In photographing the running horse, where there were no sulky wheels to set off the action of the cameras, another device was used:

Fine black threads were placed across the track [and] connected so that the armatures would release the slides [shutters] as before. The racing mare "Sally Gardner," a handsome animal, was brought out and the threads placed so as to strike her breast as she went by. The instruments were made ready, the signal given, and she came rushing down the track like a whirlwind. . . . When the mare broke the eighth or ninth thread she became aware of something across her breast, and gave a wild bound in the air, breaking the saddle girth as she left the ground. This gave a curious picture of the mare with her legs wildly spread and the broken girth swinging in the air just as it is separating.

The photographing was immediately followed by the processing of the negatives in the studio shed. Visitors were treated to a sight of them within twenty minutes of the time when the exposures were made.[9]

Other reporters wrote:

It was a brilliant success. . . . Even the thread-like tip of Mr. Marvin's whip was plainly seen in each negative, and the horse was exactly pictured. . . . Mr. Muybridge, a photographer of genius and an artist of rare skill, was the operator. He is, practically, the inventor of the process, although the design or idea was suggested by Governor Stanford, who has unstintedly supplied the means to perfect the apparatus.[10]

It is difficult to say to whom we should award the greater praise, to Governor Stanford, for the inception of an idea so original, and for the liberality with which he has supplied the funds for such a costly experiment, or to Muybridge for the energy, genius and devotion with which he has pursued his experiments, and so successfully overcome all the scientific, chemical, and mechanical difficulties encountered in labors which had no precedent, and which have so happily culminated in such

[5] *Resources of California,* San Francisco, August 1878.

[6] In *The Horse in Motion,* p. 124.

[7] San Francisco, June 22, 1878.

[8] *The Horse in Motion,* p. 125.

[9] *Pacific Rural Press,* June 22.

[10] *Examiner,* San Francisco, July 1, 1878.

a wonderful result. We hope that he will reap the benefit to which his genius and success clearly entitle him.[11]

From 1878 on through 1879 the press continued to cover the experiments at Palo Alto Farm. Stanford and Muybridge were equally praised for their part in the project: Stanford for having set the goals for the experiments, envisioned the use of photography as a scientific tool in the study of animal locomotion, succeeded in interesting the West Coast's most enterprising photographer in giving his energies to the project, and provided the financial backing required to set up the experiment, buy the cameras and lenses, and carry on the photographic work; Muybridge for having accepted Stanford's commission and its purposes, written the specifications for the experiments, coordinated the work of the various "expert engineers, electricians, mechanics," and others in "preparing the necessary machinery and appliances for taking the negatives," and set the pace for the photographic research. His charge from Stanford was to deliver sequential, instantaneous photographs illustrating various phases of the horse in motion. This he ultimately accomplished, to Stanford's complete satisfaction, between 1878 and 1881.

In later years the relationship between Muybridge and Stanford grew strained. Each made extravagant claims about the importance of his part in the success of the Palo Alto experiments. But during the 1870s San Franciscans were led to believe that neither Stanford nor Muybridge would have got very far with the project without the other. Indeed, the two saw each other as creative collaborators.

In 1878 Muybridge copyrighted and published, through Morse's gallery, a set of six cards entitled "The Horse in Motion":

1. "Abe Edginton," trotting at a 15-minute gait; 6 positions
2. "Mahomet," trotting at an 8-minute gait; 6 positions
3. "Abe Edgington," trotting at an 8-minute gait; 8 positions
4. "Abe Edgington," trotting at a 2:24-minute gait; 12 positions
5. "Occident," trotting at a 2:20-minute gait; 12 positions
6. "Sally Gardner," running at a 1:40-minute gait; 12 positions[12]

These were commercially distributed abroad as well as at home — in France as "Les Allures du Cheval," in Germany as "Das Pferd in Bewegung." A certain awe surrounded the series, for the results of the Muybridge-Stanford collaboration were now before the public, and the legend of the work at Palo Alto Farm was made palpable at last. As the cards illustrating the strides of Stanford's

famous racers found their way about the world, scientific and fashionable journals, popular magazines, and newspapers carried lengthy descriptions of the work and how it was accomplished.[13]

In San Francisco the consensus was that the method used by Muybridge "precluded all suspicion of mistakes, and insured accuracy which could not be questioned."[14] Popular fancy was caught by the fact that there was "something so complicated yet so simple and wonderful in the plan by which 'the horse took his own picture'!"[15] But the city had at least one dissenter. The following letter to the editor appeared in the August 1878 issue of the *Philadelphia Photographer:*

THE CALIFORNIA HORSE — ELECTRIC FEAT
The following will interest those who "take stock" in the wonderful horse story.

None know better than yourself that the country is full of photographic quacks vending their nostrums, deceiving the credulous and defrauding the ignorant. California is noted for its "largest pumpkins," "finest climate," and "most 'phenomenal horse" of the world. So also it has a photographer! the dexterity of whose "forefinger" invokes the aid of electricity in exposing his plate — a succession of plates, so as to photograph each particular respiration of the horse. The result is, a number of diminutive **silhouettes** *of the animal on and against a white ground or wall; all these in the particular position it pleased him to assume, as the wheels of his chariot open and close the circuits.*

[13]For example, *Scientific American,* October 19, and *La Nature,* Paris, December 14, 1878; *Fremdenblatt,* Berlin, and *Landwirtschaftliche Zeiting,* Vienna, April 26, and *The Field,* London, June 28, 1879; in Scrapbook.
[14]*Morning Call,* San Francisco, June 16, 1878.
[15]*California Spirit of the Times,* San Francisco, June 22, 1878.

90. Front of electro-shutters developed by Muybridge, with positions of panels before, during and after exposure, 1878.

[11]*Resources of California,* August 1878.
[12]Not to be confused with the 1877 card of the same title. The 4 x 8-¼ inch photographs were mounted on a slightly larger card, with an analysis of the stride printed on the back. The price of a set was $15.

*All this is new and wonderful. How could it be otherwise,
emanating as it does from this land of miracles? Photographically
speaking, it is "bosh"; but then it amused the "boys," and shows
that a horse trots part of the time and "flies" the rest, a fact of
"utmost scientific importance." Bosh again.*

Respectfully, your friend,

Wm. H. Rulofson

In the same issue the editor printed a notice of the "Horse in
Motion" pictures, concluding with this statement:

*Surely Mr. Rulofson could not have given much thought to the
subject when he called these pictures silhouettes only, and the
claims made for them as "bosh." Mr. Muybridge deserves great
credit, and has gained great notoriety for what he has done, and
we shall try to induce him to tell us more about it.*

On June 27, 1878, Muybridge applied for patents on his
"Method and Apparatus for Photographing Objects in Motion."
What he claimed as new was:

1. *The background of* L, *provided with vertical lines or gage-stripes*
   s *and horizontal stripes of lines* l, *arranged substantially as*
   a *shown and described, for the purpose of obtaining horizontal*
   and vertical measurements of the passing object, as set forth.
2. *The slides* c/d, *set by means of the lever* f, *trigger* g, *and centrally*
   pivoted lever G, *with its armature* h, *in combination with the*
   c *electro-magnets* l/l, *wires* j/k, *and metallic spring plates* m/m,
   d *constructed to operate substantially as and for the purpose*
   described.

On July 11, he filed a further application, on an "Improvement in
the Method and Apparatus for Photographing Objects in Motion."
Whereas the "contemporaneous application" dealt with an
arrangement for "operating a slide or slides for this purpose by an
electric circuit which was established or broken by the object to
be photographed as it passed in front of the camera," this second
application dealt with an arrangement "whereby the moving
object is made to operate the slide simply by mechanical means."
What he claimed as new was:

1. *The sliding plates* A/B, *provided with openings, in combination*
   with the supplemental slides 2, *arranged above and below said*
   openings, substantially as and for the purpose set forth.
2. *The sliding plates* A/B, *with the supplemental slides* 2, *in*
   combination with a releasing and trigger mechanism and a cord
   or thread secured thereto for operating the same, substantially
   as and for the purpose set forth.
3. *The improvement in the process of taking instantaneous*
   photographs of objects in motion, which consists in the
   arrangement of a tripping and releasing mechanism across the
   track along which the object to be photographed is made to

*pass, and connecting said mechanism with devices for releasing
the shutters in the camera, substantially as described.*[16]

The patents were granted to Muybridge on March 4, 1879,
presumably with no objection on the part of Leland Stanford.

During 1879 Muybridge increased the number of cameras in
the studio to 24. Some 20 other horses were photographed during
that year. In addition, studies were made of the locomotion of
the ox, dog, bull, cow, deer, goat, and boar. For these animals, whose
movements were too erratic for them to go along the prepared track
and take their own pictures by progressively breaking the threads
which triggered the shutters, Muybridge devised a clockwork
mechanism to fire the shutters, and time the exposures. In sum, the
animals were represented in such actions as walking, ambling,
cantering, pacing, trotting, running, leaping, and hauling, and the
result was a utilitarian compendium directly fulfilling Stanford's
request for analyzable data.

In August 1879 Muybridge took his first sequential photographs
of the human figure in motion, an investigation he was to pursue
extensively five years later at the University of Pennsylvania. These
photographs came about when Stanford invited to the farm three
members of the Olympic Club, a San Francisco athletic
organization. They were W. S. Lawton, superintendent of the club;
Louis Gerichton, teacher of boxing; and Louis Brandt, strong-man
of the organization.

*In order to display as completely as possible the movements of the
muscles, the athletes wore only brief trunks while performing. . . .
From 10 o'clock in the morning until 4 o'clock in the afternoon
boxing, wrestling, fencing, jumping and tumbling followed in
quick succession, and all of their intricate movements were
instantaneously and exactly photographed. . . . After the athletic
performances several photographs were taken [in] various classical
groupings.*[17]

Stanford stated his intention of having these pictures "worked up"
to cabinet-size photographs and taking them to Europe, where
he would have two life-sized oil paintings made of each, one set
of which he would present to the club.[18] Oil paintings rather than
photographs were still his sine qua non for culture.

Muybridge strongly identified with the athletes. He photographed
himself greeting them on their arrival at the farm studio and

[16] U.S. Patent Office, nos. 212,865 (June 27 application) and 212,864
(July 11 application); for further details and drawings see *Muybridge: The
Stanford Years*, pp. 114-115.

[17] *Chronicle*, San Francisco, August 9, 1879.

[18] Ibid. I have not ascertained whether the paintings were made;
presumably they were not.

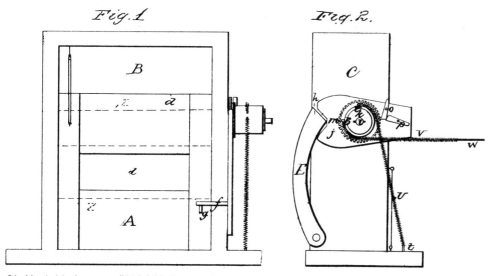

91. Muybridge's patent #212,864, for securing instantaneous photographs of rapidly moving objects incorporates a double-acting slide with a *mechanically* operated trigger which was fired as the moving object broke through a thread attached to the camera and stretched across the track, thus accomplishing the exposure.

92. Muybridge patent model of the double-acting slide in the Palo Alto experiments.

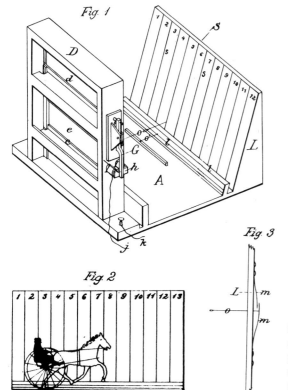

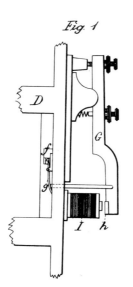

94. *Above*, Muybridge's patent model of the slide frame and "novel background" which represented the basic method and apparatus for photographic objects in motion used at Palo Alto.

93. *Left*, Muybridge's patent #212,865 for securing instantaneous photographs of rapidly moving objects incorporates a "novel background, which is graduated or marked so as to gage (sic) the position of the horse and the posture of his limbs." An accompanying sheet details an *electrically* operated trigger which was to be "established or broken by the object to be photographed as it passed in front of the camera."

included himself in the series as a fellow athlete. At the age of forty-nine he was still a fine figure of a man. Regular exercise under the guidance of the Nahl brothers had undoubtedly helped him to maintain his health in the years following the stagecoach accident, just as his work as an outdoor photographer had made it possible for him to live up to Dr. Gull's prescription of an outdoor life.

By the end of 1879 Muybridge had taken hundreds of photographs and Stanford was said to have spent about $42,000 on the project. The "series of photographic images made in rapid succession at properly regulated intervals of time, or of distance" now provided a body of data which Stanford hoped would definitely "set at rest" the many conflicting theories of animal locomotion. The analysis of the photographs and the presentation of a new and better explanation of animal locomotion from the data secured by the camera now occupied him. Newspaper accounts reflect Stanford's first steps in critical interpretation — for instance: "In figure one the horse is shown with his nose in the space nine and his left hindfoot in space three, in the act of leaving the ground. The right forefoot, which moves in unison with it, having already been raised nearly twelve inches from the ground, as is shown by the third horizontal line which is twelve inches above the track."[19] So Stanford proceeded with his analysis of the photographs, hoping to find consistent support for the conclusions the work of Muybridge had allowed him to reach.

Although the photographic work at Palo Alto Farm continued intermittently until 1881, Stanford's interest shifted after 1879 to the further problems of achieving a new theory of animal locomotion and of presenting to a wider public the results of the research. Before this was accomplished, he had shifted collaborators, calling in Dr. J. D. B. Stillman to bring his knowledge of physiology, anatomy, and scholarly writing to bear on the task — with unhappy results for Muybridge.

Meanwhile the pictures spoke for themselves. Wilkes, in the New York *Spirit of the Times,* was now writing like a man who had always believed:

There can be no doubt of the correctness of the representations, and they set several questions at rest about which even experts have been at variance. . . . Two-thirds of the photographs have a very comical effect, and some of them look more like a hobby-horse than a trotter going at full speed. There are four of them, however, which represent the horse entirely clear of the ground, showing that he is free from contact with the earth certainly one-third of the time, and these do look like a trotter. It has long been a vexed question as to whether a trotting horse was ever clear of the ground when in motion, and some lights of the turf have stubbornly argued the negative of the proposition. These gentlemen must now, as gracefully as possible, lay aside opinions held for years.

Neglecting to admit that he had been one such stubborn light of the turf, Wilkes nevertheless gracefully laid aside his previous opinions: "This series of pictures will confuse and break up all existing notions as to the trotting gait, but they substitute the truth for vague impressions arising from defective observation."[20] J. Cairns Simpson later agreed with his friend Wilkes: "If we fail to avail ourselves of the teachings of this superhuman professor [Muybridge], it will be a confession of willful perversity and an avowal of stupid, mulish ignorance."[21] The tendency was for people "in the know" to accept the pictures unreservedly and to learn what they could from them. But for a long time the general public continued to resist the evidence of the camera and regard the images of animal locomotion which had not previously been accessible to the human eye as ludicrous and incredible.

Probably the most important voice to be raised in behalf of the photographer was that of the French scientist Etienne Jules Marey. Impressed by the account of Muybridge's accomplishments which had appeared in *La Nature,* on December 18, 1878, he wrote a letter to the editor, Gaston Tissandier:

I am lost in admiration over the instantaneous photographs of Mr. Muybridge, which you published in your last number of La Nature. *Can you put me in correspondence with the author? I want to beg his aid and support to solve certain physiological problems so difficult to solve by other methods; for instance, the questions connected with the flight of birds. I was dreaming of a kind of photographic gun, seizing and portraying the bird in an attitude, or better still, a series of attitudes, displaying the successive different motions of the wing.*

Cailletet informed me he had formerly essayed something similar, with encouraging results. It is evident this would be an easy matter for Mr. Muybridge to accomplish, and what beautiful zooetropes he could give us, and we could perfectly see the true movements of all imaginable animals. It would be animated zoology. So far as artists are concerned, it would create a revolution, since we could furnish them the true attributes of motion, the position of the body in equilibrium, which no model could pose for them. . . . My enthusiasm is overflowing.[22]

[19]*Resources of California,* August 1878. Muybridge's first lectures when he demonstrated the Zoöpraxiscope (chap. 21) must have leaned heavily on Stanford's analysis.

[20]July 27, 1878.
[21]*California Spirit of the Times,* San Francisco, May 8, 1880.
[22]Translation in *Morning Call,* February 23, 1879; in Scrapbook.

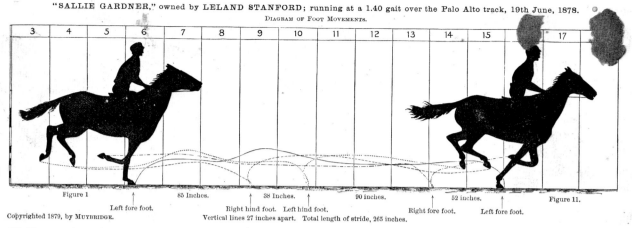

Figure 1.   85 Inches.   38 Inches.   90 inches.   52 inches.   Figure 11.

Left fore foot.   Right hind foot.   Left hind foot.   Right fore foot.   Left fore foot.

Vertical lines 27 inches apart.   Total length of stride, 265 inches.

95. The negatives of the Palo Alto photographs were made an intervals of twenty-seven inches of distance and about the twenty-fifth part of a second of time. They illustrate the consecutive positions assumed by the animal during a single stride. The exposure of each negative was calculated by Muybridge as less than the two-thousandth part of a second. This diagrammatic analysis of the stride of "Sally Gardner" was prepared for the use of Thomas Eakins.

With the appearance of Marey's letter in *La Nature*, the Stanford-Muybridge research was accorded the status of a major scientific contribution. Stanford was no longer simply an American millionaire, or the "Eisenbahnkoenig" as the Berlin press characterized him. Rather he was now Marey's own kind of ideal man, "especially interested in these inquiries and placed in favorable circumstances to undertake them," as he had defined such a man in his book *La Machine animale* in 1873.[23]

Muybridge's reply to Marey's letter was dated February 17, 1879, and printed in *La Nature* for March 22:

Please have the goodness to transmit to Professor Marey the assurance of my highest esteem and tell him that the reading of his celebrated book on animal locomotion had inspired Governor Stanford with the first idea of the solving of the problem of locomotion with the aid of photography. Stanford consulted me in this matter and, at his request, I decided to undertake the task. He asked me to follow a most complete set of experiments . . .

This exchange of letters focused scientific and artistic attention on Muybridge rather than Stanford — on the doer rather than the patron, the practitioner rather than the theorist — and was to lead to an unexpected chain of consequences which would make it possible for Muybridge and Marey to meet as creative collaborators in Paris. Soon Muybridge sent to Marey an instantaneous photograph of a flock of homing pigeons in flight, the first of a long series of studies on the flight of birds which would engage the attention of future investigators and ultimately add to the knowledge of aerial locomotion and to theories of aeronautics.

[23] In the American edition, *Animal Mechanism,* 1874, p. 161.

In 1878 the painter Thomas Eakins, in Philadelphia, began a brief exchange of correspondence with Muybridge which was to be of importance for both their professional futures. This was hinted at by an article in the *Alta California* for November 21:

The instantaneous pictures of the running and trotting horse, at full speed, taken on an original plan devised by a Californian photographic artist, with the assistance of a San Francisco capitalist, have attracted much attention in the Eastern States and Europe, and called out a number of letters from artists, anatomists, horse-fanciers, and others, all expressing the hope that other pictures of a similar character will be taken. A lecturer on anatomy in an art school wants a series showing the changes in the position of the muscles while running, thus supplying a great want of art students.

96. Thomas Eakins (1844-1916) *The Fairman Rogers Four-in-Hand* 1879. Oil on canvas. Eakins attempted to utilize the Muybridge findings in representing the movement of the horses, but Muybridge objected that the positions chosen were anachronistic for the strides represented.

The lecturer on anatomy presumably was Thomas Eakins, for there exists a series of Eakins-Muybridge letters in which Eakins, who lectured at the Pennsylvania Academy of the Fine Arts, expressed the delight of himself and Fairman Rogers, the director of the academy, in the Muybridge photographs of 1878. Eakins used the photographs to guide his representation of the horses in his 1879 painting, *A May Morning in the Park*, commissioned by Rogers, which depicts the latter's four-in-hand coach and its fashionably attired passengers being drawn along at a pleasant pace. Eakins also offered methodological suggestions. We find Muybridge writing to him on May 7, 1879:

I shall commence with the new experiments next week and we shall hope to give you something better than we before accomplished. . . . I invited Mr. Rogers to come out here during the time we shall be at work. The trip will well repay him, not only from the great interest he has manifested in the subject of our experiment but also in the pleasure he would feel in visiting our mountains and their glorious scenery and the extensive ranches and stock farms. Cannot you persuade him to come out?[24]

[24] Quoted in Gordon Hendricks, "A May Morning in the Park," *Bulletin of the Philadelphia Museum of Art*, LX, no. 285 (Spring 1965), 48-64.

21. The Zoöpraxiscope (1879–1880)

As early as July 1878 Muybridge began to lecture before California audiences on the results of the Palo Alto photographic experiments. These lectures, illustrated with lantern slides made from the instantaneous photographs, proved popular and provided Muybridge with a new and welcome source of income.

A typical program was presented before the Art Association of San Francisco on July 8. Muybridge employed two projection lanterns. As the lecture progressed, he placed in the first lantern the slide from the "Horse in Motion" series showing Occident in all twelve positions of his trotting stride. In the second lantern he placed enlargements of each of these positions, one after another. This scheme allowed for a comparison of the positions as well as a detailed analysis of each, for the single pictures were projected upon the screen nearly in life size.

On this same program Muybridge projected from one lantern the photograph of an artist's rendering of "Judge Fullerton," supposedly a representation of that horse at the height of his trotting stride, and simultaneously from the other a slide showing Occident photographed at the peak of his trotting stride. The audience burst into spontaneous laughter, readily seeing the discrepancy between the tradition a "hobbyhorse" posture of the painter's steed and the quite different but scientifically accurate representation caught by the camera. Thus, by projecting slides which showed contrasts and comparisons, Muybridge sought to educate the audience — or, rather, reeducate their eyes — to the facts of animal movement, and to demonstrate how artists had traditionally relied upon convention rather than fact in delineating rapid motion.

Muybridge usually showed about sixty such slides at a program.

His commentary was at first based on Stanford's analysis of the pictures, but soon he had formalized his own observations as well. The press stated that "in these automatic-electric photographs Mr. Muybridge instructs the world."[1]

The programs continued through August and September. When the novelty of the horse pictures wore off, Muybridge varied the fare with view slides, shown about 20 feet square, of Alaska, the Yosemite Valley, Central America, of the "Panorama of San Francisco." Presently attendance declined and he ceased to appear on a regular schedule, giving showings only when the spirit moved him. He carried his program to outlying cities — Sacramento and Stockton.[2] Then the analysis of motion ceased to hold the attention of the West Coast.

But Muybridge was not a man to remain long on any one plateau. The next step was synthesis. Between 1878 and 1879, scientific journals in the United States and abroad were digesting the meaning of the Palo Alto experiments and predicting where Muybridge's instantaneous, analytical photographs of motion might lead. The editor of the *Scientific American* suggested that the serial pictures from "The Horse in Motion" (as published in the magazine) might be cut out and mounted on strips for use in the scientific toy known as the zoetrope.[3] This optical instrument reached the peak of its popularity in the 1860s and 1870s. Available in both disk and cylinder forms, it was a kind of viewer in which drawings, prepared to represent stages in a sequence of motion, could be placed and whirled around

[1] *Examiner*, San Francisco, July 2, 1878.
[2] *Chronicle*, San Francisco, August 29, 1878.
[3] Issue of October 8, 1878.

to give the illusion of continuous movement. Like the kaleidoscope, the stereoscope, and the microscope, it was an "educational toy" suitable for both children and grown-ups, and permissible as an instructive Sabbath pastime: along with the demonstration of an optical principle, the persistence of vision, it offered the possibility of a kind of sober entertainment.[4]

In December 1878, Marey had written of the "beautiful zoetropes" that Muybridge might provide. In *L'Illustration*, Paris, January 25, 1879, it was reported by Emile Duhousset, who had written books on horses and their gaits, that he had mounted the Muybridge photographs in a zoetrope to good effect. In the same issue, bands of silhouettes for the zoetrope, made from the photographs, were offered for 10 francs, with the observation that, whereas Muybridge "decomposed" motion in his instantaneous photographs, the effect of their use in the zoetrope would be to recompose it. In *The Field*, London, on June 28, appeared a comment by the editor, W. B. Tegetmeier, that "Representations of animals in rapid motion are always conventional, never real, [but] if the ten stages in the stride of the racer could be as it were fused together, so as to be seen in rapid succession, the appearance of the horse in action should, if they are correct, be reproduced." He stated that he had already mounted Muybridge's pictures in a zoetrope with satisfactory results and was awaiting the construction of a praxinoscope especially adapted to them. Tegetmeier seems later to have gone further and offered the zoetrope bands for sale in England under his own copyright.[5] On July 9, Fairman Rogers mentioned in an article that Thomas Eakins had utilized the phenakistoscope to synthesize Wachter's drawings of 1862 illustrating the gallop. He added that now he had himself "constructed a large metal zoetrope with various appliances for making it a scientific instrument," and went on:

The idea was of course a very natural one, and it had already occurred to Gov. Stanford and Mr. Muybridge, who had independently done the same thing. The photographs are not exactly adapted for immediate use in the zoetrope. They are too small, and most of them show no interior modelling, but are mere silhouettes, in which the near and off legs [of the horse] cannot be readily distinguished from each other. . . . To obtain a perfectly satisfactory result, drawings must be based upon the information given by the photographs. . . . To do this, Mr. Eakins plotted carefully, with due attention to all the conditions of the problem, the successive positions of the photographs and constructed, most ingeniously, the trajectories. . . . When the figures thus made are put in the zoetrope, a perfect representation of the motion is obtained. . . . The value of these investigations to the artist is very great.[6]

The machine developed by Muybridge in 1879 went beyond anything used by Duhousset, Tegetmeier, or Eakins. Working at Stanford's suggestion and with his blessing, Muybridge constructed his first viewer, a device based on Wheatstone's reflecting stereoscope and adapted, he said, from a model that he found in the *Boy's Playbook of Science*.[7] This viewer has vanished without a trace. It was soon succeeded by what Muybridge called initially the Zoögyroscope[8] and later the Zoöpraxiscope. The latter instrument is the one on which Muybridge's fame as an early exhibitor of motion pictures is founded.[9]

The Zoöpraxiscope combined a projecting lantern, rotating disks on which appeared a limited number of silhouettes, hand-painted over Muybridge's sequential photographs; and a counterrotating slotted disk, geared to operate at equal speed, which acted as a kind of shutter and gave the effect of intermittent movement, as in the phenakistoscope.[10] The two advances over what Duhousset, Tegetmeier, and Eakins were doing consisted of the use of a projecting machine and the use of images directly made from instantaneous, unposed photographs.

As early as 1853, the Austrian officer Franz von Uchatius had combined the use of disks with a projecting lantern. Such an

[4] The zoetrope was based on the phenakistoscope, invented in 1832 by the Belgian physicist Plateau, who developed the stroboscopic method of studying motion by looking through slots in a revolving disk. In the same year the similar stroboscope was invented independently in Austria by Stampfer. In 1860, Desvignes suggested the showing of a series of stereo-scopic views in a revolving cylinder; instruments of this sort were called stereotropes.

[5] A zoetrope band, "The Gallop, from Tegetmeier on the Paces of the Horse," is in the Scrapbook, with clippings from *L'Illustration* and *The Field*.

[6] Newspaper clipping in Scrapbook.

[7] By J. H. Pepper, London, 1860; a copy is in the library of the Academy of Motion Picture Arts and Sciences, Beverly Hills, Calif. Muybridge refers to this viewer in *Animals in Motion*, p. 14 (Dover edition).

[8] *News Letter*, San Francisco, May 8, 1880.

[9] The final instrument is in the Public Library, Kingston-on-Thames. The Science Museum, London, as mentioned earlier, has a copy. A working Zoöpraxiscope is in the International Museum of Photography, Rochester, N.Y. For the Muybridge exhibition at the Stanford Museum of Art in 1972, David Beach constructed another one.

[10] In *Muybridge: The Stanford Years*, p. 71, Anita Mozley suggests that Stanford and Muybridge "intended to synthesize the analytical photographs even before an experimental method for taking them had been devised." She bases this idea on the fact that "a zoetrope with thirteen slots uses twelve images to convey forward motion, and that twelve cameras were ordered for the study."

instrument, the "projecting phenakistoscope," was patented in the United States by A. B. Brown in 1869[11] and was used by Heyl, of Philadelphia, for projecting his sequence of posed photographs of the waltz in 1870. The synthesis and projection of images of motion upon a screen, therefore, was a legacy to Muybridge from previous experimenters; but the use of the phenakistoscope for projecting photographic sequences of rapid motion was entirely his contribution. He alone had the method and apparatus for producing the sequences of analytic photographs of rapid motion required for such projection.

Muybridge wrote of the Zoöpraxiscope:

Pursuing this scheme, [I] arranged, in the same consecutive order, on some glass discs, a number of equidistant phases of certain movements; each series, as before, illustrated one or more complete and recurring acts of motion, or a combination of them: for example, an athlete turning a somersault on horseback, while the animal was cantering; a horse making a few strides of the gallop, a leap over a hurdle, another few strides, another leap, and so on; or a group of galloping horses.

Suitable gearing of an apparatus constructed for the purpose caused one of these glass discs, when attached to a central shaft, to revolve in front of the condensing lens of a projecting lantern, parallel with, and close to another disc fixed to a tubular shaft which encircled the other, and around which it rotated in the contrary direction. The latter disc was of sheet-metal, in which, near its periphery, radiating from its centre, were long narrow perforations, the number of which had a definite relation to the number of phases in the one or more lines of motion on the glass disc — the same number, one or two more, or one or two less — according to the sequence of phases, the intended direction of the movement, or the variations desired in the apparent rate of speed.

The discs being of large size, small portions only of their surfaces — showing one phase of each of the circles of moving animals — were in front of the condenser at the same instant. . . .

To this instrument [I] gave the name of Zoöpraxiscope; it is the first apparatus ever used, or constructed, for synthetically demonstrating movements analytically photographed from life, and in its resulting effects is the prototype of all the various instruments which, under a variety of names, are used for a similar purpose at the present day.[12]

This intricate and marvelous machine thus combined for the first time the projecting lantern, the transparent positive made from instantaneous photographs (heavily outlined and often completely covered with opaque paint to heighten the contrast),

[11] A picture of Brown's device appears in C. W. Ceram, *Archaeology of the Cinema,* New York: Harcourt, 1965, facing p. 73, where it is juxtaposed to Muybridge's Zoöpraxiscope.
[12] *Animals in Motion,* p. 14.

the revolving disk of Plateau (see note 4), and the counterrevolving, slotted disk that acted as an intermittent shutter.

The Zoöpraxiscope was given its debut at Mayfield Grange during a private party in the fall of 1879. As Muybridge put the machine in operation, projecting 24 consecutive phases in the stride of one of Stanford's favorite horses, he remarked, "There, Governor, you have a representation of Hawthorn galloping at a 1:42 gait."

Stanford studied the image on the screen a few moments, catching at once the rhythm of the horse's gait. "I think you must be mistaken in the name of the animal, Mr. Muybridge," he replied. "That is certainly not the gait of Hawthorn but of Anderson."

Stanford was right. For "Anderson" had been substituted at the track for "Hawthorn" on the day that the photographs were taken. Muybridge had not known this. The fact that Stanford recognized the difference between the two horses was testimony both of his acute observation and of the excellence of Muybridge's Zoöpraxiscope.[13]

Alexander Barclay, formerly keeper of the Department of Chemistry and Photography at the Science Museum, South Kensington, and a keen student of Muybridge's work, has suggested that there were, in fact, two Zoöpraxiscopes:

The early hand-drawn images were in the form of black silhouettes, [and] the plates and discs were heavy and cumbersome. They do not fit the machine at Kingston-upon-Thames which probably represents a later adaptation, or possibly an improvement on the earlier model. The possibility of adaptation is rather borne out by the horizontally projecting arms at the sides of the lantern, which do not appear to be necessary for the successful use of the instrument, at any rate in its present form. They may possibly have formed parts of a science lantern.

The existing instrument employs glass discs of 12 inch diameter, bearing hand coloured transparent diagrams, suitably elongated. The number of phases of motion on the discs is kept to within certain limits, allowing the use of a single shutter with 13 slots which are adjustable in size. The discs are turned by a handle closely resembling that of a hand sewing machine, from which indeed it may have been obtained. Discs and shutter are simply geared to operate at equal speed, though in opposite directions. Adjustments are provided for centering the edge of the discs correctly in the beam of light, which at that time was provided by the "lime light." The glass discs are quickly changed and held in position by a three-pronged clamp and screw behind the shutter. This was a great improvement

[13] Clark, pp. 367-368.

97. *Top left,* an advertisement for the Zoetrope or "Wheel of Life," the optical toy in *drum* form, in which a sequence of drawings viewed through the slits at the upper edge took on the illusion of continuous, lifelike motions when the drum was rotated.

98. *Top right,* the Phenakistoscope, an optical toy in *disc* form, in which a sequence of drawings on one side is viewed (against a mirror) through slots on the other side. In another form, the need for the mirror was eliminated by utilizing two counter-rotating discs to create the illusion of motion

99. *Lower left,* Muybridge's motion-picture projector, the Zoopraxiscope, combining elements of the magic-lantern slide projector, the optical principle of the persistence of vision in the counter-rotating discs of the Phenakistoscope, and the preparation of images taken from instantaneous, sequential photographs and mounted for projection on glass.

100. *Lower right,* glass discs prepared by Muybridge for projection in the Zoopraxiscope, 1879 and after.

on the earlier apparatus and must have saved considerable time.
No intermittent mechanism was necessary with this type
of instrument, all parts moving continuously. The amount
of movement portrayed was, however, strictly limited.[14]

Muybridge never claimed to be the inventor of his Zoöpraxiscope, and never patented it, in the United States or elsewhere. He did claim it to be the prototype instrument for "synthetically demonstrating movements analytically photographed from life." Certainly it remained the only commercially demonstrated motion picture machine for more than a decade, or until Thomas A. Edison mass-produced his Kinetoscope, which was not a projector.

San Franciscans were apprised of the new machine when the *California Spirit of the Times,* on March 27, 1880, announced the "invention" of an "instrument which Mr. Muybridge has christened the zoogyroscope. . . . It consists of two discs about 18 inches in diameter, one being of glass on which there are figures copied from those taken by the camera." On May 4, the photographer demonstrated the Zoöpraxiscope before members of the San Francisco Art Association, showing horses running, trotting, and jumping; the athletes and their performances; and the bull, deer, and dog, along with the flying birds that Marey had so admired, in analytical form. In reports the next day, the *Call* exclaimed that "Nothing was wanting but the clatter of hoofs upon the turf and an occasional breath of steam to make the spectator believe he had before him the flesh and blood steeds," while the *Alta California* declared: "Mr. Muybridge has laid the foundation of a new method of entertaining the people, and we predict that his instantaneous, photographic, magic-lantern zoetrope will make the rounds of the civilized world."

In a negative vein, the San Francisco *News Letter* on May 8 claimed that a local artist, Jules Tavernier, had "suggested the idea of *adapting* the series of pictures to the toy," and that Muybridge had applied for a patent on the Zoöpraxiscope which had been denied. Describing the demonstration, the paper commented:

The pictures shown by Mr. Muybridge of horses **not in motion** *are clear and sharp, while those of the same horse* **in motion** *are clumsy, stiff and uncouth — in fact, they seem to have been* indicated *by the camera, and* **made** *by the retoucher, and badly made, too. The propulsion of the horse, along with a stiff and jerky motion of*

[14] Letter to Haas, February 4, 1958.

the limbs, as are these pictures when shown by the zoescope, is not enough to portray the "horse in motion." It is no more graceful, and but little less natural, than the ring of hobby-horses we rode in childhood. Much has yet to be done before a fair exhibit is made of what is here clumsily attempted.[15]

Many detractors up to the present day have sought to discredit not only Muybridge's Palo Alto photographs as "mere silhouettes," but also the Zoöpraxiscope as being primitive in the extreme and thus of no consequence for the history of motion pictures.

The photographs speak for themselves. Testimony about the Zoöpraxiscope (other than that it drew audiences for fifteen years and was variously reviewed by the press) is harder to come by. In 1930, Ernest Webster, who as a boy had traveled with Muybridge on his lecture tours, declared that the projected images "did NOT flicker painfully as did the early cinematograph, but moved smoothly." This testimony is supported in a letter by the former borough librarian of Kingston-on-Thames, Harry Cross:

In July 1946 the **Daily Express** *assembled an excellent exhibition at Dorland House, London, "Fifty Years of Films," which was attended by thousands of people. . . . We lent the zoopraxiscope and other material. The zoopraxiscope was actually shown working during the whole period of the exhibition — about six weeks. It is a tribute to Muybridge's skill that the machine, electrically operated, worked without a hitch for the whole period the show was open, 11:00 a.m. to 7:00 p.m. each day, including Sundays.*[16]

Whatever its limitations, the Zoöpraxiscope did a pioneering job of synthesizing motion. In 1879 and 1880 it must, to some, have seemed a minor miracle.

Today, one may still see Muybridge's Zoöpraxiscope at his birthplace. It stands in lonely splendor, regal and somber, in its glass case in the Public Library. Within recent years Thom Anderson, of Los Angeles, has undertaken to resynthesize the Palo Alto sequences on motion picture film. As one after another of Muybridge's subjects appears to move upon the screen, one feels the spell of his photography and the logic of his method.[17]

[15] Emphasis in original.
[16] Letter to Janet Pendegast Leigh, about 1946; Haas collection. The testimony of Webster is in a clipping from the *Gazette* (not further identified), August 1, 1930, laid in the Scrapbook by the librarian.
[17] Thom Anderson, "Eadweard Muybridge," *Film Culture,* Summer 1966.

PORTFOLIO IV
Palo Alto 1878–1883

101. The "experiment track" at Palo Alto.

102. The Palo Alto Stock Rancho.

103. *Above,* Frankie leaping, 1879

104. *Left,* Studies of foreshortenings.

105. Running high leap.

106. Athlete running.

107. Greyhound running.

108. *Mahomet Running*, 1879.

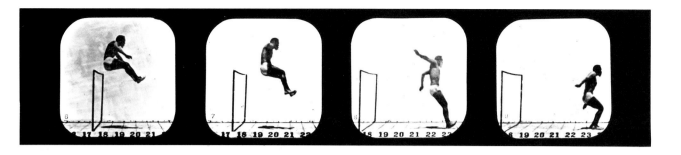

109. A Muybridge composite photograph of a running herd of horses at Stanford's Palo Alto farm.

PIGEONS.

Photographed at Palo Alto, 1879.

THE subjects of flight and soaring present so many intricate problems that the author is reluctantly compelled to relinquish his attempt to elucidate them. His investigation, however, brought to light some facts which, although they had been theorized upon, had never been proved.

Phases 5, 6, 7, 16, 17, and 18 of the cockatoo, series 79, demonstrate that the primary feathers of a bird's wing, although interlocked in the downward stroke, are separated, and their thin edges turned in the direction of their movement during the recovery. This partial revolution of the primary

237

110. Photograph of birds in flight, sent by Muybridge to Professor Etienne-Jules Marey in Paris in 1879, at the beginning of their life-long professional friendship and collaboration.

111. Residence of Leland Stanford on San Francisco's Nob Hill (right) the interiors of which were photographed by Muybridge (see pages 106-108); the residence of Mark Hopkins (left), one of Stanford's "Big Four" railroad-king partners, shown under construction, with the tower from which Muybridge photographed his spectacular "Panoramas of San Francisco from the California Street Hill" 1876/1877. (See pages 85-92.)

22. Fame Abroad: Paris (1881~1882)

In 1880 and 1881 the San Francisco press took frequent note of the Stanford-Muybridge activities. In the clippings kept by Muybridge we read of his giving a "private exhibition of his art accompanied by a lucid lecture" in the ballroom of the Stanford mansion on Nob Hill. No doubt the Zoöpraxiscope was in use. Opinions varied as to whether his estimate of 1/5,000 of a second for his instantaneous exposures was accurate, and whether Leland Stanford had spent $40,000 on "his hobby," or much more. One newspaper commented that people who could not accept the findings of the camera were "hardshells," another that Muybridge's motion studies would not "greatly affect art."[1]

Early in 1881 a newspaper reported that Stanford had "imported a horse's skeleton from New York," and that the skeleton had been "carefully photographed in each of the positions of a horse trotting." It added that the photographs of horses in motion at the Palo Alto Farm were being prepared for publication "in a large and costly volume" and also "for use in the zoogyroscope, which it is Mr. Stanford's intention, it is understood, to exhibit before the scientific bodies of the East, England and Europe."[2] A few months later it was reportedly the "intention of Governor Stanford to send the entire equipment of electro-photographic apparatus to Europe and continue the experiments there, and also to entertain the various art and scientific societies with a series of private entertainments," where the "intelligent and lucid descriptions by the inventor himself" would add to the audience's enjoyment.[3]

Meanwhile, events were taking place in Paris which were to have a profound effect upon Muybridge's professional future and the thus far amicable relationship between him and Leland Stanford.

In 1879 Stanford had taken his wife and their young son to Europe for an extended stay. The chief purpose was to visit European artists and commission family portraits. While Muybridge was lecturing and exhibiting the results of his Palo Alto work in California, Leland Stanford was studio-hopping in Paris. The painter he chose to do Mrs. Stanford's portrait was Léon Bonnat,

the "French Lenbach," an exceedingly conscientious artist who had painted a whole gallery of celebrated personages from Victor Hugo to Pasteur. His large and excellent ceremonial portrait of Mrs. Stanford was completed in 1881.[4]

The painter whom Leland Stanford wished for his own portrait was, however, Jean Louis Ernest Meissonier, an even more scrupulous artist than Bonnat. His "whole long, rich and fruitful career," wrote one of his biographers, "may be summed up as a successful and varied application of one great principle: devout and inflexible respect for reality."[5] Stanford's factual nature warmed to this approach to the arts. Moreover, Meissonier also was a passionate observer of animal locomotion, famous for his sweeping historical canvases in which horses played a conspicuous part. It was well known that he had "expended a fortune and years of his life in his attempts to solve the problem of fixing the attitude of animals in motion at a given moment" on his canvases.[6] He had studied the motion of horses from the window of a private car that was constructed at his own expense, sketching rapidly as his subjects galloped alongside the track. Even so, in his masterpiece, *Friedland, 1807,* painted for the New York merchant prince A. T. Stewart, Meissonier had represented Napoleon's steed in an attitude which critics ridiculed and pronounced impossible.

Stanford first visited Meissonier in 1879, and it was Stewart who introduced him. The meeting was not, at the outset, auspicious, for Meissonier was prosperous and could well afford to take an independent stand. When it was proposed that Meissonier should paint Stanford's portrait, he refused point blank. The checkbook in Stanford's hands only irritated him further.

But Stanford was a man of infinite skill and patience in getting his own way. Realizing that he must do something to win Meissonier's attention, he carefully baited a trap. As the master led the two American capitalists around his studio, carefully explaining how he had used his exact knowledge of equine motion in painting his recent canvases, Stanford asked him to sketch the accurate posture of a trotting horse. Meissonier stepped to the easel and with a few dextrous touches produced a drawing.

[1] A different sort of motion was the subject of a series of photographs of the solar eclipse of January 11, 1880. Muybridge took exposures two and three minutes apart at the height of the eclipse. *Muybridge: The Stanford Years,* pp. 74-75.

[2] *Examiner,* San Francisco, February 16, 1881; in Scrapbook. This article was written by Muybridge, according to testimony by J. B. D. Stillman (see chap. 24).

[3] *Evening Post,* San Francisco, May 3, 1881.

[4] The portrait is in the Stanford University Museum of Art.

[5] *Meissonier,* "Masters in Art" series, Boston: Bates and Guild Co., 1904, p.28.

[6] Ibid., For a discussion see Françoise Forster-Hahn, "The Study of Movement in Science and Art," in *Muybridge: The Stanford Years,* pp. 85-109.

Stanford contemplated the results. "Now," he said, "make me a sketch of that same horse when he shall have progressed twelve inches further on."

Meissonier was indeed caught. He went to the easel again and, with some hesitation, made a second sketch. He stepped back, looked at it critically, rubbed it out, made another, and three times repeated the same operation. Then, rubbing out the lines of his last attempt, he said, "I cannot do it."

Now it was Stanford's turn to play the expert. He showed Meissonier some of the Muybridge photographs and told him in detail about the Palo Alto experiments. "I was dumbfounded," Meissonier reported later. "I was no longer in business with an American millionaire. Here was something I could build on. I promised him his portrait." Perhaps Stanford left the studio completely happy, but Meissonier spent a sleepless night, vowing to himself that he would never paint a horse again.[7]

The portrait of Leland Stanford was painted in 1881.[8] In it, Meissonier placed at Stanford's elbow the open volume of Muybridge photographs that summarized the Palo Alto experiments. This album, bearing the title *The Attitudes of Animals in Motion* and the patron's name in gilt letters, was Stanford's dividend from the experiments, presented by the photographer in these dedicatory words:

Hon. Leland Stanford:

SIR: Herewith please find the photographs illustrating the attitudes of Animals in Motion executed by me according to your instruction at Palo Alto in 1878 and 1879.

Muybridge

Menlo Park, 15th May, 1881[9]

[7]Vallery Gréard, *Meissonier,* New York, 1897, pp. 194-195.

[8]Now in the Stanford University Museum of Art.

[9]Presumably this is the copy held in the Rare Books and Special Collections, Stanford University Libraries. The full title is *The Attitudes of Animals in Motion: A Series of Photographs Illustrating the Consecutive Positions Assumed by Animals in Performing Various Movements.* The book contains 203 albumen prints from wet-plate collodion negatives, with the statement: "Executed at Palo Alto, California, in 1878 and 1879. Copyright 1881, by Muybridge." The individual pages are untitled, bearing only Muybridge's copyright stamp, and are preceded by an index and his introduction.

   "It is not known how many copies of this book Muybridge printed. There must have been at least five: the one that appears in the Meissonier painting [and] the four that Muybridge sold in London in 1882. . . . The book was, at any rate, handmade. No reproductive process was used for the photographs. There was no factory setup at Palo Alto, and there is no publisher named. Muybridge printed the five (at least) sets of 203 photographs himself. It was a prodigious work.

   "The photographs . . . have an archetypal quality, a tense awkwardness that is apparent in any art before the finesse that accompanies foreseeable

During the long sittings for the portrait Meissonier and Stanford became fast friends. Now Meissonier wanted something from Stanford, and he baited his trap as well. Playing upon Stanford's pride in the experiments, he proposed that Muybridge be brought to Paris to elaborate upon the story of the motion photographs, and that Muybridge and Marey should work on further experiments together under Stanford's patronage. To cement the matter, he offered to call together a number of eminent scientists and artists to view the projections of the Zoöpraxiscope and hear Muybridge's comments on them at first hand. In the end Stanford agreed to underwrite the cost of Muybridge's trip.

In San Francisco, meanwhile, Muybridge was having a productive time. Besides giving lectures, he prepared a few further copies of *The Attitudes of Animals in Motion,* which he copyrighted in his own name in the spring of 1881. In July he filed application for a patent on a "Picture-Feeding Device for Magic Lanterns," which was granted in December.[10] In August he filed application on a "Method of and Apparatus for Photographing Changing or Moving Object," essentially a means for activating a circuit breaker which operated the shutters of a camera at desired intervals of time. This patent was granted in June 1883.[11] In September he applied for a reissue of the letters patent for the "Method of and Apparatus for Photographing Objects in Motion." This was granted on December 6.

All together, a consolidation and fulfillment of Muybridge's West Coast projects was taking place, or seemingly so. Stanford's friend Dr. J. B. D. Stillman was proceeding with an elaborate analysis of the locomotive machinery of the horse.[12] Stillman proposed a commercial publication of the Palo Alto findings and to this plan Muybridge agreed, assuming that his role in the experiments would be given due recognition. With this, at best a loose understanding, the project slipped out of his hands.

En route to Europe, Muybridge paused in New York, where

results sets in. Muybridge was experimenting in 1878-79; he was at the height of his interest in the doing of the work." Anita Ventura Mozley, in *Muybridge: The Stanford Years,* p. 60.

[10]No. 251,127.

[11]No. 279,878.

[12]Stillman, a Gold Rush physician, was the author of *Seeking the Golden Fleece,* a memoir of those times. He settled in San Francisco in 1849, in a home "made from the boards of dry-goods boxes." Henry Harris, *California's Medical Story,* San Francisco: Stacey, 1932, p. 82. He took part in the organization of the Medico-Chirurgical Association, edited the *California Medical Gazette,* and was a close friend of Stanford from the latter's earliest days in Sacramento.

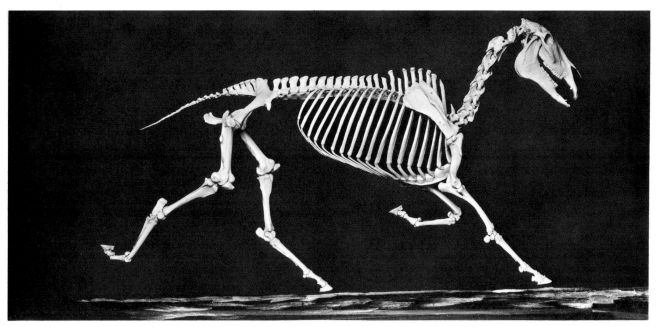

112. Muybridge, "Horse's skeleton in a trotting position," c. 1880. From *The Attitudes of Animals in Motion*, 1881.

113. Eadweard Muybridge during the first year of his fame abroad, 1881.

114. Jean-Louis-Ernest Meissonier (1815-1891) *Leland Stanford*, 1881. Oil on canvas. At Stanford's left elbow lies an opened volume of Muybridge's *The Attitudes of Animals in Motion*.

he put in storage the battery of cameras used for taking the analytical photographs at Palo Alto. The Zoöpraxiscope and the magic lantern, the disks and the slides, he took abroad with him. In London he made arrangements with the *British Journal of Photography* for that journal to handle the sale of copies of *The Attitudes of Animals in Motion* which he had also brought along, the price of an album to be twenty pounds.[13]

In September, Muybridge arrived in Paris. Here, for the next few months, he was rewarded with his first taste of undiluted glory. Nearly three years had passed since Etienne Jules Marey had first seen the photographs by Muybridge in *La Nature.* Now the two men met face to face and became devoted colleagues and lasting friends. On September 26, Marey gave a reception at his new home, to which he invited many distinguished Frenchmen and foreigners, with Eadweard Muybridge as the guest of honor.[14]

At this gathering, Muybridge showed his analytical photographs in the magic lantern, and then the disks were put in motion in the Zoöpraxiscope. Because Muybridge did not speak French, Marey commented on the pictures. To judge from a newspaper account, the reactions were wildly enthusiastic for a scholarly group. The performance of the Zoöpraxiscope, in particular, was greeted with astonishment, the apparently moving pictures suggesting a "chasse infernale" or a "défilé diabolique."[15] Muybridge concluded the presentation by showing the photographs of birds for which his host had wished in 1878.

Under Muybridge's influence Marey gave up his former graphic method of recording motion and turned to photography. For a while the two men collaborated, with two notable outcomes. First, Marey "substituted for Mr. Muybridge's apparatus a single one that gives upon the same plate the successive positions of a man or animal at the different instants that he is passing in front of the black screen."[16] This procedure resulted in the development of "Marey's wheel," or "Marey's photographic gun,"

a portable camera with a single circular revolving plate on which consecutive exposures were recorded at regulated intervals of time and distance. These multiple but often overlapping photographs, taken from a single point of view, although in effect quite different from those Muybridge achieved with his battery of cameras, were truly innovative visual images. Second, Muybridge had an opportunity to experiment with rapid gelatin dry-plate photography. He found it excellent and promptly gave up the more cumbersome wet-plate process. In his enthusiasm for this newer procedure (in which he credited Europe with being far ahead of the United States), he wrote to Stanford asking that publication of the Stanford-Muybridge-Stillman book be held up until he could provide a new series of illustrations made with dry plates. Stanford, however, expressed no interest in delaying the book, now entrusted to Stillman, for that purpose.[17]

On November 26 the art world of Paris was invited to meet Muybridge. Meissonier, who had recently finished Stanford's portrait, now played host, in his characteristic grand manner, at an entertainment for two hundred guests in his studio and residence.[18] Again the applause for Muybridge's pictures showed that his work was favorably judged by men of the highest discernment. His audience had expanded far beyond that of the San Franciscans whom he had sought to interest in the past; now he was faced with international recognition and acclaim. Meissonier, who translated Muybridge's remarks into French, stated at the conclusion of the showing his belief that Muybridge had made new resources available to artists through his photographs, and that a new era was now open to art.[19]

In December, Muybridge was asked to appear before the Cercle de l'Union Artistique. Meissonier again served as interpreter. Muybridge's informal humor was much appreciated. He spoke simply and directly, welcomed questions about his method, and behaved in no way like a lion. He professed himself to be only at the beginning of his work.[20]

During the six months that Muybridge was in Paris, Stanford's patronage of him waned. That some changes in feeling occurred on both sides can be seen in the subsequent events surrounding the

[13] As noted in the journal on August 19; in Scrapbook. The cameras and the sum of $2,000 (see chap. 24) appear to have been Muybridge's financial reward for his part in the project. The sale of the *Attitudes* albums is noted by Muybridge in a draft letter of May 2, 1892 (see chap. 28).

[14] *Le Globe,* Paris, September 27, 1881; in Scrapbook. The newspaper mentions, among others, Helmholtz, Bjerknes, Brown-Séquard, Mascart, d'Arsonval, Duhousset, Nadar, and Tissandier.

[15] Ibid.

[16] *Nature,* London, May 25, 1882. Both Muybridge and Eakins experimented with cameras based on the Marey principle. The *British Journal of Photography,* June 9, 1882, reported that Muybridge had shown some of Marey's photographs of motion early in 1882 and that these were "comparatively unfinished" in character.

[17] Stillman's deposition, August 7, 1883; in the Huntington Collection, George Arents Research Library, Syracuse University.

[18] *Le Figaro,* Paris, November 27, 1881; in Scrapbook. This mainly artistic company included Gérôme, Cabanel, Dumas fils, J. L. C. Garnier, Aimé Millet, Neuville, Bonnat, Detaille, Augier, Ridgway Knight, Goupil, Lefebvre, Claretie, Albert Wolff, Guillaume, and Saint-Marceaux.

[19] *Galignani's Messenger,* Paris, November 30; in Scrapbook.

[20] *American Register,* Paris, December 3; in Scrapbook.

115. Title page of *The Attitudes of Animals in Motion*, 1881.

116. Muybridge's patent for a picture-feeding device, which he used in presenting his slide and motion picture shows both in California and in Europe.

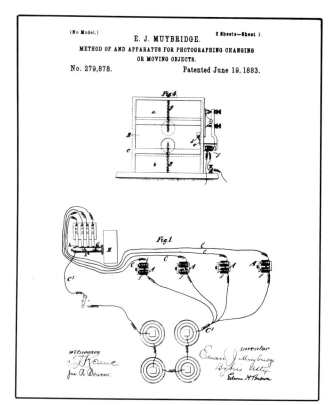

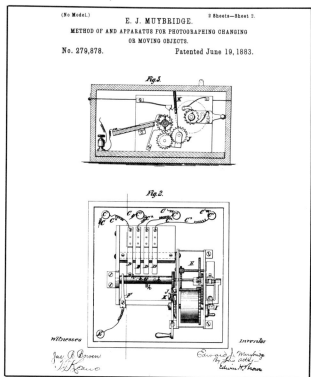

117. Muybridge's patent for an electrical timer, which he used at Palo Alto in those instances where the subject did not trigger the exposure automatically or electrically.

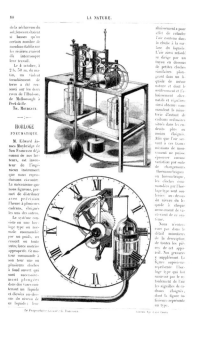

118. Pneumatic clock, presumably invented by Muybridge in San Francisco in 1879 or before, discussed in the French magazine *La Nature*.

publication of the book prepared by Stillman, *The Horse in Motion,* which was soon to become a cause célèbre.

For Muybridge, the prospective loss of Stanford's support had to be offset by the discovery of a new patron. Marey and Meissonier for a time sought to interest another important capitalist in collaborating on a huge new work on animal locomotion.[21] This might have happened, had not events next brought fame to Muybridge in his native land and led him to a wearisome lawsuit in the United States.

[21] Described by Muybridge in a letter to Shay, December 23; in Huntington Collection (see n. 17), quoted in *Muybridge: The Stanford Years,* pp. 124-125.

23. Fame Abroad: London (1882)

The attention shown to Muybridge in Paris in the fall of 1881 was noted in the British press. Detailed reports of his lectures and accomplishments had built a certain audience for him in England even before he returned there to lecture in March 1882. Moreover, he came to London armed with letters of recommendation from Meissonier to Sir Lawrence Alma-Tadema and to Henry Stacy Marks of the Royal Academy. He had also a letter from Sam Ward, the American politician and bon vivant, to the Earl of Rosebery.

"The Royal Institution — the most sedate, bewigged and conservative of bodies," reported the Philadelphia *Times,* "has held a meeting to consider whether the exhibition of photographs representing men and animals in motion is of a nature sufficiently calm and scientific to transpire before their grave and reverend selves. The Council has come to the conclusion that it is so."[1] On March 13, Muybridge presented his illustrated lecture before the Royal Institution. The audience that Monday afternoon included the "greatest scientific lights of the Kingdom, with a rare spice of aristocracy thrown in." Royalty was present in the persons of "the coming King and Queen, their children and their brother." There were also the Dukes of Westminster, Sutherland, Argyll, and Richmond, the Marquis of Salisbury, Lord Claude Hamilton, Sir Frederick Pollock, Sir Frederick Leighton, Professors Tyndall, Gladstone, and Huxley, and the poet laureate, Alfred Tennyson.[2]

The *Photographic News* reported the event in loving detail:

MR. MUYBRIDGE AT THE ROYAL INSTITUTION

Before a distinguished audience, which included H. R. H. the Prince of Wales, the Princess of Wales, and the three young Princesses, the Duke of Edinburgh — a distinguished photographer,

[1] March 26, 1882, from a London report dated March 11; in Scrapbook.
[2] Ibid.

it may be remembered — the Poet Laureate, the President of the Royal Society, and most of the managing body of the Royal Institution, Mr. Muybridge, of San Francisco, gave, on Monday, his first public demonstration in this country. Mr. Muybridge might well be proud of the reception accorded him, for it would have been difficult to add to the éclat of such first appearance, and throughout his lecture he was welcomed by a warmth that was as hearty as it was spontaneous.

Mr. Muybridge wisely left his wonderful pictures to speak for him, instead of making the occasion the subject of a long oration. He showed his photographs one after another on the screen by the aid of an electric lantern, and modestly explained them in clear but plain language. In this way the demonstration was at once rendered entertaining as well as interesting.

Mr. Muybridge first explained his plan of securing such rapid pictures of animals in motion. He showed a representation of his "studio" to begin with; it was like that portion of a race-course to be found opposite the grandstand. This latter building was, in effect, a camera stand, and a very grand one, into the bargain, for it contained twenty-four cameras in a row, the lenses a foot apart, all looking on to the course. As the animal passed, these cameras, with their instantaneous shutters, were fired off one after another by electricity. Thin linen threads, breast high, and a foot apart, were stretched across the course, and as the animal broke these threads, they, being connected, each of them, with a camera, brought about the exposure. The instantaneous shutter in each case simply consisted of two little planks, one to move upwards, and the other to move downwards, in front of the lens by rubber springs; the tension of these latter is very great — equal to 100 lb., Mr. Muybridge said — and the exposure was calculated to be not more than 1/5000 of a second. Whether this calculation is correct or no, certain it is that the spokes of a trotting carriage shown were very sharp, and there was hardly a movement visible in any of the animal pictures.

We may mention here that all his photographs were taken on wet plates, for they were secured four years ago. Iron was employed in their development, and no additional care or particular method was had recourse to.

Mr. Muybridge, by way of comparison, first threw on the screen a series of artists' sketches of the horse in motion, some of them old-world designs of the Egyptians and Greeks, some very modern, including the principal animal from Rosa Bonheur's well-known "Horse Fair." In no single instance had he been able to discover a correct drawing of the horse in motion, and, to prove his statement, he then threw on the screen several series of pictures representing the different positions taken up by a horse as he walks, trots, ambles, canters, or gallops. One thing was very plain from Mr. Muybridge's pictures, namely, that when a horse has two of his feet suspended between two supporting feet, the suspended feet are **invariably** *lateral;* that is to say, both suspended feet are on the same side of the animal. This, no painter — ancient or modern — had ever discovered. Then the amble was found to be different from the canter, and the canter very different again from the gallop; although most people imagined that, to perform all these, the horse used his legs in the same fashion. Mr. Muybridge was at some difficulty to describe the amble, and it seemed at one time as if it would be necessary to call upon Mr. Tennyson to give a definition of it in his well known lines: "Property, property, property!"[3] but he succeeded subsequently in defining the step very satisfactorily afterwards by means of his pictures.

After Mr. Muybridge had shown his audience the quaint and (apparently) impossible positions that the horse assumes in his different gaits, he then most ingeniously combined the pictures on the screen, showing them one after another so rapidly, that the audience had before them the galloping horse, the trotting horse, etc. Nay, Mr. Muybridge, by means of his zoepracticoscope, showed the horse taking a hurdle — how it lifted itself for the spring, and how it lightly dropped upon its feet again. This pleasing display was the essence of life and reality. A new world of sights and wonders was, indeed, opened by photography, which was not less astounding because it was truth itself.

After these life-like pictures, it needed not Mr. Muybridge's dictum that to use a mild term it was "absurd" to see a galloping horse depicted with all four feet off the ground, a simple impossibility. And if this held good of one horse, what must be said of ten horses, thus painted, as was the case in Frith's "Derby Day," which Mr. Muybridge projected on the screen by way of comparison, and which the clever photographer described as a miracle.

Mr. Muybridge modestly calls his series of animals in motion — they include horse, dog, deer, bull, pig, etc. — simply preliminary results. They contain little or no half-tone, and are only proof of what may be done. What he desires now to secure, if he only receives sufficient encouragement, is a series of photographic "pictures," and these, with the experience he has now acquired, and with the gelatine process to help him, should be well within his reach. We only trust this encouragement will be forthcoming, and that Mr. Muybridge will be tempted to carry on the difficult work he has commenced with such genuine success.

[3] The rhythm of the words matches that of the ambling horse.

"I should like to see your boxing pictures," said the Prince of Wales to Mr. Muybridge . . . when the galloping horse, the running deer, the trotting bull, the halting pig, and the racing dogs had successively crossed the screen in life-like measure.

"I shall be very happy to show them, your Royal Highness," responded the clever photographer. . . . "I don't know that these pictures teach us anything very useful," said Mr. Muybridge, "but they are generally found amusing."

There were promptly thrown upon the screen the photographs of two athletes who pounded away at one another "to the infinite delight of the audience in general and the Prince of Wales in particular."[4] An extra meeting was arranged hurriedly for the same evening to accomodate the audience overflow of the afternoon.[5]

On Tuesday of that week, Muybridge lectured before members of the Royal Academy of Arts at Burlington House. The London correspondent of the San Francisco *Call* wrote of this lecture:

If you in California have any State pride, you must take pleasure in the amazingly brilliant success which has this week been achieved in London by Mr. Muybridge. . . . In all my long experience of London life I cannot recall a single instance where such warm tributes of admiration for merit have been unstintingly given by the greatest of the land. . . . All classes of people here have interested themselves in Mr. Muybridge's photographs. . . . To me, I confess, it was a sight of pride to behold a countryman of mine installed as an instructor within the sacred walls of the great temple of fine arts, there to give the fruits of his knowledge and the sum and substance of his investigations to such listeners as Sir Frederick Leighton, Alma-Tadema, Marks, Orchardson, Vicat Cole, and in fact the whole body of R.A.s, for the Academicians had rallied there almost to a man. . . . I sat next to Sir Frederick Leighton, who occupied the chair during the whole exhibition, and was very much interested in his remarks of surprise upon the extraordinary curvatures of the horse's hoofs. . . . He imitated it with his hand and arm in explanation to the various artists gathered near him. Certain it is that if any artist, before the advent of Muybridge's photographs, had the temerity to paint horses in the positions which the man from Palo Alto has shown to be those which these animals assume when in motion, that same artist would have been reproached for curious drawing. Now I should not be in the least surprised if next year's batch of paintings at the Salon and Royal Academy were to show the influence of Muybridge's photographs in the most

[4] London, March 17; in Scrapbook.

[5] A summary of Muybridge's presentation was printed by the Royal Institution as *Syllabus of a Course of Two Lectures on the Science of Animal Locomotion in Its Relation to Design in Art,* London, April 1882, 12 pp.

pronounced manner. Meissonier told Muybridge that he had given him entirely new lights on the positions of horses.

Alma-Tadema is also most enthusiastic in his praise of the new discovery; and after the exhibition was over the other evening, Sir Frederick Leighton went upon the platform, and in the most cordial language thanked Mr. Muybridge for the valuable information which he had afforded him and his brother artists. Thus Mr. Muybridge is launched upon the sea of London celebrity. Let us hope he will not be spoiled by it, as a certain California literary man has been. I do not fancy Muybridge is one of the kind who get spoiled by flattery. There seems too much hard sense and practical thought there for anything of this sort. There is money in his invention, in various ways. I believe if he were to "hire a hall" and give exhibitions twice a day at a shilling entrance fee, Mr. Muybridge would clear enough money during the coming summer to greatly assist him in the pursuance of the researches in the field where he has already made such curious and unexpected discoveries. The "send off" he has obtained in the shape of his two wonderfully brilliant audiences at the Royal Institution and the Royal Academy are sufficient in themselves to insure the attendance of thousands of curiosity-seekers, anxious to see what a thing could be which was patronized not only by royalty, but by that very close and conservative body, the Royal Academy of Fine Arts. Added to this fact, it must be remembered that England is a land where all classes of people love and cherish dogs and horses, and anything new relating to those animals is sure of attracting attention.

I have written concerning Mr. Muybridge's invention at great length this week to all the various newspapers with which I am connected, and again I say that California has reason to be proud of this clever photographer. With true American courage he delivered his explanatory lecture before the high mightinesses who assembled to hear him on two occasions, and his remarks were fitting, lucid, and often enlivened by humor of good taste.[6]

Whatever personal gratification Muybridge got from such acclaim, his public behavior was modest in the extreme. His thoughts were clearly on the future. At the conclusion of his lecture for the Savage Club, on March 18, he offered to place his entire equipment and his own experience gratis at the disposal

[6]*Morning Call,* April 9; in Scrapbook.

of any society or gentleman disposed to pursue further the subject of animal locomotion. The bid for patronage was not taken up, but Muybridge was loudly applauded and extended an honorary membership in the club — all the more pleasant because it came "immediately after the Prince of Wales had accepted the same distinction."[7]

Between April and June, Muybridge delivered further lectures at Eton College, the Society of Arts, the South Kensington Science and Art Department, the Royal Artillery Institute, and the Liverpool Art Club.[8] The press was uniformly complimentary. George Sala, in the *Illustrated London News,* declared: ". . . had Muybridge exhibited his 'Zoopraxiscope' three hundred years ago, he would have been burnt for a wizard."[9]

The correspondent of the Philadelphia *Times* gives us a glimpse of Muybridge, now at the age of fifty-two years:

In the midst of his Old World triumphs Mr. Muybridge has found time to drop in at my quarters on several occasions for a friendly chat. Like all people who amount to something, the California artist bears the traces of genius in his face and general get-up. As to the latter it is as **artistique au possible***; the loosely tied neck ribbon, the velvet coat, the grey felt sombrero — these might be called Californian, were they not the true artistic style of the London and Paris* **ateliers.** *With grey hair carelessly tossed back from an intellectual forehead, bright flashing eyes and a pleasant mouth, Mr. Muybridge must himself make an interesting subject for a photograph, whether in motion or repose.[10]*

Muybridge might have continued to bask in the recognition that he was receiving. Of a sudden, however, his pride and his sense of justice were shocked, and his reputation was put in question, by the treatment accorded him in the book issued under Stillman's name.

[7]*Photographic News,* March 24; in Scrapbook.
[8]A transcript of one of the lectures, including the comments of the chairman and Muybridge's modest, informative response, was printed in the *Journal of the Society of Arts,* June 23, pp. 838-843; in Scrapbook.
[9]March 28; in Scrapbook.
[10]March 26; in Scrapbook.

24. *The Horse in Motion* (1882-1883)

While Muybridge was enjoying his success in Paris, the book on the Stanford-Muybridge findings was being put into readiness for printing by Dr. J. B. D. Stillman. As early as October 24, 1881, the Boston publishing firm of James R. Osgood and Company was in correspondence with Stillman to settle the details of the title page of *The Horse in Motion.*[1] Neither Stanford nor Stillman had consulted Muybridge about the final form of the book. The American edition appeared in February 1882, copyrighted by Stanford, and the English edition shortly thereafter, copyrighted by Stillman.

Whether Muybridge had seen a copy of the book by March 7, 1882, is not known, but on that date he wrote to Stillman as if he thought its publication was still a long way in the future:

You are I suppose still writing away: You perhaps recollect what I originally told you about the time it would take; and, if you succeed in getting the work in the market before 1883 I shall consider you very fortunate. Who have you arranged with to publish it?[2]

If Muybridge had not yet seen the book, his final question would indicate how much Stanford and Stillman had kept him in the dark. If, on the other hand, he had seen a copy, the question might covertly suggest legal implications. In the letter he reminded Stillman that Stanford had previously been offered the chance to "acquire the copyrights to the photographs," but had never favored Muybridge with a reply: "having heard nothing further in relation to it[,] I suppose the idea of making arrangements for pictorial illustration has been abandoned." Clearly, Muybridge was reasserting his rights to the use of his photographs. Because they were copyrighted in his name, he assumed that they would not be utilized in any manner without his consent or remuneration.

Almost simultaneously Muybridge must have seen a copy of *The Horse in Motion* and discovered that the book had been completed and published without his knowledge, that his name did not appear on the title page as he had reason to expect, and that his photographs had been used and even misused in the text without his consent.

Only five of Muybridge's photographs were actually reproduced. The other illustrations (aside from the nine color plates of

anatomical drawings by William Hahn, a San Francisco artist trained in Düsseldorf) were 91 photolithographs of drawings made from Muybridge photographs. There was a reason for this, according to Stillman:

Many of the photographs reproduced in the photolithographs, and used in this volume to analyze the paces, were imperfect in lights and shades, and others, when the subjects were dark colored, were in silhouette, to which all were reduced. The outlines are quite perfect, and the details in other aspects are quite unimportant to the study of the movements.[3]

Thus, no original Muybridge prints appeared in *The Horse In Motion* at all. Of his pictures there were only reproductive illustrations: the five heliotype reproductions, and the 91 photolithographic illustrations which had been greatly reduced in quality through drawing — some to mere silhouettes.

Muybridge's publications had always been in the form of original prints, as in the case of *The Attitudes of Animals in Motion.* In this new publication he had expected his original prints to be used. Now he found that the reproductive processes used in *The Horse in Motion* negated the direct data that his cameras had supplied, and this without his knowledge or permission. The blow to his pride was enormous.

Muybridge apparently wrote then to the Osgood firm, questioning the copyright claims of both Stillman and Stanford, and putting forth his own claims under the copyright granted him in 1881 on *The Attitudes of Animals in Motion,* for James Osgood reported to Stillman on March 18, 1882: "Gov. Stanford has authorized us to instruct the London publishers to disregard the claims of Muybridge (about which we telegraphed you) and we have accordingly done so."[4] Stillman, however, anticipating legal complications, transferred his copyright on the English edition to Stanford. He wrote to Osgood on April 10:

I telegraphed to you today at the request of Gov. Stanford when I told him of what had been done in the matter of the English copy right of The Horse in Motion. I was satisfied myself that the copy right in my name was wrong and the error should have been corrected and could not be corrected by committing another.

The proprietorship is not in me but in Gov. Stanford alone and it should appear so in the book. In a suit at law this may give rise to unpleasant complications.

[1] Osgood to Stillman; in Stanford University Archives.
[2] Stanford University Archives.

[3] *The Horse in Motion,* pp. 114-115.
[4] Stanford University Archives.

With regard to the claims of Muybridge that the illustrations in silhouette are an infringement of his copyright. I have this to say that I can swear that they were all taken at the order of Gov. Stanford who paid all the expenses, furnished all the apparatus and material and Muybridge furnished me with all the copies from which the plates were executed knowing that they were to be used for the purpose to which they were to be applied. He [Stanford] also furnished him with the magic lanterns and apparatus which he is now using to amuse the audiences in England and [with] the money he used to travel and exhibit the movements of animals, and he imposed upon the Governor the idea that he possessed the most delicate chemicals ever used to produce the results when in fact he was far behind the times and processes were in use for years far more delicate and which he did not know of until he went to Europe and he wrote to me when I was in Boston to delay the work until he could take a new set of photographs by the dry process of which he had just learned. Muybridge wrote for me a long account of the history of the enterprise in which he gave [himself?] all the credit of the suggestions to the use of electricity in the process of taking the pictures. In my hearing he advised the Governor to make the illustrations very elaborate [so] that the book should be a monument to his fame like Audubon's work on Ornithology, and if his advice had been followed the work would not have been completed in two years and at a cost of $50,000.

He wanted me to go to England to get it executed as he did not believe it could be done well enough in America, but the Governor wanted the whole work done in his own country where the experiments had been made. [5]

Two days after the letter was written, Stillman advised Osgood by telegraph from San Francisco to ask Trübner, the London publisher of the book, to withhold the English registration of it. This Osgood did by cable, simultaneously dispatching a form for Stanford's signature which would settle the copyright in his name rather than Stillman's. On April 18, Osgood informed Stillman: "A New York lawyer in Muybridge's behalf [has] notified us that he [Muybridge] claims American as well as English copyright." Osgood asked for Stanford's guarantee to "hold us harmless as against Muybridge, for any claims he may have." [6] Stanford thereupon telegraphed Osgood that he would so indemnify them.

In the April 20 issue of *Nature*, London, appeared the announcement of a new American book, *The Horse in Motion*, described as a handsome and richly illustrated volume by "J. D. B. Stillman, A.M., M.D.," whose investigations had been "executed and published under the auspices of Mr. Leland Stanford, of Palo Alto Farm, California." An extract from Stanford's preface to the book was quoted. In it, Stanford's

description of how the book came about greatly underplayed Muybridge's contribution. [7] In the next issue, April 27, Muybridge responded. He claimed that the preface inaccurately described his role in the project:

*In **Nature**, Vol. XXV. p. 591, you notice the publication of a work entitled "The Horse in Motion," by Dr. Stillman, and remark: "the following extract from Mr. Stanford's preface shows the exact part taken by each of those concerned in the investigation." Will you permit me to say, if the subsequently quoted "extract" from Mr. Stanford's preface is suffered to pass uncontradicted, it will do me a great injustice and irreparable injury. At the suggestion of a gentleman now residing in San Francisco, Mr. Stanford asked me if it was possible to photograph a favorite horse at his full speed. I invented the means employed, submitted the result to Mr. Stanford, and accomplished the work for his private gratification, without remuneration. I subsequently suggested, invented, and patented the more elaborate system of investigation, Mr. Stanford paying the actual necessary disbursements, **exclusive** of the value of my time, **or** my personal expenses. I patented the apparatus and copyrighted the resulting photographs for my own exclusive benefit. Upon the completion of the work, Mr. Stanford presented me with the apparatus. Never having asked or received any payment for the photographs, other than as mentioned, I accepted this as a voluntary gift: the apparatus under my patents being worthless for use to anyone but myself. These are the facts; and on the basis of these I am preparing to assert my rights.* [8]

Two months later Muybridge sailed for the United States to protect his rights as a professional photographer. Upon arriving in New York, on July 4, he sought counsel from the law firm of Allen, Hemenway, and Savage. Then he went to Boston, where he called upon Osgood and Company to advise them personally that he would shortly bring suit.

The case of Muybridge vs. Osgood was heard in the federal circuit court, beginning on September 14. Through his counsel Muybridge claimed to be the author and proprietor of *The Attitudes of Animals in Motion*, a book which had been properly deposited for copyright with the Library of Congress in 1881. He claimed to be the author and proprietor of the photographs which made up that book (the Palo Alto photographs) and of the negatives as well — with the sole right of vending them.

Muybridge alleged that the defendants, Osgood and Company, had contrived and intended to injure him by printing,

[5] Stanford University Archives.
[6] Stanford University Archives.
[7] Clipping in Scrapbook.
[8] In Scrapbook; emphasis in original.

publishing, and exhibiting for sale *The Horse in Motion,* and
that this was a violation of and infringement of his copyrights.
He believed that the sale of his own work, *The Attitudes of
Animals in Motion,* already advertised for sale in Great Britain,
had been hindered by the publication of *The Horse in Motion,*
and that the sale of his photographs would continue to be
diminished. He prayed the court to restrain the defendants by
injunction from offering *The Horse in Motion,* for further sale. In
addition he asked for an accounting of sales of the book to
date, for all unsold copies to be surrendered to him, and for
Osgood and Company to pay the costs of his suit.[9]

Osgood and Company, in the respondent's answer to
Muybridge, claimed merely to be acting as agents for the account
of Leland Stanford, whose name, they pointed out, appeared
on the title page of *The Horse in Motion,* and who, they said,
was the "real owner and proprietor" of the work. Since they
denied responsibility, having accepted the work from Stanford
in good faith, and a preliminary investigation proving nothing
to the contrary, the suit was never brought to trial. It was
dismissed without prejudice or costs.

In October, Muybridge began a direct attack on Stanford. He
brought a suit by attachment, naming $50,000 in damages.
The Boston *Evening Transcript* noticed the action and commented
on October 21: "The case will be interesting as casting some
light on the question whether a poor scientific investigator has
any rights that our plutocracy is bound to respect." This appeal
for sympathy in Muybridge's behalf brought forth a peppery
response, but an unsigned one. The *Transcript* was accused of
making it appear that Muybridge was the real originator of *The
Horse in Motion* and that Governor Stanford was attempting to
steal the honors. The anonymous writer intimated that should
the case ever come to trial, the public would form a different
opinion: "The facts are, I think, demonstrable that the idea
of instantaneous photography as applied to animal motion came
from Mr. Stanford, that he employed Mr. Muybridge to carry out
his idea, and furnished him with ample means to prosecute all
experiments which he might find necessary; that he also paid Mr.
Muybridge for his time and labor. That work brought to a
conclusion, Mr. Stanford employed other competent talent to
interpret the results of the photographs, and to harmonize them
with the anatomy and physiology of the horse."[10]

After an extensive period of deposition taking, Stanford's

lawyer made a motion that judgment be rendered for the
defendant. This was granted on February 13, 1885. Thus Muybridge
ultimately lost his case.[11]

The trial brought much evidence to light as to the relationship
between Stanford and Muybridge from 1872 to 1881. At the
beginning of the Palo Alto experiments, the two were close friends.
Muybridge was welcomed at the Stanford home, and in the
evenings "they would sit together sometimes for several hours
talking and discussing." In San Francisco, Muybridge "would call
at the office and see Governor Stanford at any time." During
the experiments Muybridge lived at Palo Alto Farm and his
personal and professional expenses there were paid by Stanford
without question. Muybridge was said virtually to have had carte
blanche. And yet, the business arrangements were loose.
Muybridge would never set a definite fee for his professional
services, expecting that Stanford would ultimately reward him
handsomely. Stanford, for his part, allowed Muybridge to
copyright the photographs and to take out patents in his own
name, intending that what he could earn from them should be his.

The arrangements troubled at least one of the men who
assisted Muybridge in preparing the experiments. John D. Isaacs,
an electrical engineer, wrote on February 26, 1879, to Stanford's
personal secretary, Frank Shay:

*I write hurriedly to ask a favor of you. You recollect the
Electrical Photographing apparatus which we got up to take
Occident's picture with — there may be a controversy between
Muybridge and myself about the patent. Please write me as
soon as convenient all that you recollect from the beginning that
bears on the subject. . . .*

*P.S. Did you understand that Muybridge invented the machine
or that I did?*

In his deposition Isaacs later claimed that he had confronted
Muybridge at Morse's gallery and told him that he would sue
him. Isaacs stated that he was prevented from doing this by Arthur
Brown, his superior in the workshops of the Central Pacific
Railraod Company. Brown knew that the work was done for
Stanford and paid for by him, and believed that Muybridge as
Stanford's agent was therefore under his protection.

Another matter could have led to deep misunderstanding
between Stanford and Muybridge, but was seemingly resolved in
the photographer's favor. Early in 1880, Muybridge heard that
a man named Miles, of Mountainville, New York, was "exhibiting

[9] E. J. Muybridge vs. James R. Osgood and Co.; suit filed in the U.S. Circuit
Court, Massachusetts District, September 20, 1882; Equity docket, no. 1928.
[10] *Evening Transcript,* October 27; in Scrapbook.

[11] E. J. Muybridge vs. Leland Stanford. The case is not on record. The
account here is based on depositions and letters in the Huntington Collection,
George Arents Research Library, Syracuse University.

by means of a magic lantern, certain photographic pictures, the production of Mr. E. J. Muybridge in connection with certain lectures delivered [by Miles] on the subject of animal locomotion." Through his lawyer, Muybridge informed Miles that he had no right to do this, and that if he did not desist, legal proceedings would be started against him. Miles apparently appealed to Stanford in the matter. This resulted in a letter of apology by Frank Shay which indicated that Muybridge's demand had been made without Stanford's knowledge: "Instead of his objecting to your using the pictures, he is glad that you have done so. Muybridge is only his employee and he thought that he was doing a service in sending the notice you received. He understands the Governor's wishes now." On July 28 of that year, however, Muybridge sent Miles an even stronger demand through his lawyer, and one can only conclude that Stanford had meanwhile reversed his opinion and chosen to support Muybridge in his suit.

These were mere preludes to the later difficulties. At one point Muybridge offered to sign over to Stanford all his patents and copyrights connected with the experiments, but the gesture was refused. Muybridge's claims were thereby strengthened.

Not so easily resolved had been Muybridge's discontent over the appointment of Stillman to write *The Horse in Motion*. An even more privileged member of the Stanford circle than Muybridge, Stillman lived in the Stanford home during the writing of the book. From the start, Muybridge was uncomfortable with him. Muybridge's 35-page account of his work at Palo Alto, which Stillman had requested for the book, was set aside by Stillman as being "ungrammatical, redundant, and full of hyperbole, which would make the whole thing ridiculous." In this matter, Frank Shay took Stillman's side. Muybridge then prepared a shorter version, which Stillman altered without his knowledge. Muybridge complained to Shay about Stanford's choice of Stillman as a writer; Stanford was offended by this, and Muybridge was overruled. Even before his trip abroad, Muybridge was beginning to lose influence with his patron.

For several months the idea and hope of making a European trip for Stanford had been in Muybridge's mind. The depositions of the trial tell that when the trip became a possibility, Muybridge packed his equipment and sent it ahead to New York, pending Stanford's instructions. While in New York himself, on May 30, 1881, Muybridge learned just what money value Stanford apparently placed on the nearly ten years of photographic work that he had done for him. The sum of $2,000 was given to him. The amount was, moreover, determined by Ariel Lathrop, Stanford's brother-in-law, and Frank Shay. It must have seemed paltry to Muybridge, who had counted upon a far more handsome settlement.[12]

In Paris, although Muybridge put a bold face on it, his relations with Stanford continued to slip. He tried to interest Stanford in supporting new photographic experiments abroad — his discovery of the superior results of the dry-plate method of photography gave him a talking point. But Stanford was not well and apparently not in a mood for discussions. Indeed, this is why he had chosen to return home in September, thus missing Marey's reception. However, Muybridge saw him off in friendly fashion and after a while wrote to Frank Shay: "I have been waiting the disposition of the governor since the 1st October. I believe he proposes to return next Spring; by that time I shall have to be in full operation experimenting with new subjects."[13] When it became apparent that Stanford was not picking up his option to finance further experiments, Muybridge tried to apply one last bit of friendly pressure by indicating to Shay that he intended to seek financial backing other than Stanford's in a proposed collaboration of Meissonier, Marey, himself, and a "capitalist" friend:

One of the conditions of the agreement is, that Meissonier is to have control of the results, and that I shall assign to him my present American and European copyrights and also those I make next season. In consideration of which I shall receive payment for the times I was working in connection with their production, and at my ordinary rate of payment for work in California, this will of course be quite a sum. M. Meissonier himself is not actuated by any selfish motives, neither do I suppose is his friend (who the "friend" is I do not know) for he assures me he is very rich; but I really believe and so does M. Meissonier it will be an investment that will pay for itself, and very probably a profitable one.[14]

This playing-off of Stanford against an unknown supporter had only negative effects. Earlier in the same letter Muybridge

---

[12] Information about the payment of $2,000 and its determination by Lathrop and Shay is in Shay's deposition, July 23, 1883. The date of Muybridge's receipt for the money is May 30, 1881.

It is not clear when Muybridge left for Europe or arrived there. Rumors that he and Stanford would take the pictures abroad were noted in the *Examiner*, San Francisco, February 6. The dedicatory words in *The Attitudes of Animals in Motion* would place Muybridge still in California as of May 15. The patent applications probably were handled by his lawyer and their dates would not establish his whereabouts. By August 19, however, he was in London and had made arrangements for sale of the *Attitudes* albums, and by September 26 (Marey's party) he must have been in Paris for several days at least.

[13] Paris, November 28, 1881; Stanford University Archives.

[14] Paris, December 23; Stanford University Archives.

tactlessly remarked that the new experiments would "throw all those executed at Palo Alto altogether in the shade." But already Stanford and Stillman had chosen to publish *The Horse in Motion* without Muybridge's name on the title page.

The depositions gathered for the trial, E. J. Muybridge vs. Leland Stanford, give an even clearer picture of the events that led up to the patenting (in December 1881) of Muybridge's "Method and Apparatus for Photographing Objects in Motion," about which so many claims and counterclaims have since been made. For example, we learn that after the Scoville cameras and Dallmeyer lenses were received at Palo Alto Farm in 1878, Muybridge prepared a "crude model" of his proposed swift-action shutter system for his apparatus and took it, at Stanford's suggestion, to the chief engineer of the Central Pacific Railroad Company, Samuel Montague, for help in converting the idea into a workable mechanism for taking instantaneous, analytical photographs of objects in motion. Montague called in Arthur Brown, who "had in his immediate employ skilled mechanics and artisans of various kinds" at the Central Pacific shops in Oakland, requesting him to take charge of the matter in accordance with Stanford's desires. Brown proposed to build the required fast-shutter mechanism with "some mechanical contrivance to work automatically, as the horse passes along by levers or some means, to set [the shutters] off as it went along." Brown then called in John D. Isaacs, who proposed the use of electricity and "took an active part in setting up this new apparatus." Isaacs made the first working drawings, but the practical electrical work, which was adapted to Muybridge's crude model and built into the final working model, was done by Paul Seiler of the California Electrical Works in San Francisco. The San Francisco Telegraph Supply Company supplied the electromagnets.

Thus the whole scheme was a cooperative working out, by specialists, on a practical level, of Muybridge's original idea as presented to Montague with the crude model. It can be said, therefore, that Muybridge originated the method, and that Isaacs originated the idea of applying electricity to it. The facts in the case, recorded at the trial, were to have importance much later, when motion picture history turned aside myth for verifiable data.

If Muybridge had been privy to the Stanford-Stillman correspondence, he would have found the following clear statement of Stanford's position:

. . . Muybridge has commenced a suit by attachment in Boston, levying on all the books, and charging that I have, by the publication of the book, injured his professional reputation. He wants damages to the extent of $50,000 and claims that the idea of taking photographs of horses in motion, originated with him, and not with me, and that I set up that claim in the book.

When I first spoke to Muybridge about the matter, he said it could not be done. I insisted, and he made his trials. He has often stated this to others, and I think there will be no difficulty in defeating his suit, and showing that his merit, such as it is, was in carrying out my suggestions. You will probably remember his having said so to you, as he was in the habit of saying so often to others, and I think it was completely set forth in the sketch that he gave me at one time, to put into the book as an appendix. I think the fame we have given him, has turned his head.[15]

Through his attorney, Stanford claimed that, being interested in the study of animal locomotion, he had "solicited and employed" Muybridge as an expert photographer; that he had, further, employed "expert engineers, electricians, mechanics, assistants and laborers" to assist in the project; and that to him personally belonged "all the cameras, plates, paper, chemicals, machinery, apparatus, appliances, models, subjects, skill and labor," including the skill and labor of Eadweard Muybridge. In short, Stanford considered himself the owner and proprietor of both the photographs and the negatives prepared by Muybridge. He honestly felt that he had a perfect right to make use of them as he saw fit. But he was dealing with a man who never considered himself to be anyone's "employee." During the murder trial Muybridge had more than once insisted that he was not "in the employ of Bradley and Rulofson," but was conducting a branch of the business on his own account. He would not be patronized, even by a patron.

In the suit of attachment Muybridge therefore claimed that when he accepted Stanford's proposal to try to photograph animals in motion, Stanford had liberally agreed to place the resources of the stock-breeding farm at his disposal and to reimburse him for the expenses of his investigations, upon the condition of his supplying Stanford, for private use, a few copies of the contemplated results. For this reason, neither the 1872 nor the 1873 photographs had been commercially distributed by Muybridge; nor were the 1877 pictures or later Palo Alto photographs put on the market until all Stanford's conditions had been met. Since Stanford apparently made no objection to the coyprighting of the "Horse in Motion" card series of 1878 or the photographs in *The Attitudes of Animals in Motion*, Muybridge's version of the matter would seem to have some validity. But Stanford put it differently: "Out of good

[15] Stanford to Stillman, October 23, 1882; Stanford University Archives.

119. Muybridge, *The Horse in Motion*, a photographic card of the painting by Koch, based on the 1877 photograph of "Occident" taken in Sacramento.

120. *Top right*, reverse of photographic card *The Horse in Motion*, 1877, announcing an additional six-card set *The Action of the Horse* photographed in Palo Alto in 1878.

121. *La Nature*, December 14, 1878.
Heliographic reproductions of Muybridge's instantaneous Palo Alto Photographs.
The first European publication of the Stanford-Muybridge experiments.

122. A parody of "The Horse in Motion"
in the San Francisco Illustrated Wasp, July 27, 1878.

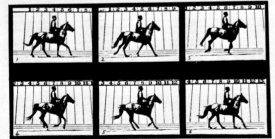

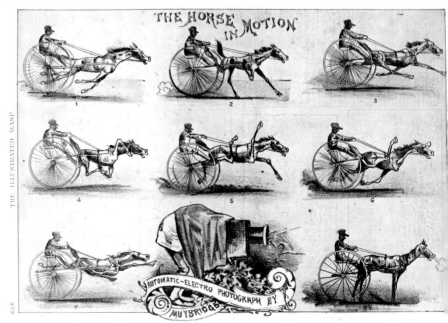

123. Title page of *The Horse in Motion*, 1882, the book commissioned by Leland Stanford and written by Dr. J. D. B. Stillman, based on Muybridge's photographs but giving him no credit for them on the title page.

124. From *The Horse in Motion*, 1882 — a lithographic drawing based on an original Muybridge photograph. Considered by Muybridge a distortion of his work. (See page 123, bottom.)

125. Plate XIX from *The Horse in Motion*, 1882 — a Muybridge photograph reduced to a "mere silhouette" by an illustrator. In quality, furthest from an original Muybridge print, and considered by Muybridge to be such a distortion of his work as to be damaging to his professional reputation.

126. Plate XIII from *The Horse in Motion*, 1882 — a heliotype reproduction of an original Muybridge photograph. In quality, closest to an original Muybridge print, but Muybridge would have preferred original photographs tipped into the book instead.

127. Another parody, from *The Judge*, June 3, 1882. The caption reads, "A HORSE RACE – NOT A BURLESQUE. The actions of race-horses by instantaneous photography. It may seem funny, but it is true to life nevertheless. What becomes of the gracefull steed?"

will for the complainant in part, and in part as a matter of convenience, I allowed copyrights of some of said negatives and photographs to be taken in the name of the complainant."

Then there was the matter of the title page. Before he left for Paris, Muybridge said, Stillman and he had agreed that the title page should read: "The Horse in Motion / As demonstrated by a series of photographs by Muybridge / With an attempt to elucidate the theory of animal locomotion by Dr. J. D. B. Stillman / Published under the auspices of Leland Stanford." Stanford, however, had given his sanction to a second version suggested by Stillman: "The Horse in Motion / As shown by instantaneous photographs / With a study in animal mechanics founded on anatomy and the revelations of the camera / In which is demonstrated the theory of quadrupedal locomotion / by Dr. J. D. B. Stillman / Published under the auspices of Leland Stanford." Not even Osgood and Company had approved this wording, but Stanford had insisted upon it. The omission of Muybridge's name from the title page was patently dishonest. Muybridge did not believe that Stanford had condoned the change until the facts came out at the trial.

Whatever the merits of his case, Muybridge finally lost his suit against Leland Stanford just as he had lost his case against Osgood. But *The Horse in Motion* had a singularly bad time of it, too. In the first printing, plates had been jumbled. Reviews (even those paid for by Stanford) were plainly lukewarm. These first 2,000 copies cost Stanford more than $6,000. When a second printing was issued, West Coast booksellers refused to stock the book because of the narrow discount offered. Finally Stillman had

to recommend to Stanford that the sale price of the book be lowered.

Stillman seems to have come out of the project in a rather confused and apprehensive state of mind. He had not been very effective in managing *The Horse in Motion*, from first to last. If Stillman had not had Leland Stanford to protect him, it is likely that Muybridge would have had his way. Muybridge was capable of writing the entire text, arranging the illustrations, and bringing *The Horse in Motion* to publication by himself. This is probably what he wanted to do, but Stanford had come to regard Stillman as his man, and he protected him to the end: "Don't allow the matters to worry you. If the people don't buy the book it is their misfortune as well as ours. As a money matter if I am not called upon to pay more, it is of the past."[16]

Throughout his life it seemed that loss, adversity, and all manner of setbacks served to move Muybridge forward rather than impede him. During the long months while the suits were pending, his lectures in the United States were a great success. On October 19, 1882, he appeared at the Massachusetts Institute of Technology. The electric light was used to illuminate the Zoöpraxiscope. On November 28 he spoke before members of the National Academy of Design. About the turn of the year he

[16] January 5, 1883; Stanford University Archives. Clark (p.279) reports the fate of the book bluntly: "It was taken off the publisher's list and the stock on hand was thrown on the market for what it would bring." From him we learn also (p.370) that during the writing of the book "two of Stanford's fine animals were sacrificed upon the altar of scientific research. They were dissected by Dr. Stillman."

128. Advertisement for a series of lectures by Muybridge.

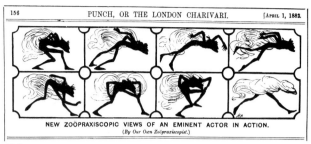

129.

made arrangements with Kelley's Musical and Literary Bureau, Boston, to undertake regular lecture engagements at a substantial fee. On January 9, 1883, he lectured at the Union League Club of New York.

He endeavored to interest new sponsors in undertaking the more detailed series of experiments that he had designed with Meissonier and Marey in Paris. R. C. Johnson, formerly of San Francisco, a wealthy patron of art and the mysterious "capitalist" sponsor referred to in Paris, was probably frightened off by Leland Stanford; he no longer felt equal to financing the project. Walter Armstrong, art critic of the *London Art Journal*, agreed to act as a sponsor in Johnson's stead, but he could contribute nothing in the way of money. Meanwhile the project took on larger scope in Muybridge's mind. A formidable outlay

would be required. He approached publishing houses for support, but none would take the risk.

Then, suddenly, Muybridge's luck changed. In Philadelphia, Fairman Rogers — the wealthy art patron, horseman, and amateur photographer who had commissioned Thomas Eakins to paint *A May Morning in the Park* in 1879, taking into account Muybridge's photographic findings — succeeded in interesting a number of prominent fellow Pennsylvanians in Muybridge's new proposal. Rogers approached the provost of the University of Pennsylvania, Dr. William Pepper, with the suggestion that money be raised to allow Muybridge to conduct his work on the campus. Enthusiastic about the idea, Pepper formed a committee of trustees and friends of the university for the purpose of bringing Muybridge to Philadelphia.

Thomas Eakins was a persuasive member of the committee. In correspondence with Muybridge in 1878 he had suggested several refinements of method which Muybridge adopted. Eakins then made drawings from the "Horse in Motion" series for use in the zoetrope at the Pennsylvania Academy of the Fine Arts, and went on to suggest the photographing of human muscular action as well, which Muybridge began to do in Palo Alto in August 1879. A stubborn advocate in the use of the live nude model in teaching, Eakins had recently lost his job at the academy after two female students fainted at the sight of a nude male model in his class and circulated a petition against him. The idea that Muybridge might produce a vast series of studies showing the human figure, clothed and unclothed, appealed to Eakins strongly at the moment. He was himself an excellent photographer, and perhaps saw himself as a potential collaborator in the new project.

In February 1883, Muybridge lectured in Philadelphia at the Academy of the Fine Arts and also at the Academy of Music. The committee attended. Negotiations began, and went on through the spring and summer. Finally, in a lecture at the Swain School, New Bedford, Massachusetts, Muybridge was able to announce that he would soon make an extensive series of new experiments for the University of Pennsylvania, upon which $20,000 would be expended. After completing a series of lectures in Boston in September, he moved his base of operations to Philadelphia.

During the latter part of 1883, Muybridge, now with the status of an academic researcher, went about the business of preparing his laboratory at the university for the start of the most systematic and comprehensive study of human and animal locomotion ever undertaken.

PART SIX:
Elaboration and Public Acclaim

25. The University of Pennsylvania (1884-1885)

While lecturing in several American cities in 1882 and 1883, Eadweard Muybridge issued a printed prospectus which made known his ideas for an elaborate new investigation, to focus on the "Attitudes of Man, the Horse, and other Animals in Motion." He proposed to take photographs, "in the immediate vicinity of New York, upon a tract of ground possessing the requisite facilities for Photography," of "Men, Horses, Dogs, Oxen, and other domesticated and Wild Animals, executing various movements at different rates of speed," for a publication of 100 plates. Each plate would include multiple photographs, bringing the total to 2,000. Subscribers would make their own selections among the plates.[1]

Muybridge proposed Illustrating "Men . . . nude or draped . . . while walking, running leaping, wrestling, boxing, fencing, military exercising, rowing, and while polo, base-ball and racquet playing," "Ladies playing at Lawn Tennis, dancing, and other exercises of muscular action and graceful movement," "Birds, on the wing," and "Seals and other marine mammals." Of much significance was his new interest in photographing the story element in human action: "Attention will be given to photographing Actors, while performing their respective parts," and "accurately recording the successive attitudes, oscillations and movements of the human body in health and disease," including

the "successive phases of the Heart and Lungs while in action, with an apparatus I have invented for the purpose." The work was also to contain examples of the action of men and horses "as represented by the Ancients and many of the most distinguished artists of modern times, copied from the originals in the Museums, Picture Galleries and libraries of Europe."[2]

This mammoth project was Muybridge's answer to the withdrawal of Stanford's patronage. Meanwhile Stanford's *The Horse in Motion* was selling poorly. Its rambling text and myriad typographical errors were bringing down rather heavy criticism on the volume and the editor, Dr. Stillman. One wishes that Stanford had put the writing of the text into Muybridge's hands when one reads his convincing and ordered prose in the prospectus. Here Muybridge displayed also a showman's flair, promising a "standard work of reference," in an "edition de luxe," and stipulating: "for each copy of the work subscribed for, the subscriber will be entitled to send a horse, or other animal or subject to my studio for a special photographic analysis of its movements, which will be illustrated without extra charge." All this was marvelous promotion in 1883, and it eventually hit a proper target — the aspiring University of Pennsylvania.

William Pepper, provost from 1881 to 1894, had from the beginning of his tenure advanced the University of Pennsylvania as a great center for research. Also he was one of a small number of American college presidents of his day blessed with rare

---

[1] *Prospectus of a New and Elaborate Work upon the Attitudes of Man, the Horse, and Other Animals in Motion, by Muybridge,* New York: Scoville Manufacturing Co., April 1883; in Scrapbook.

[2] Ibid.

administrative abilities. Under his direction the university hospital expanded its staff and areas of specialization; the veterinary college was started; departments of philosophy and physical education and courses in natural history and paleontology were added; and a graduate department was opened for women. Pepper believed that he was building for a glorious future when he succeeded in attracting outstanding researchers to his campus or when he promoted an important piece of work and saw that it was carried out under scientific controls. Often dipping into his personal fortune to sustain projects in which he was especially interested, he was also a master in persuading trustees and friends of the university to make contributions for research.

Impressed by the prospectus, Pepper called together a committee, whose members he succeeded in interesting in Muybridge's program of photographic research. Besides himself, the committee consisted of Charles C. Harrison, Thomas Hockley, Samuel Dickson, Edward H. Coates, and the Philadelphia publisher J. B. Lippincott. These men became the guarantors of the Muybridge project, each prepared to advance $5,000 as required, and each to have his money secured "by the subscription list of the proposed publication," which Muybridge was to "bring up to the point where it will cover the amount advanced."[3]

Joshua Ballinger Lippincott — whose interest in the "lower animals" had already been shown in repeated gifts to the veterinary college — was much interested in Muybridge's work and thought that his firm might undertake to publish the results of the research. On August 9, 1883, when Muybridge was formally invited to come to the university, Lippincott advanced the first $5,000.

It was stipulated by the guarantors that the conduct of the research should rest in the hands of the university, and that a commission of faculty members should be appointed to supervise Muybridge's endeavors. The members of this commission were: Pepper, the provost; Coates, chairman of the instructional committee at the Pennsylvania Academy of the Fine Arts; Joseph Leidy, professor of anatomy; George F. Barker, professor of physics; Rush Huidekoper, professor of veterinary anatomy and pathology; William D. Marks, professor of dynamical engineering; Thomas Eakins, of the Academy of the Fine Arts; and Harrison Allen, emeritus professor of physiology. Coates was named chairman of the commission, and Allen its secretary. On September 3, Muybridge accepted all the conditions proposed by the guarantors and the supervisory commission as "entirely reasonable."[4]

[3] Muybridge to Pepper, September 3, 1883; in University of Pennsylvania Library (courtesy Neda M. Westlake).
[4] Ibid.

The work was to be carried on "in the enclosure of the Veterinary Department" during the spring and summer of 1884. Preparations therefore went on throughout the preceding fall and winter. A laboratory was set up in the basement of Biological Hall. Here Muybridge designed and ordered the equipment required for the outdoor work, and drafted the university's prospectus and subscription sheet for *Animal Locomotion* (as the eventual publication was called). Before the sheet was circulated, 63 subscriptions at $100 had been obtained, and by February 1884 at least 133 "Libraries, Institutions, and well known Artists, Scientists, and Dilettante" had responded. Thus nearly half the money required to cover the guarantors' $30,000 was pledged before the actual photographing was begun.[5]

Next, Muybridge's open-air studio was set up in the courtyard of Veterinary Hall and Hospital, where a high temporary fence completed the enclosure. The studio was arranged around a track of walk, some 120 feet long, covered with "corrugated rubber flooring," along which the model moved when progressive motion was to be illustrated. It was described as follows:

The studio through which this great defile of life-studies passed was a fenced space open to the sky. A screen, before which the object moved reticulated in small squares of 2 inches and large ones of 19¾ (5 and 50 centimeters), whose net-work appears on the back-ground of some illustrations, faced a "battery" of from 12 to 24 cameras.

Except for the fencing, necessitated by the use of many nude models, the scheme thus far was not unlike that of the Palo Alto studio. There were, however, certain elaborations and refinements:

At right angles stood another row [of cameras] arranged perpendicularly, and for many movements a third set was employed. Each act was therefore raked fore and aft as well as registered in passage, and was often covered from top to bottom besides. Sloping white screens "threw up" the under lights. Beyond all, there was above neither roof, glass, nor sky-light, nothing but the clean and open sky.[6]

This elaborate scheme implied a comparable research plan. Forty of the "largest and most magnificent camera lenses ever made" were ordered from England. Twenty-four of these were placed into cameras in a building, or "camera house" fronting the track. This constituted the "lateral battery."

[5] Copies of the prospectus, in two versions, December 1883 and February 1884, are in the Scrapbook. This was the precursor of the *Prospectus and Catalogue of Plates* that Lippincott published in 1887 (see chap. 26) when the work was done.
[6] Talcott Williams, "Animal Locomotion: Muybridge's Photographs," *The Century*, July 1887.

130. Veterinary Department of the University of Pennsylvania showing the yard in which Muybridge's outside studio was constructed in 1884.

131. Plan of the photographic studio at the University of Pennsylvania showing the track along which the models passed from left to right, the camera shed for the lateral shots and the portable fore and aft camera batteries.

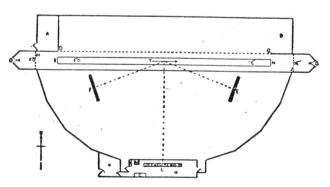

"Immediately in front of each of these cameras was placed an electro-photographic exposer," or shutter. These were fired, at predetermined intervals, by an "exposing motor," electrically controlled, which was an improvement on that used at Palo Alto. In addition to the lateral battery, two portable batteries of twelve cameras each were designed for "front" and "rear" foreshortenings.[7]

Muybridge, standing in the director's position, could fire his cameras in a number of ways — singly, or in various combinations and sequences. Maximally, for twelve exposures at least, three sets of photographs of the subject taken from different angles could be secured.

Since the exposing motor could be adjusted to vary the interval between exposures, Muybridge had considerable control over the duration of his sequences. To ensure scientific accuracy, an electrically operated tuning fork, vibrating at 100 times a second, was also connected to the circuit. As each exposure was made, the movement of the fork was exaggerated and its record left on a sheet of blackened paper. From the number of vibrations recorded, the length of each exposure and the time between each exposure could be verified. Tests of the accuracy of the time intervals between exposures were made by photographing a white spot painted on a black disk moving at a known speed. The chronographic record of the tuning fork, the commission decided, agreed with the results of these tests, and the accuracy of the procedure was confirmed.

As the photographic work got under way in the spring of 1884, the Veterinary Department, the Academy of Fine Arts, and the Zoological Society of Philadelphia cooperated in choosing the subjects and actions most likely to meet the requirements of veterinary surgeons and of artists, physiologists, and naturalists — all who might be interested in the movement of quadrupeds and birds, and of human beings executing the actions incidental to ordinary muscular exercise in work and play.

The first subjects were human beings, draped or nude. They were depicted walking, running, turning, ascending and descending inclines, jumping, crawling, hopping, dancing, stooping, carrying, lifting, sitting, rising, kneeling, dressing, ironing, washing, drinking, sweeping, raking, and "courtesying." Athletes were depicted playing baseball and cricket, fencing, and so on. Artisans were shown blacksmithing, laying bricks, shoeing a horse, farming, mining, and gardening. A guardsman went through the

movements of armed drill. The "exercises of graceful movement" by women included waltzing, dropping handkerchiefs, flirting with fans, getting in and out of bed, in and out of hammocks, opening parasols, and playing lawn tennis. All this Muybridge had promised to explore in his original prospectus. He later described his models in detail:

The female models were chosen from all classes of society. Number 1, is a widow, aged thirty-five, somewhat slender and above the medium height; 3 is married, and heavily built; 4 to 13 inclusive, 15 and 19, are unmarried, of ages varying from seventeen to twenty-four; of these, 11 is slender; the others of medium height and build; 14, 16, and 93, are married; 20, is unmarried, and weighs three hundred and forty pounds.

The male models were also described:

The greater number of those engaged in walking, running, jumping, and other athletic games are students or graduates of the University of Pennsylvania, — young men aged from eighteen to twenty-four — each one of whom has a well-earned record in the particular feat selected for illustration. . . . The Models 52, 64, 65, and 66 are teachers in their respective professions; 60 is a well drilled member of the State Militia; 51, a well known instructor in art; 95 an ex-athlete, aged about sixty; 22 a mulatto and professional pugilist; 27, 28, and 29, boys aged thirteen to fifteen; 42 and 49, public acrobats; [while] 92 and 94 were patients of the University of Philadelphia Hospitals, selected to illustrate abnormal locomotion. . . . The mechanics are experts in their particular trades, and the laborers are accustomed to the work in which they are represented as being engaged.[8]

The photographing of the human figure was carried out quietly, but not secretively, in the outdoor studio. Muybridge had the greatest difficulty in persuading the mechanics, at any price, to go through the motions of their trade in a nude condition. Among those males who willingly posed in various stages of undress were the fencing master Bonaffron, the artist Eakins, and Muybridge himself, the "ex-athlete."

Members of the press were much taken with the series of the young men who illustrated baseball pitching and batting. They wrote that nothing was absent from the photographs. The camera had caught life itself, particularly that breathless moment "when the intense strain of expectancy dissolved from the face of the batter and turned into a broad and conscious grin of content as his bat swung around to meet the coming ball."[9]

[7] Eadweard Muybridge, *Descriptive Zoöpraxography, or the Science of Animal Locomotion Made Popular,* Philadelphia: University of Pennsylvania, 1893, p. 15; hereafter cited as *Descriptive Zoöpraxography.*

[8] Eadweard Muybridge, *Prospectus and Catalogue of Plates* (for *Animal Locomotion*), Philadelphia: Lippincott, 1887, pp. 12-13.

[9] *The Pennsylvanian* (student newspaper at the university), September 28, 1886; in Scrapbook.

The Science of

Animal Locomotion

(Zoopraxography)

An Electro-Photographic Investigation of

Consecutive Phases of Animal Movements

By

Eadweard Muybridge

Executed and Published under the Auspices of the

University of Pennsylvania

Description of the Apparatus
Results of the Investigation
Diagrams
Prospectus
List of Subscribers

Eadweard Muybridge
University of Pennsylvania,
Philadelphia
or
Henrietta Street
Covent Garden
London

132. Title page of *Prospectus for Animal Locomotion*, 1887.

133. Dry-plate-holders for the batteries of twelve cameras used in the Pennsylvania experiments, 1884-1885.

Muybridge had encountered some difficulty in securing the proper female models. He felt that artists' models were, for the most part, ignorant and not well-bred; as a consequence their movements were apt not to be graceful. The gamut finally ran from society matrons to the première danseuse of a Philadelphia theater. The women were often photographed entirely nude. Sometimes they were clothed with a light, transparent drapery from the waist to the knees, or a long, flowing robe of diaphanous texture which permitted the action of the limbs to be seen as well as the conformation of the folds of the drapery.

The nudity was justified at the time as being for the sake of science and art. But there were many who were made a bit tense by the revelations of the camera, and who expressed their nervousness in various ways. An instance was reported by the Philadelphia artist Thomas P. Anshutz after he attended a Muybridge lecture at the university with some of his students from the Academy of the Fine Arts. During the intermission a gentleman escorted his lady across the hall. One of the students, reminded by this of the parade of Muybridge's models which he had just seen moving across the screen, shouted,

"Oh, mom, there goes our Willie!" The art student's remark brought down the house.[10]

The work in the photographic laboratory itself went on with the utmost serenity and decorum. A local reporter described the procedure very clearly:

A beautiful young girl, who is a professional artist's model in New York, was photographed several hundred times this afternoon. She was of almost faultless figure and her drapery was a loose covering that allowed the muscular action to be distinctly seen. At a word from Mr. Muybridge she left the dressing room in a corner of the enclosure, and walked rapidly to a little platform towards which the thirty-six cameras were pointed. The photographer held the stick commanding the thirty-six batteries in his hand, and at another word of command from him the model stepped forward, placed a chair in position, seated herself, crossed one leg over the other, and began fanning herself. These various movements occupied three seconds in execution and every successive muscular movement was photographed from three different standpoints.

[10] Anschutz to J. Lurie Wallace, August 7, 1884; in University of Pennsylvania Library (courtesy Dr. William Homer).

At another sitting, she performed a pirouette and twelve successive impressions of her motion were obtained from the three different points of view.[11]

Anshutz, kept one of his students informed of the progress of the photographic sessions:

Muybridge as you know is carrying on his scheme over at the University. He has a small enclosure. . . . Muybridge has also a machine for taking views on one plate, of moving objects, by opening and closing the camera rapidly at the rate of about 100 exposures per second. This shows the moving object not as a continuous smear but shows one clear view at every 2 or 3 inches of advance. The exposures are made by two large discs with openings cut around their circumferences. They run in opposite directions and are geared to run very fast, the exposure is while the two openings meet. The lens remains uncapped until the object has reached the edge of the plate. . . .

Eakins, Godley and I were out there yesterday trying a machine. Eakins had made from the above design except he had only one wheel We sewed some bright balls on Godley and ran him down the track. The result was not very good although you could see the position of the buttons at every part of the step.

But afterwards Muybridge took him with his machine and got a very good result even showing his black clothes.

Eakins is on the committee which superintends Muybridge. He is of course much interested in the experiments. Muybridge has not made very rapid progress and the University people seem to be losing faith in him. But he showed good results yesterday on the machine. (18 June 1884)

The photographing of models takes place at intervals. But we have made no set as good as that hurried work of ours when we did the hypo deed.(7 August)

You want to keep posted on the Muybridge business. Well, he is making some very nice photographs of men and women doing things. Such as throwing, jumping, stepping down and up etc.

These are all made as I crudely explained on one plate. So that it shows the figure at intervals of a few inches as it goes through the movement. These images, of course frequently overlap but do not seem to confuse on that account. The work is, of course, done with one lens. . . . He has not yet done any work with his series lenses and I hear they do not work. The shutters are too clumsy and slow. The University people are dissatisfied with the affair as he cannot give them the result they expected. Which was to photograph the walk of diseased people paralytics, etc. So that by means of the zoopraxiscope (help!!!) they could show their peculiarities to the medical student. This it seems however cannot be done even with the best known contrivances. So they would like to fire the whole concern but they have gone too far to back out. . . .

Eakins, Seiss and I went out to make photographs of Buffalo Bill's bucking horses. But the results of the experiments we made

were so poor, that we went home again without accomplishing our end. . . .

The study of movement is a good thing even by the aid of photography, but I have no desire to become an electrician in order to make my own photographs, and so I do not feel a very lively interest in the matter. (? August)

The Muybridge work progresses. Muybridge is during this month working at a zoological gardens with his apparatus. Seiss saw him photographing the camels and elk.

Eakins and Godely and I tried our hands at some jumping and running things the other day with moderate success. . . .

The correct way and I think the only way to get good results, is to have the whole yard roofed over and hung with black velvet or something similar, and then admit the sunlight through a broad slit just where the figure is. In this case there would be nothing to fog the plate which could be on a running figure and then forced up in the developer. This cannot now be done for it forces the background up faster than the figures. (25 August)[12]

The Anshutz letters give information not only about Muybridge's work, but also about Eakins's parallel experiments with a "wheel" camera like Marey's, though of his own design and manufacture. In 1884 Eakins was obtaining some tolerably good results. As time went on, however, he left the study of motion to Muybridge and returned to his earlier use of the camera for recording his family, friends, and students, together with the Arcadian scenes of nudes and other studies of models which were to bear importantly on his painting.[13] Muybridge himself made some use of the photographic gun favored by Marey; but as soon as his batteries of cameras were working well, he used them almost exclusively in his work at the university.

Some animal photographs were taken on the campus, others at two new centers of operation now santioned by the commission — the Zoological Gardens, where Anschutz's students had seen the camels and elk photographed in August 1884, and the Gentlemen's Driving Park, in Belmont, near Philadelphia. In 1885 Muybridge took his portable cameras and backgrounds to these locations, which were used in photographing "birds and horses, and also wild animals when possible to do so."

At the Zoological Gardens, Muybridge's work became a matter of public interest. Philadelphia newspapers carried daily accounts of the temperamental behavior of the birds and beasts during the picture taking.[14] On the first day, activities focused

[11] *Times,* Philadelphia, August 2,.1885; in Scrapbook.

[12] Letters to Wallace, dates as indicated in text; University of Pennsylvania Library.

[13] For the influence of Muybridge's work on Eakins see Gordon Hendricks, "A May Morning in the Park," *Bulletin of the Philadelphia Museum of Art,* LX, no. 285 (Spring 1965), 48-64.

[14] Based on accounts in the *Press* and *Evening Telegraph,* Philadelphia, middle to end of August 1885; in Scrapbook.

around the birdhouse. The temperature was above 100 degrees, and breezes were shut off by the brick wall of the birdhouse itself and by the fences around the enclosure.

The first subjects were the pigeons. Mr. Murray, the keeper, brought them out in a basket. A black Antwerp pigeon was first placed in a trap at the edge of the portable screen. Murray held the trap shut with a string until, at Muybridge's signal, he let it go and the trap fell. Muybridge and his two assistants were poised for quick work. Everyone waited for the bird to shoot out, but he was not to be seen. He proved to be a very independent creature and suited himself about coming out. Grass and sticks were thrown at the trap, but they didn't annoy the pigeon into flight. Finally, when all the coaxing had failed, the pigeon came out of his own accord, suddenly flew straight up into the air, and got away without having his picture taken at all.

The same fate awaited the next trial. A silver and blue hen, one of the handsomest Murray had, was dropped into the trap. When it was opened, the bird got away too quickly again. All this loss of time rendered the success of the day very questionable.

The third trial was more satisfactory. The pigeon flew directly across the background screen, gave two great flaps of its wings, and was gone in a flash. The time during the bird's flight across the screen, a distance of some twelve feet, was estimated by Muybridge at one-twentieth of a second. In that short time the electrical machine went off "like a miniature Gatling gun," and while the bird passed across the dazzling white muslin background, 25 separate and distinct photographic views were taken of him, from side and rear.

On this first day a fact was discovered which had not been known before — that a pigeon in the air flaps its wings 10 times in a second, or 600 times in a minute. This went to prove also that the noise made by the flapping of the pigeon's wings as it leaves the ground is caused by their coming together over his back only, instead of "alternatively at the sides and over the back too."

The *Evening Telegraph*'s reporter much enjoyed describing these novel activities: "Mr. Muybridge . . . got the cameras ready. This involves as much preparation as loading a Gatling gun, only it is much more tedious. The Professor, protected from the sun by an old straw hat, walks about the field like a Western stock farmer. He fixes the slides, gives out orders, like the mate of a schooner in a gale, and when everything is ready the Professor sits on a small beer keg, holding an electric key in his hand, and orders up the birds."

134. Clockwork timing mechanism or "exposing motor" used by Muybridge in the University of Pennsylvania experiments, 1884-1885.

"What kind of bird shall we call, sir?" the keeper asked, with one eye on a crow and the other on a red-tailed hawk, both held with a cord fastened to a leg.

"Give us the hawk," said Muybridge.

Murray grabbed the bird by the tail and held it by the wings at the edge of the screen. "Fly the bird," said Muybridge. Then away the hawk sailed, until it reached the end of the string, to be drawn back for another trial.

On the first day the subjects included also a crow, a fish hawk, and finally an owl. The sleepy owl blinked his eyes in a manner that seemed to say, "You needn't think you are going to take my picture." Muybridge photographed him anyway, and the owl, as a reporter said, "went into the rogues' gallery along with the rest of them." Subsequently there were studies of the cockatoo, vulture, American eagle, ostrich, adjutant stork and swan.

A reporter, on hand when Muybridge brought the horizontal cameras around to the Bengal tiger, told how the cautious keeper mounted the top of the cage with a long pole and poked at the beast. The cameras were placed close to the bars, in order not to photograph them. The tiger stared at the little black alpaca curtains of the cameras, then went away and lay down in a corner. Now the keeper crept to a point above the tiger and held the pole in readiness. Muybridge signaled to his assistants and called "Now!" The keeper jabbed the tiger, whose rising motion was broken in twelve different ways. Another jab followed, and the cameras caught twelve exposures of the tiger's impatient stride.

Muybridge had special problems in getting pictures of the big lion, George. Because there was not enough light in the lion house, it was necessary to bring in the broad white background screen. George and his companion, Princess, were let out into the little yard at the back of their quarters. While their attention was engaged by the preparations in progress on the asphalt walk outside, the screen was lowered to cover the wall behind them. The wagon containing the electric battery was drawn up, and the cameras with their 24 staring glass lenses were put in position. George sat in the center of the yard, watching every movement attentively, and Princess, with true feminine and feline curiosity, was standing with her nose between the bars and switching her tail.

As Muybridge announced that everything was all right, George rose and walked to the bars beside Princess. Then the animals turned and stopped short in amazement. The white screen had been let down over the door to their den. George immediately made an investigation to discover what had become of the door, in the course of which, with the help of Princess, the screen was torn away. Having satisfied themselves that the opening was still there, they took no more interest in the proceedings and lay down peacefully to sleep.

A second screen was lowered, once more the instruments were made ready, and the keeper went to work with his pole. George was poked in the ribs until he howled. He and Princess stalked about the yard, lashing their tails. At this point Muybridge pressed the electric spring, there was a click and a whirr, and the pictures were taken at last.

In these and other ways, with the help of the superintendent and keepers at the Zoological Gardens, Muybridge and his two assistants succeeded in photographing such wild and domesticated animals as the mule, ass, ox, hog, goat, oryx, Virginia deer, elk, eland, antelope, giraffe, buffalo, gnu, dog, cat, lion, tiger, jaguar, elephant, Egyptian camel, Bactrian camel, guanaco, raccoon, capybara, baboon, sloth, rhinoceros, and kangaroo. Several splendid pictures were also obtained of a five-foot reptile of the harmless variety known as the pine snake.

Because Muybridge was neither a physiologist nor an anatomist, the analyses of these photographs of animal locomotion were entrusted to two members of the university faculty — the instructor in nervous diseases and the professor of comparative anatomy and zoology. Some surprising findings emerged. It was discovered that a man crawling on his hands and knees matched the walk of the lion and horse in sequence of footfalls; that the giraffe walked differently from the horse; and that the elephant and the raccoon, which seemed unlike in their manner of walking, were yet alike in the sequence of footfalls, the fore foot invariably following the hind foot on the same side. The walk of the giraffe was extraordinary; the same sequence applied, but no less than eight changes in the curvature of the body were made in a single stride, twice upon laterals and twice upon diagonals. One might have thought that the rhinoceros, from its bulk and clumsiness, was the least likely to support iself on laterals, yet the photographs showed that was the case: the animal lifted its fore foot before the hind foot touched the ground, leaving the body supported by laterals. An interesting observation was made in analyzing the photographs of the movement of a bird's wing. Each feather seemed to have a separate motion. When the wing was lifted, each feather was found to turn on edge, as an oar is "feathered" between strokes.

All during August 1885 the intense heat and light acted adversely upon the sensitive dry-plates upon which the photographs were taken. The evaporation quickly destroyed their effectiveness. When the instantaneous process was tried in direct sunlight, this drawback became serious.

The photographic team was glad to move on to the Gentlemen's Driving Park, where Muybridge intended to photograph the horse again, confident that he could surpass his earlier work at Palo Alto. Many very successful equine pictures had already been taken at the campus studio: "Johnson Hauling," "Elberon with Rider," the handsome nude rider series of "Pandora Jumping a Hurdle," and others. The park at Belmont provided for larger ranges of movement, and the portable screens were carried there, along with simpler and lighter portable photographic equipment that Muybridge had developed for the purpose. Here were taken such subjects as "Nellie Rose with Sulky," "Reuben with Sulky," "Pronto with Rider," "Annie G. with Jockey," and "Daisy Jumping a Hurdle," among others. The excellence of these photographs, taken in the fall of 1885, led to an extensive analysis of animal locomotion into "eight different regular systems of progressive motion" — the walk, amble, trot, rack (or pace), canter, transverse-gallop, rotatory-gallop, and ricochet.[15] The new dry-plates made possible an amount of

15 Muybridge's "Prelude to Analyses" in *Animals in Motion,* p. 26 (in Dover edition).

detail unattainable before in instantaneous photography. Greatly surpassing the Palo Alto photographs, the results nevertheless made clear the pioneering accomplishment of the earlier work.

In the summer of 1885 Muybridge photographed also (with a "wheel" camera) a number of clinical subjects brought to him by members of the university's faculty. Having established various characteristics of normal movement with the batteries of serial cameras, he now sought by another method to clarify, for medical purposes, the characteristics of abnormal

movements. The final catalogue of plates listed more than two dozen such studies: "Spastic gait (hysterical); walking," "Epilepsy; walking," "Locomotor ataxia; walking," "Artificially induced convulsions," and so on.

It was estimated that some 20,000 negatives were produced during the experiments in 1884 and 1885 at Philadelphia. Muybridge and his assistants were to spend the next few months arranging them into the series of 781 plates that would become his major contribution to science and art, *Animal Locomotion.*

26. *Animal Locomotion* (1886-1889)

From the late fall of 1885 through the spring of 1886, Muybridge was preparing his work for publication. In March, a student reporter visited him in Biological Hall and saw the "private laboratories" under his guidance. The reporter found Muybridge "diffident in communication" until he was assured that his explanations and statements would not appear in print. Agreeing that it was not "expedient or judicious" to "court untimely publicity," the reporter refrained from presenting an "unvarnished recital of actual sights and experiences that would be an astonishing but delightful revelation" to readers of the campus newspaper. What he wrote, however, gives an interesting view of Muybridge and his methods.

It may be stated . . . that the work on the subject of **Animal Locomotion,** *on which he is still busily engaged, will be published within a year. It will be accompanied by about twelve hundred plates, carbon reprints from the twenty-six thousand photographs already taken. Several hundred of the foremost scientists and educational institutions, both at home and abroad, are already subscribers.*

The working laboratories are in Biological Hall. In one, several assistants are constantly preparing the delicate photographic plates; in another, the developing, etc., of the negatives is in process; and in another, presided over by a pretty young lady with a wealth of golden hair, the multitudinous plates are arranged and classified. Here is seen the unique zoopraxiscope, for the reproduction of the actual locomotion from photographs.

Mr. Muybridge looks and talks like a philosopher. He is a genial gentleman in the prime of life, and, although his beard is long and white, and hair and eyebrows shaggy, his countenance is ruddy, clean-cut and intellectual. He is intensely enthusiastic in his work, and takes a genuine pleasure in explaining his theories and apparatus to interested friends.[1]

[1] *The Pennsylvanian,* March 16, 1886; in Scrapbook.

The guarantors met at about this same time to review policy. They had been summoned by Provost Pepper in response to a letter from the chairman of the guarantors' committee, Edward Coates, Coates, who proposed an agenda of items relating to the coming publication:

Memorandum
1. Examine 781 plates
2. Consider publication of 562 human figure.
3. Consider Muybridge catalogue
4. Contract with Forbes Co. and Photogravure Co.
5. Copyright England and America
6. New subscription circular — 500 names
7. No duplicate prints to be selected
8. Treatises by Parker, Allen, Eakins, Muybridge, French
9. Letterpress by Lippincott Co. and size of page with view of separate publication
10. Shall any time record be given upon the plates?

In the letter Coates posed a major problem:

The human figure series should I think be carefully examined and considered. If the work is to be published at all the usual question as to the study of the nude in Art and Science must be answered Yes. Otherwise the greater number of the 562 series would be excluded. At the same time there are **probably** *some lines to be drawn with regard to some of the plates. That there will be objections in some quarters to the publication would seem to be most likely if not inevitable. Mr. Dickson may be quite right as to the undesirability of conciliating one enemy but I am inclined to believe this point worthy of consideration at least.*[2]

[2] To Pepper, September 27, 1886; in University of Pennsylvania Library.

135. Tickets for Muybridge's public lectures in various American cities.

The issue of the nude in art was dealt with affirmatively by the guarantors, although this was the same issue over which poor Eakins was to lose his job when the Academy of the Fine Arts chose to deal with it negatively. The only concession agreed to by the guarantors was that in the catalogue of the plates, from which subscribers were to make their choices, models were clearly to be indicated as nude, semi-nude, or draped. Thus, subscribers could know ahead of time what they were ordering and the moral burden would be upon them.

Craige Lippincott appeared before the guarantors on behalf of his recently deceased father, J. B. Lippincott, whose original contribution of $5,000 had permitted the purchase of photographic lenses in London. "It was verbally understood," he indicated to Pepper, "that if [J. B. Lippincott] advanced the money for the lenses, our house should have the privilege of publishing Mr. Muybridge's work."[3] The guarantors were willing to abide by this understanding, but the project had taken on such scope in the past year that publication through the ordinary channels of the book trade no longer seemed feasible. It was finally decided that the Lippincott company would publish the prospectus and catalogues of plates (as was done in 1887), while the plates themselves would be distributed by the printer, the Photogravure Company of New York, acting as agent for the committee. The plates would be bound in volumes, cased in portfolios, or supplied separately, to fill orders as the subscribers might choose. The lenses, which were now no longer necessary, would be sold to reimburse Craige Lippincott for his father's advance. Muybridge proposed to "canvas for subscriptions" himself, and to write a new prospectus for that purpose in the name of the University of Pennsylvania.

The aforementioned student reporter interviewed Muybridge again, in September 1886, and found him considerably more loquacious:

"The work of photography is all completed," continued Mr. Muybridge, "the positive plates are fully prepared and merely waiting reproduction. I have written a lengthy introduction, and my colleague, Dr. Andrew J. Parker, of the University, is at work on the descriptive text for the plates." "Then how soon will the full work be published?" "Not later than next Spring, provided the requisite number of subscriptions are secured, to assure a financial success. There must be at least five hundred at not less than $100 apiece. This is the lowest subscription, and includes the book and one hundred plates, selected by the subscriber out of the total seven hundred and eighty-one. Each

[3] Lippincott to Pepper, October 26, 1886; University of Pennsylvania Library.

*additional plate will cost a dollar, but, of course, there will
be a special reduction to those taking the whole series, as many
of our subscribers have signified their intention of doing."*

*A large number of subscriptions, mostly unsolicited, has already
been received, but more are still needed to cover the aggregate
cost of production, which will be not less than $40,000. Among
a long list of subscribers — all of whom will be mentioned in
the appendix of the work — we noted names of many of the most
prominent scientific men and institutions, both at home and
abroad. Harvard is down for two copies, besides individual
subscribers, such as Prof. Agassiz, several copies are taken by
Johns Hopkins, Princeton, Yale, Cornell, in fact, nearly all the
American Colleges. On the foreign list were Oxford, London and
Cambridge names, royal societies, the Imperial Library and
the Agricultural College of Berlin, Lord Rosebery, and unsolicited
subscriptions from the Khedive of Egypt and the Emperor of
China.*

The reporter ventured to predict that the work's "completion and
publication will be a deserving honor to our University and a
practical contribution to the scientific world."[4]

Specimen plates for *Animal Locomotion* were being prepared
for subscribers in January 1887. By October, proof impressions
had been deposited in Philadelphia, New York, Washington, and
Boston, where subscribers could examine them and make their
selections. Copies of the *Prospectus and Catalogue of Plates*
appeared shortly thereafter. This pamphlet contained a subscription
blank with serial numbers for all of the plates so that subscribers
could indicate the plates desired. To judge from the subscriptions
that came in, the *Prospectus and Catalogue of Plates* found its way
into the far corners of the world.

In the early fall of 1887, Muybridge began an extensive lecture
tour. His accomplishments at the University of Pennsylvania had
been given advance acclaim in a lengthy critical article in the
Century magazine for July, which reviewed the entire project, its
goals, and its methods. The article, was illustrated with photographic reproductions of several Muybridge plates — of animals,
birds, children, and, more importantly, nude male figures. This
notice in the *Century* produced a kind of breakthrough of popular
interest in the project, in the personality of Muybridge as a
creative figure of considerable stature, and in a more objective,
less prudish attitude toward the nude as a subject for scientific
and artistic study.[5]

In its grandest form, *Animal Locomotion: An Electro-
Photographic Investigation of Consecutive Phases of Animal
Movements, 1872-1885* consisted of 781 plates, 19 1/8 x 24 3/8

inches overall, of males, females, children, wild animals, horses,
domestic animals, and birds. Besides the excellence of the
production, very gratifying to Muybridge must have been the
credit given to him in the words following the title: "By Eadweard
Muybridge." The work was indicated as having been "Published
under the Auspices of the University of Pennsylvania" at Philadelphia
in 1887.

Very few of the complete sets of the plates were sold, either
bound or in portfolios — perhaps 40 in all. This was, of course,
because of the necessarily high cost, $600. Far more subscribers
ordered selections of "100 unbound plates in a leather portfolio
for $100." If all the institutional and individual subscribers listed
by Muybridge in the *Prospectus and Catalogue of Plates* of
January 1887 really paid up, the income before publication was
well in excess of $24,000. If the entire cost of the project
came to $40,000 as Muybridge said it did, he was obliged to
seek additional subscriptions for almost the same amount as was
pledged before publication. Presumably it was with this in mind
that he planned a three-year world tour and started giving public
lectures (with the Zoöpraxiscope) that took him over the United
States and eventually abroad.

The pattern of Muybridge's travels is difficult to follow. In
September 1887 he lectured in Albany; in December in Pittsburgh,
at the studio of the sculptor and painter Thomas Shields Clark;
and also in December at the Art Museum, Chicago. In February
1888 he gave an exhibition and lecture before a number of artists
at the studio of William Merritt Chase in New York, and perhaps
also at the Union League Club. By June he had lectured in
Milwaukee and was expecting to visit Madison, Minneapolis, St.
Louis, and Denver. He kept in touch with the University of
Pennsylvania, explaining at one point: "[These] lectures will not
be paid for, but I considered it desirable to accept invitations, as
of indirect benefit to the University and — Animal Locomotion."
Another letter stated: "I did pretty well in Chicago. 14 ($100)
subscribers, and 2 complete series ($600 each) and expect some
more when I return."[6]

Reviews of *Animal Locomotion* now began to come in, and
were favorable and extensive. (These were based on examination
copies available in New York and elsewhere.) The review in *The
Nation* was particularly perceptive:

*The result of years of labor and of large expenditure of
money is at last laid before the public in this magnificent work.
The result is one which Mr. Muybridge and the University*

---

[4] *The Pennsylvanian,* September 28, 1886; in Scrapbook.

[5] Talcott Williams, "Animal Locomotion: Muybridge's Photographs."

[6] To Jesse Burk, February 7 and June 22, 1888; in University of
Pennsylvania Library. Burk was secretary to Pepper.

*of Pennsylvania, as well as those concerned either in the actual
investigations or in the supply of funds for carrying them on,
may well be proud, and the work should belong to every
scientific and artistic institution in the country and in the world.*

*The words of the title must be taken in the widest sense.
By far the greater number of plates are devoted to the human
"animal," while the "locomotion" illustrated includes almost
every action of which bones and muscles are capable. It is well
known that Mr. Muybridge's investigations began in the
attempt to demonstrate the falsity of some commonly accepted
and traditional methods of depicting the gaits of the horse.
To show how far his work has outgrown this narrow aim, it is
only necessary to state that, out of the 781 plates he has now
published, only 95 are devoted to the horse, and only 124 to
other animals and to birds, while the other 562 are devoted
to men, women and children, nude, semi-nude, and draped,
walking, running, dancing, getting up and lying down,
wrestling, boxing, leaping and playing at athletic games — in
short, acting before our eyes the animal life of man.*

*Here we have the naked, absolute fact: here, for the first
time, human eyes may see just how the human body moves in
the performance of its functions, how backs bend and hips
balance and muscles strain and swell. This is not an art,
but it is a mine of facts of nature that no artist can afford to
neglect. How would Signorelli, that enthusiast of movement
and anatomy who drew his dead son naked, or Michael
Angelo or Benvenuto, who thought the crupper "a beautiful
bone," have revelled in such volumes as these! How splendid
nature is! Here are dancing girls graceful enough to delight the
soul of Raphael; athletes with heroic movement that would
fire the spirit of Buonarotti: foreshortenings, and flowing contours
to satisfy Tintoret: and all with the indisputable stamp of fact,
painted for us by the same sun that illumined these glowing
chests and cut sharp shadows under the edges of swelling muscles.
Thus to see the natural man in his own motion under nature's
light is a lesson to humanity of its own glory that the Puritan
and the ascetic, the contemner of the nude and the ignorer of art,
would do well to study.*

*For, any impression to the contrary notwithstanding, these
plates are beautiful. There are certain phases of movement that
seem awkward, certain transient movements when the limbs
assume positions which none has ever seen, and which strike the
eye by their strangeness; but follow the whole action
through its various phases, and you will find it free and noble;
study the attitude at the culminating moment of an action, and
you will find it superb. No one need copy the posture of
some of these photographs, or imagine that because a phase of
action is proved to exist it is therefore fit for immediate
reproduction in art. . . . The use of these records of transient
phases of motion is to show how the body passes from an earlier
to a later phase, through what changes it passes from rest up
to the culminating moment of action and back again to rest: and
the artist's true method of study is to master the whole
movement, and then to select for representation the one or*

*two phases that most nearly convey the sense of this movement
as a whole. He may even do well to throw away his photographs
altogether, the action once understood, and express it by a
pose not actually found in any one of them, but conveying
better than any of them, taken separately, the total results of the
series. For the end of art is not record but expression.*

*So studied, the most interesting revelation that the camera
has given us is not, perhaps, that art has been occasionally wrong,
but rather that it has been so generally right. In turning over
these plates, one is constantly struck with the recurrence of
attitudes made famous in immortal sculpture or painting. Here
is John of Bologna's Mercury; here is a fragment from the
Parthenon; here is a figure of Michael Angelo's or Raphael's
or Tintoret's — until one is filled with wonder at the power of
the eye or brain that saw or divined actions and movements that
have waited until now for proof of their verity. Even in the
representation of the lower animals, always less carefully
observed, this is true. The full-spread gallop of the horse in
sporting prints is gone, but the dog has it: the canter of the horse
of the Parthenon is true! and in the first equestrian statue modelled
in modern times Donatello has rendered the walk with an accuracy
unsurpassable. It is only the moderns and the weaklings that
suffer. The Greeks and the great masters of the Renaissance saw
truly and well.*

*There is not space, nor is there any need, to go into detail.
Least has been done in the investigation of the flight of birds,
where the difficulties were peculiarly great: what has been done
shows the marvellous observative faculties of the Japanese,
who have rendered bird-flight more truly than the artists of all
other races. But the presentation of human and quadrupedal action
is bewilderingly abundant and complete, and we cannot more
fittingly conclude our review than by repeating our recommendation
to all artistic and scientific bodies, and indeed to all private persons
who can afford to do so, to subscribe at least for the one hundred
plates that make up a "copy" of the work, and for as many more
as they can compass the means for. Communication may be
addressed to Mr. Eadweard Muybridge, in care of the University of
Pennsylvania.*[7]

The review shows that there was, by 1888, a notable advance
in the interest of artists in Muybridge's work and its meaning
for them. The scientific revelations were taken for granted; the
wonder of the work now seemed to be in the shift of vision that
it brought about for the artist, who "for the first time . . .
may see just how the human body moves in the performance
of its functions," in transient movements "which none has ever
seen." The artist's proper use of the Muybridge photographs

[7]New York, January 19, 1888. The author is not known. For other
reviews see *Lippincott's Magazine,* February 1886; *Public Ledger,*
Philadelphia, November 10, 1887; *Dispatch,* Pittsburgh, December 26,
1887; *Times,* New York, March 5, 1888; and *Scientific American,* March 17,
1888.

was wisely defined: "The artist's true method of study is to master the whole movement. . . . For the end of art is not record but expression."

This was always Muybridge's position about the relation of his photographs to the artist's work. In 1887 Meissonier told him of painting a second version of *Friedland, 1807* (in water color) in order to correct the errors in his past observations of horses in motion.[8] Meissonier subsequently made a similarly executed version of his *1812* so that the depiction of animal movement would be consistent with Muybridge's findings and worthy of his "highest artistic knowledge." In 1888 it was reported that the artist Frederic Remington, "who has lived among the cowboys and knows a horse as he knows his master," had "forsworn conventions" and "accepted the statement of the camera as a guide in future."[9]

All this was a considerable advance over Thomas Eakins's earlier attempt to apply the Palo Alto findings. Commenting on the Eakins painting *A May Morning in the Park,* Muybridge said:

[8] Reported by Charles M. Kurtz in a letter printed in the *Evening Post,* New York, March 26, 1887; in Scrapbook; reprinted in *Muybridge: The Stanford Years,* pp. 127-128.

[9] In the *Eagle,* Brooklyn, New York, January 29, 1888.

Like many other discoveries, the truths revealed by the camera were misinterpreted by some men and applied in such a fashion as to excite ridicule. In this way the beauty and usefulness of the experiments have been somewhat obscured. A painter in Philadelphia, for instance, made a picture of a four-in-hand in which the four horses were drawn according to positions which have been revealed as really those of a trotting horse, yet in effect completely absurd. Had he been consistent, this artist must have painted the wheels with every spoke definable as if at rest. That, however, taken in conjunction with the strange posture of the hoofs and legs of the horses, would have brought the whole team to a dead standstill. He was therefore compelled to show motion by the wheels which he did in the ordinary fashion by giving a blur where the instantaneous photographs would have showed each spoke at rest. The horses looked as if struck by a petrifying disease in their places; the coach was also stationary, in sympathy with the team, but the wheels were whirling like the pinborne fireworks sacred to St. Catherine.[10]

Muybridge's lecture "The Science of Animal Locomotion in Its Relation to Design and Art," later to be incorporated in the text for his *Animals in Motion,* showed him conversant with the history of the visual arts and clear in his analysis of the

[10] *Times,* New York, March 5, 1888.

136. Some of the subscribers to *Animal Locomotion* — a sample page from *Descriptive Zoopraxography,* 1893. Names of outstanding military men, physicists, biologists, physiologists, anatomists, painters, sculptors and authors were traced by Muybridge for reproduction from the original signatures on the subscription book in his possession.

approach of artists, over a sweep of centuries, to the representation of motion. His ability to communicate with artists in their own terms was bound to have effect. Among the subscribers to *Animal Locomotion* appear the names of such eminent American artists as John George Brown, R. Swain Gifford, Eastman Johnson, John La Farge, Thomas Moran, Enoch Wood Perry, John Rogers, Augustus Saint-Gaudens, Launt Thompson, and Louis Comfort Tiffany. Uncounted artists and illustrators attended his lectures and responded to the challenge of his revelations in their professional work.

Also among the subscribers were two American painters residing abroad, Whistler and Ridgway Knight, and a number of European artists, including Meissonier, Bonnat, Bouguereau, Carolus-Duran, Detaille, Gérôme, Puvis de Chavannes, Rodin, J. G. Vibert, Karl Becker, Kaulbach, Knaus, Lenbach, Adolph Menzel, Johannes Schilling, Hans Thoma, Alma-Tadema, W. P. Frith, George du Maurier, Holman Hunt, Leighton, Millais, Orchardson, E. J. Poynter, and Watts. Edgar Degas, although not a subscriber, is known to have followed Muybridge's work closely. Of the painters, those noted for their battle scenes showed the most direct influence and then, as at home, the illustrators and sculptors, aside from the particular interest shown, among the Americans, by Thomas Eakins.[11]

A monograph, *Animal Locomotion: The Muybridge Work at the University of Pennsylvania — The Method and the Result*, was printed by Lippincott and issued by the university in the fall of 1888. The 136-page text contained a prefatory note in which Provost Pepper stated: "In 1883 it was found that Mr. E. Muybridge . . . was the first successfully to apply instantaneous photography to the study of Animal Motion," that the university had therefore wanted him to develop an extended study, and that the result had "fully justified the action of the University, as well as the expenditure of time and money." He predicted that Muybridge's work would be "of lasting service to art and science," and commented on the "mass of novel material" that had been turned up, estimating that much time would still be required to subject it to critical examination. There followed three extended essays:

"The Mechanism of Instantaneous Photography," by William D. Marks, Whitney professor of dynamical engineering at the university; "Materials for a Memoir on Animal Locomotion," by Harrison Allen, emeritus professor of physiology; and "A Study of Some Normal and Abnormal Movements Photographed by Muybridge," by Francis X. Dercum, instructor in nervous diseases.

Muybridge's Philadelphia investigations had far-reaching effects. His deliberate focus on the transient aspects of behavior in both man and animals foreshadowed much in the twentieth century that would be concerned with rapid motion on the earth and rapid motion above it: phenomena of motion, change, and flux; man as a dynamic organism in an expanding universe; kinetic applications of the machine — the automobile, the motion picture machine, the flying machine.

Particularly in the investigations had man been able to step out of his time-space cage and move. He moved free and naked into the *plein air*, into open universe. In less than a decade, Isadora Duncan began her career, bare footed, bare to the shoulder, bare legged to the knee — moving across the stages of the world like one of Muybridge's female models in "transparent drapery" come to life. As Muybridge had liberated the nude model to move in photographs, so Duncan liberated the dance from the prudish clichés of the pre-Muybridge visual world. Gertrude Stein, who also knew of the Muybridge experiments and of Duncan's breakthrough from her early years in California, came to characterize the "composition" of the twentieth century as "a space of time filled with moving." In the first decade of the century she began her literary innovations, based on cinematic techniques, in which "Each statement made is uniquely felt, uniquely formed in the present, and is succeeded by another, slightly different, like the successive frames of a film that build an image which seems to prolong itself in the present for a given period of time."[12] This was a liberation of language from its Aristotelian structures which emphasized the static, and a new use of language to describe the process character of reality and its moment-to-moment novelty. Even the visual arts, from Duchamp's *Nude Descending a Staircase* to Tinguely's self-destroying sculptures, from the animated film to the serial painting of today, traveled a trajectory implicit in *Animal Locomotion* — that penetration of the core of motion which the human eye could not fathom unaided, but which Muybridge with the camera comprehensively revealed.

---

[11] The names of subscribers are taken from the 1891 printing of the *Prospectus and Catalogue of Plates.* It is to be understood that a subscriber did not necessarily order the entire series; an order for a few plates, or a single plate, was counted as a subscription.

Degas's interest is noted by Françoise Forster-Hahn in *Muybridge: The Stanford Years,* p. 101 (references on p. 108, n. 46).

Eakins deliberately blurs the moving form to suggest motion in *Courtship* (1878) and *Spinning* (1881) as well as in the *May Morning.* Examples of his use of "arrested motion" are the *Swimming Hole* (1883) and the *Concert Singer* (1892).

[12] My comment in Robert B. Haas, ed., *A Primer for the Gradual Understanding of Gertrude Stein,* Los Angeles: Black Sparrow Press, 1971, p. 49.

PORTFOLIO V
Philadelphia (1884–1885)

137. Ascending incline. Descending incline. The Model is Muybridge.

138. Jumping a hurdle.

139. Cockatoo, flying.

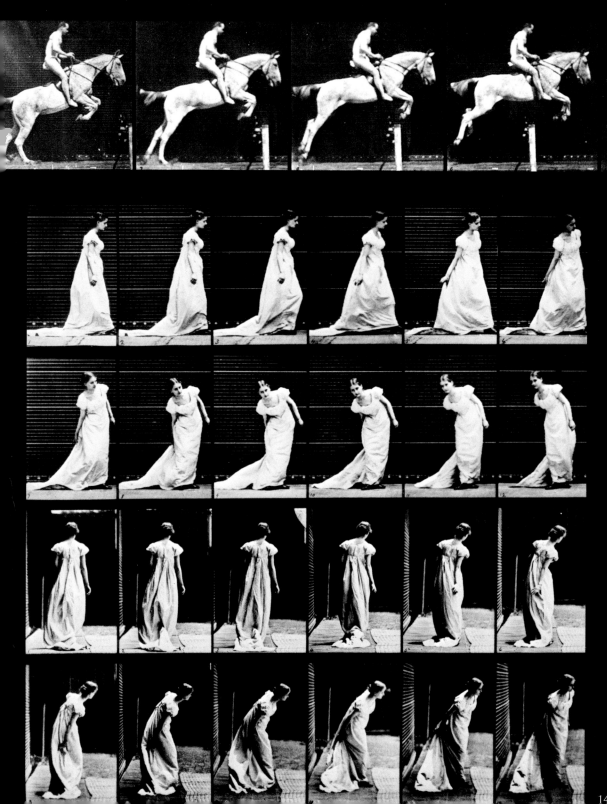

140. Stooping to arrange train, and turning

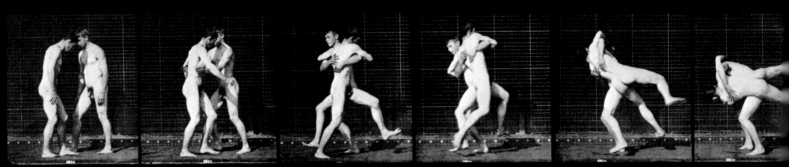

141. Wrestling, lock.

142. Mule; performing mule. Detail

143. Contortions on the ground. Detail.

144. Double amputee moving.

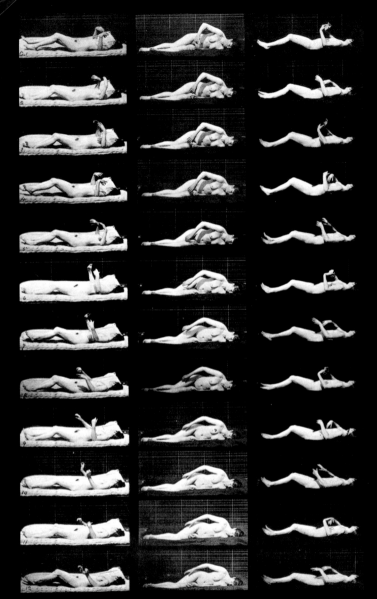

145. Artificially induced convulsions; A, B, C, while lying.

146. Woman and child, banquet to 12.

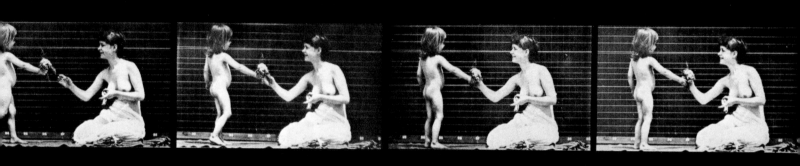

27. European Tour (1889–1892)

Eight years after his first London season, Muybridge again lectured before the Royal Institution and the Royal Society. Evidently *Animal Locomotion* had convinced these august bodies that Muybridge was not sailing under false colors in claiming his proper credit for the work. He was considered the sole author of the electrophotographic studies of motion undertaken both at Palo Alto and at Philadelphia.

He now lectured on "The Science of Animal Locomotion in Its Relation to Design in Art," having assembled a sizable number of slide examples of delineations of motion through the ages — works of prehistoric man, the Egyptians, Assyrians, Etruscans, Greeks, Romans, and Byzantines, and of artists of medieval and modern times.[1] In the two years that followed, he delivered this lecture sixty or more times, before audiences in England, Ireland, and Scotland.

Ernest Webster, a young man from Berkhamsted with a taste for mechanics, traveled with Muybridge. They had previously met at the Royal Academy showing of 1882. In 1889 Webster went along with Muybridge to manage the Zoöpraxiscope. He remembered the tour as a "very enjoyable one" which caused the "greatest interest in all the towns we visited."[2] The itinerary included Bath, Birmingham, Bristol, Dublin, Dundee, Edinburgh, Glasgow, Gloucester, Hull, Ipswich, Leeds, Liverpool, Manchester, Newcastle, Nottingham, Plymouth, Sheffield, and York.

On the front cover of its issue for May 25, 1889, the *London Illustrated News* depicted "Mr. Muybridge Showing His Instantaneous Photographs of Animal Motion." We see him entering his sixtieth year, with high forehead, impressive white beard, and the gestures of a prophet, in formal attire.[3] In Paris in 1881 he had dressed like an elegant Bohemian. In Philadelphia he had been careless of his appearance. Pepper once advised him, "Now dress up!" "What is the matter?" asked Muybridge. Pepper pointed to his hat with a hole in it through which unruly wisps of his hair were showing. "Yes," said Muybridge, "but I didn't know it." Usually when engrossed in photographic work he affected the dress of the Western outdoors. Now the role of public lecturer demanded dignity of costume and he adopted it. This fitted with his reserve as a private person. Friends and colleagues thought he was a bachelor. He never referred to his marriage.

Aside from the gray hair and white beard, evidences of age appear in the sequence of nude photographs taken of himself at Philadelphia — the "ex-athlete" model in *Animal Locomotion*. The muscualr body is about to go soft, and there is the suspicion of a troublesome hernia.

Among the institutions of Great Britain where he was invited to lecture (besides the Royal Institution and the Royal Society) were the Royal Academy of Arts, the Royal College of Surgeons, the Royal Geographical Society, the Zoölogical Society, the art and science schools of the South Kensington Museum, the school of military engineering at Chatham, and the University of Oxford. Charterhouse, Cheltenham, Clifton, Eton, Haileybury, Lancing, Marlborough, Rossal, Rugby, Tiverton, Uppingham, Wellington, and Yorkshire were among the schools he addressed.[4] Yet only a decade before, his lectures in California had met with but moderate success, and some had been so poorly attended that he failed to return for scheduled second appearances.

After a brief return to Philadelphia to report to the guarantors the results of his canvassing for subscriptions abroad, Muybridge went again to Europe.

The lectures which I have recently had the honor of giving at many of the best known Institutions of Art, Science, and Literature in Great Britain and Ireland, on the Movements of Animals, especially in their relation to Design in Art, seem to have awakened so much interest and enthusiasm [that] in nearly every instance where I have given lectures, I have been invited to give one or more others on the same subject during the season of 1890-91.

I have therefore arranged to continue my stay in England and during this season shall be open to lecture engagements. It may perhaps not be irrelevant for me to say that the apparently abstruse subject of Animal Locomotion, is, in these lectures treated in a **popular** *manner, and the demonstrations of the Movements of Animals and Birds are as attractive to the Child as to the Savant, or as the Saturday Review expresses it, "They appeal to every class and condition of humanity" being as well suited for exhibition in the drawing-room as in the theatre of a college.*

Kindly permit me therefore to direct your attention to the accompanying prospectus and to say that I shall be delighted to place my services at your disposal for a course, or for a single lecture, should you be inclined to avail yourself of them.[5]

[1] The slides are in the Science Museum, London. Muybridge issued a prospectus, under the lecture title, in January 1890; copy in Scrapbook.

[2] Ernest Webster, "The First 'Movies,' " *The Gazette,* London, August 1, 1938.

[3] The cover picture is reproduced in *Muybridge: The Stanford Years*, p. 93.

[4] As stated in the prospectus (n. 1, above).

[5] Draft of letter soliciting engagements, in Scrapbook.

147. "Mr. Muybridge showing his Instantaneous Photographs of Animal Motion at the Royal Society," *Illustrated London News,* May 25, 1889.

By the spring of 1891 Muybridge was lecturing on the continent. We find him in Berlin and Munich, and then in Rome, where he secured engagements with the French Academy and the International Society of Artists, both of which became subscribers for *Animal Locomotion.* "Being in Rome on Sunday," he wrote, "I deemed it the proper thing to go to St. Peter's and reverentially kiss the black image of [the] blessed Apostle's toe as is the custom of all true believers in his papal descendant." From Rome he went to Naples, and from Naples took a pleasure trip to Vesuvius and Pompeii. He reported that he had visited nearly all the important universities of Italy and South Germany, and had "everywhere obtained for the University of Pennsylvania a recognition of its enlightened and liberal policy. In July he was back in Berlin. He now spoke Italian, German, and French "with equal fluency."[6]

The universities on Muybridge's subscription list were those of Oxford, Berlin, Paris, Munich, Naples, Tübingen, Würzburg, Geneva, Freiburg, Basel, Halle, Jena, Göttingen, Bonn, Strassburg, Vienna, Heidelberg, Prague, Genoa, Zurich, Pisa, Innsbruck, Budapest, Florence, and Padua. Scientists such as Helmholtz, Bunsen, Virchow, Ludwig, and Du Bois-Reymond, among others, permitted the reproduction of their signatures as subscribers, as did "nearly all the notable artists" of England, France, Germany, and Italy.[7] To each subscriber a copy of the *Prospectus and Catalogue of Plates* was sent by the University of Pennsylvania (to those abroad through Lippincott's London office), for selection of the desired plates, which then were shipped from New York by the Photogravure Company.

Meissonier died on January 31, 1891. More than any other man, he had stood faithfully by Muybridge as a patron and friend. He had been a warm advocate of Muybridge's work before the most distinguished artists and scientists of Europe. He had humbly taken from him the revelations of his cameras, always seeking to build from this knowledge a more perfect and accurate art. In his great vitality and success as an artist, Meissonier had supplied the missing role of the admired father in Muybridge's later life, especially after Stanford withdrew his patronage. With Meissonier's death, the secure and solid world of personal and professional recognition that Muybridge had built for himself began to show signs of stress.

[6] Letter to Jesse Burk, July 15, 1891.
[7] From a leaflet describing his lectures, London, January 1890; in Scrapbook.

28. Father and Son (1892)

The financial rewards of the European tour, when Muybridge's "equitable commission" on the sales of *Animal Locomotion* was subtracted, were not sufficient to repay fully the guarantors in Philadelphia. Sales, however, had been steady, and the deficit had been reduced by nearly $20,000. Each guarantor was still "out" about $2,000 at the end of the year 1891.

Now Muybridge was again in Philadelphia, where it was agreed that he should turn his canvassing labors in another direction and prepare for a lecture tour of the Orient in 1892.[1] In the spring he traveled to California, expecting before long to embark for Japan.

In February Muybridge was planning for a stop-over in California, partly to renew his acquaintance with the city he had not visited for a decade, partly to relish a little the fame he had earned during his ten years of absence, partly to visit Floredo (now 18 years old) about whose future he would have to make some decisions, and partly, as we know from the following letter, to explore the possibility of finding a professional position for himself at another institution of higher learning:

To/ President David Starr Jordan AM, MD.
Leland Stanford Junior University
Palo Alto/California

Dear Sir.

Although I have not the pleasure of your personal acquaintance, I may not be wrong in assuming that you know something of my work, and that my first experiments of Animal Locomotion were made with the co-operation of Senator Stanford.

I am now happy to say that after several years of privations, and laborious exertions, I have recovered the position — at least in reputation — from which I was displaced by the publication of "The Horse in Motion by J D B Stillman"; and have completed under the auspices of this University a comparatively exhaustive investigation of Animal Movements, and I avail myself of the opportunity to send you two pamphlets on the subject which I think will interest you. I have recently seen both Mr. and Mrs. Stanford, and was very much gratified with the renewed assurance by Mrs. Stanford of her belief that the interest and attention I succeeded in obtaining for my work by the Senator, during a period of great mental anxiety was mainly instrumental in saving his life.

I am now being urged by many men, eminent in various branches of Science — among them are Professors Helmholtz, S P Langley, Ray Lankester & Sir Wm Thomson and Sir John Lubbock and Mr Edison — to undertake an investigation of the flight of insects; they being impressed with the belief that a comprehensive knowledge of the subject will be of much interest and value in many ways, and materially assist in a solution of the problem of aerial navigation.

With this object in view I have devised an apparatus which will be capable of photographing a dozen or more consecutive phases of a single vibration of the wing of an Insect in flight; even assuming that the number of vibrations exceed 500 in a second, which is far in excess of what Professor Helmholtz believes to be possible with a common house fly.

Finding that both Mr & Mrs Stanford maintain an apparent undiminished interest in this subject, will you kindly permit me to inquire whether it is within the province of the Leland Stanford Junior University to prosecute or aid in any marked degree, original research; and whether you would approve — or better be willing to promote and assist such an investigation as I propose.

It was an agreeable surprise to me while recently travelling in Europe to find that the University of Pennsylvania was chiefly known there through its association with investigations of Animal Locomotion.

I have made no mention of this matter in any way to Mr Stanford, preferring to first communicate with you, and to afford you an opportunity of proposing it to him should you feel so inclined. I believe the work can be more successfully carried on in California than anywhere else, and it would be some satisfaction to me and it might be so also to Mr Stanford that the investigation of this subject of Motion should be completed, where it was commenced.

> *I am*
> *Dear Sir*
> *Yours Faithfully*[2]

The response from President Jordan could not have been favorable, for Muybridge was not either then nor later invited to become a faculty member of the University. His search for patronage, and perhaps for the father behind the patron, was destined, as always, to end in apparent failure.

Nevertheless, in the spring of 1892 Muybridge travelled to California expecting before long to embark from there for Japan.

Many familiar things had altered in the decade that Muybridge had been away from San Francisco. The old photographic crowd had largely disappeared — Selleck had retired from business; Rulofson had died from a fall off the roof of his gallery, in mysterious circumstances; Bradley had retired in financial ruin. The *Chronicle* now occupied a ten-story building on Market Street and was introducing a sensational new kind of journalism.

[1] Preparations for a lecture tour through Australia and India are mentioned in *Descriptive Zoöpraxography*, p. 1.

[2] Written from the University of Pennsylvania, February 11, 1892. Letter discovered at Stanford University, 1974. Courtesy of Anita V. Mozley.

The editor, Michel de Young, had just been appointed by President Harrison as a national commissioner-at-large to represent the United States at the coming World's Columbian Exposition in Chicago. Leland Stanford was now a United States senator, residing in Washington. He and Mrs. Stanford had recently endowed the Leland Stanford Junior University on their Palo Alto property as a memorial to their beloved Leland, Jr., who had died unexpectedly in Florence in 1884. Twelve spelndid buildings and the Memorial Church had been constructed when the university was opened in 1891, with an expected endowment of twenty million dollars. It was rumored that Leland Stanford was in poor health and much in need of rest and relaxation.

Seeking to bring himself to the attention of President Jordan again, Muybridge appears to have offered to lecture at Stanford on an informal basis sometime in April. As the event neared, either he or his friends had second thoughts about his reception at Palo Alto on that basis. He tested the likelihood of an official welcome in a second letter to President Jordan:

My dear Sir.

A conversation which I, this morning had with one of the Trustees of your University, has led me to question the advisability of my coming to Palo Alto, prepared to give a Lecture on the Science of Animal Locomotion, without first having received a formal invitation from you to do so.

I was induced to offer my services to you for one or a course of Lectures, — First, in the belief that it would afford both Mr and Mrs Stanford pleasure to attend one of them, — Second, with the hope that you, your professors, and your students might be pleased to have an opportunity of studying some facts about animal movements but little understood; and Third, because I shall naturally feel some gratification in giving my first Lecture in this Course on the same ground where my first experiments in analysis were made; and I shall be delighted to learn that it is agreeable to you, and to Mr and Mrs Stanford that I should do so.

Dr. Harkness has done me the honor to invite me to Lecture at the Academy of Sciences, which I have accepted with the understanding that your University has the prior claim.

Will you kindly let me know what — if any — evening will be agreeable for the Lecture to be given, and I will immediately inform Dr. Harkness who will make his announcement accordingly.

> *I am*
> *my dear Sir*
> *Yours Faithfully* [3]

[3] Written from Room 755, Palace Hotel, San Francisco, April 5, 1892. Letter discovered at Stanford University, 1974. Courtesy of Anita V. Mozley. Muybridge asked Jordan to kindly address his reply c/o Art Association since there was "much delay in the delivery of letters at this hotel.'

There is no record that President Jordan responded with an official invitation. For Muybridge this was not only an immediate turn-down, but also clear evidence that he had no future at the University or under father Stanford's aegis as he had hoped.

During his next four months in California, Muybridge had additional and frustrating evidence that any personal or legal appeals he might make to Stanford or to Stanford's associates at Palo Alto would be humiliatingly rebuffed.

The draft of a letter in his handwriting, dated May 2, 1892, at San Francisco, still exists. The intended letter, if Stanford actually saw it, must have reopened old wounds.

My Dear Sir: In the spring of the year 1872 in Sacramento, you asked me if it was possible to photograph from a lateral point of view, your horse Occident while trotting at full speed; as you wished to confirm a theory that a horse trotting at full speed must necessarily be clear of the ground for a portion of his stride.

I need not remind you that in a few days I established the truth of this theory to your and my own satisfaction, if not to the satisfaction of the world.

On the 7 August 1877 in a letter (a copy of which I have before me) [4] *I suggested to you a plan for making a series of electro-photographs, automatically, by which the consecutive phases of a single stride could be successfully photographed. Being much interested in this subject, I offered to supply you with what copies of the results you required for your personal use, if you would pay the actual expenses of obtaining them — omitting any payment in money for my time.*

You accepted my proposition, and from a few days after the date of my letter, until the spring of 1881, or for more than three years, my time was devoted almost exclusively to superintending the construction of the apparatus or the execution of the work.

In the summer of 1878 I published and copyrighted under the title of

> *The Horse in Motion*
> *by*
> *Muybridge*

six photographs of your horses, each illustrating consecutive phases of the Trot, Gallop, etc.

I delivered to you a large number of these photographs with the above title printed on the mounts thereof, but very few were sold.

In consequence of the interest which you manifested in the work, it was then arranged that I should continue my work, with 24 cameras instead of 12 the results of which, as you state in the preface to the book, published under your auspices — were not originally intended for publication by you.

Finding, however that my system of investigating Animal

[4] This letter has not been found.

Locomotion began to attract some attention, it was agreed and arranged that my photographs should be reproduced and published in book form.

It was your professed, and I believed your sincere desire to recognize my devotion to the work by extending a knowledge of it to the world, and by that means to bring me not only fame, but something more substantial, in the shape of that which too often fails to accompany fame, these or words to that effect, were frequently used by you.

During the winter of 1880-81 "J D B Stillman MD" (who was not present at a single experiment of motion) — at your request commenced to examine and write a description of my photographs. While engaged in this work, Stillman submitted to me the title page of the proposed book, which, taking my original copyrighted title as his key, was substantially as follows.

THE HORSE IN MOTION
as demonstrated by a series of photographs

BY MUYBRIDGE
With an attempt to elucidate the theory of Animal Locomotion

BY J. D. B. STILLMAN MD
Published under the auspices of

LELAND STANFORD

This title page was satisfactory to me and had this book been published it might have been of some assistance in obtaining for me the reward which you expressed your belief and desire I should have.

Early in the year 1882 I gave a Lecture at the Royal Institution of Great Britain, when I took the opportunity of giving you, what I think you will consider was full and generous acknowledgement for your co-operation and assistance in my work.

This lecture brought me into contact with many persons distinguished in Science or Art or holding the highest ranks in Society.

Mr. Spottiswoode — the President of the Royal Society of London invited me to prepare a monograph on Animal Locomotion to be published in the "Proceedings" of the Society, and promised to provide the funds for an exhaustive investigation of the subject to be made under the auspices of the Society.

I was invited to give several public and private repetitions of the Lecture given at the Royal Institution. And altogether a brilliant and profitable career seemed opened to me in London.

In response to the invitation by the President I wrote a monograph on Animal Locomotion, and submitted it to the Council of the Royal Society.

This monograph was examined, accepted and a day appointed for its presentation to the Fellows, and for its being placed in the records of the Society.

I have in my possession a proof sheet of my monograph,

printed by the Society, (as is its custom) before being place[d] on the record of its "Proceedings."

About three days before the time appointed for the reception of my monograph by the Fellows, I received a note requesting my presence at the Rooms of the Society.

Upon my arrival I was conducted to the Council Chamber and was asked by the President in the presence of the assembled Council, if I knew anything about a book then on the table having on its title page, the following

THE HORSE IN MOTION
by

J D B STILLMAN MD
Published under the auspices of

LELAND STANFORD

there being no reference thereon to Muybridge.

I was asked whether this book contained the results of the photographic investigation of which I had **professed** *to be the author. That being admitted I was invited to explain to the Council how it was that my name did not appear on the Title Page, in accordance with my profession.*

No explanation of mine could avail in the face of the evidence on the title page, and in the book before the Council, I had no proof to support my assertions. My monograph was refused a place on the records of the Royal Society until I could prove to the satisfaction of the Council my claim to be considered its original author, and until this day it remains unrecorded from lack of evidence which would be acceptable to the Council, which evidence is at your command.

The doors of the Royal Society were thus closed against me, and in consequence of this action, the invitations which had been extended to me were immediately cancelled, and my promising career in London was thus brought to a disastrous close.

My available funds being exhausted I was compelled to sell the four original photographic copies of

"The Horse in Motion"

which I had printed at your request, and for your purposes, and with the proceeds of their sale I returned to America. [5]

I will not now trouble you with any details of other and subsequent happenings more than to say that in consequence of this publication of

"THE HORSE IN MOTION"
by

J D B STILLMAN MD

[5] Muybridge must be referring to the four albums of *The Attitudes of Animals in Motion.*

I for two years vainly sought assistance to pursue my researches until at last through the influence of Dr. William Pepper, and other gentlemen (who had made due enquiries as to my position in the matter) I was instructed by the University of Pennsylvania to make a comprehensive investigation of the subject of Animal Locomotion. A few of the results of this investigation, you have seen. I have patiently waited during eleven years without bringing this matter to your attention, but I think that the time has arrived when in justice both to you and to myself I ought to do so.

With many of the facts which I have related you are already familiar and I do not believe you will question the accuracy of my statements in regard to the others, they are however all susceptible of conclusive proof.[6]

I am, Dear Sir, Yours Faithfully

Whether Stanford received the letter is unknown. Another matter was troubling Muybridge, and he endeavored to approach Stanford about it in a letter of August 5 from San Francisco:

THE HONORABLE LELAND STANFORD, Palo Alto
You will please deliver to Mr. John T. Doyle several boxes of goods belonging to me, and marked with my name, which were left by me with your permission, at Palo Alto when I went to Europe in 1881. These boxes contain apparatus and other property which belonged to me, — or the greater part thereof — before I commenced my work at Palo Alto.

EADWEARD J. MUYBRIDGE

MEMORANDUM
I applied for these boxes through Geo. D. Morse, and also through Arthur Rodgers in 1882 when Mr. Ariel Lathrop through some unknown cause refused to deliver them. I applied again personally in July 1892, to Mr. Lathrop for said boxes, and without assigning any reason, other than that he did not know that I left any boxes at Palo Alto, he declined to give me permission to take them away.[7]

Apparently Stanford remained adamant, for the boxes never reached Muybridge, who probably interpreted the treatment given his request as a personal rejection. The boxes subsequently were given at some time to Doyle, probably after Stanford's death in 1893.

Muybridge had another personal matter to attend to in California. In 1884, the year when young Leland Stanford, Jr., died, Muybridge had taken Floredo Helios Muybridge from the Protestant Orphan Asylum in San Francisco and sent him to live at the Haggin ranch near Sacramento. There Floredo was placed

[6] The draft letter is in the Bancroft Library.
[7] The letter to Stanford, August 5, 1893, and the memorandum are in the Bancroft Library.

148. Floredo Helios Muybridge (1874-1944) the ill-fated son of Flora Muybridge who throughout his life claimed Eadweard Muybridge to be his real father. In his early life he worked as a stable boy at Haggin Grant, then in the Southern Pacific Railroad shops. After that he became a gardener until his accidental death.

with the family of David Buck, a harness maker at the ranch. Mrs. Buck employed him first as a houseboy and treated him with a mother's concern. Despite his ambiguous background and tragic early childhood, Floredo was a responsive boy and a good worker, but he did not seem to develop intellectually. When Mrs. Buck divorced her husband and married Carsten Tietjen (whose brother Albert had been present at Muybridge's first attempts to photograph Occident), she and Tietjen continued the care of Floredo, who was employed as an errand boy on the Haggin ranch and, when he grew older, as a jockey and caretaker of animals.[8]

[8] For the data here, given in conversation, I am grateful to Frank Tietjen, of Sacramento, who was a close friend of Floredo. Frank was the son of Carsten Tietjen.

Muybridge had been away from the boy for eleven years. His trip to the West Coast coincided with Floredo's eighteenth year, and he spent some time with him at Sacramento. Floredo had been brought up to think of Muybridge as his father, and, indeed, Muybridge had given Floredo his name and provided for his support. Seeing now how limited a personality Floredo had come to be, and how little desire he had for further education or accomplishment, Muybridge decided to terminate his responsibility. He had kept money on deposit at a bank in San Francisco for Floredo's education. This he now made over to two Kingston cousins, changing his will to exclude Floredo, who was of an age when he could support himself by his own labors. Muybridge made him a gift of a handsome gold watch and an excellent photograph of himself.[9] He left California and never saw Floredo again. Despite the fact that Floredo had developed a striking resemblance to Muybridge, the man whom he called father rejected him.

Floredo may well have been Muybridge's son. The love affair between Flora and Larkyns cannot be doubted, and it is true also that they chose to think of him as their child. At the time of the murder (and perhaps before it) Muybridge evidently assumed that he was not the father. But he and Flora lived together both up to the time of Floredo's birth and after that. The question of paternity thus remains unanswerable.

Mrs. Tietjen brought up Floredo as a Catholic. She taught him to honor Flora and Muybridge as his parents, and refused to believe the story of his bastardy. She had known Flora. She stuck to her convictions about Flora's innocence and taught Floredo the facts as she understood them. After Muybridge's death, she encouraged Floredo to sue for a share of the estate.

Fatherhood was clearly a problem for Eadweard Muybridge. His own father died early. The father replacements who figured in his life — Selleck, Stanford, Meissonier, Marey, the guarantors, and the university — all aided him at first and then failed him in some way, leaving him (or perhaps stimulating him) to go on alone to new heights of accomplishment. Muybridge played the father role to Floredo after the same model, apparently the only one he knew. He helped as long as he honestly could, then turned his back.

Floredo Helios Muybridge survived the blow, which may not have greatly affected him. He survived for fifty-two more years, living his own kind of happy-go-lucky life. When he left the ranch, he became a gardener and handy-man in town, and was a well-known "character" in Sacramento. Occasionally, when he had been drinking a little too much, he would bend the ear of any willing listener and confide that he was the son of a famous photographer.[10] In his seventieth year he was struck down by an automobile, fatally, while on his way to work. The obituary column of the Sacramento *Bee* contained a notice: "MUYBRIDGE — In this city, February 1, 1944, Floredo Muybridge, a native of San Francisco . . ."

[9] Both items kept by Frank Tietjen.

[10] Information given to Janet Leigh by Frances Garroutte, Woodland, Calif., April 7, 1948.

29. World's Columbian Exposition: Zoopraxiscope and Kinetoscope   (1893)

While attending to painful personal matters in California, Muybridge received an unexpected offer. The Fine Arts Commission of the World's Columbian Exposition, which was to be held at Chicago in 1893, invited him to present a series of popular lectures on animal locomotion.[1] This prospect seemed so attractive that he put off the lecture tour in the Orient and planned instead his participation in the "quadri-centennial celebration of the grandest and most accidental discovery the world's annals will ever record"[2] — the discovery of America by Christopher Columbus.

Construction work on the exposition's "White City" had been under way since 1891, on a site of some 700 acres along the shores of Lake Michigan. The dedication of the major buildings took place on October 21, 1893, in a ceremony "so impressively grand as to be without equal and beyond comparison" and "in

[1] *Descriptive Zoöpraxography*, p. 1.

[2] *A Week at the Fair, Illustrating Exhibits and Wonders of the World's Columbian Exposition*, Chicago: Rand, McNally, 1893.

the presence of an audience amounting to a quarter of a million, gathered from every civilized nation on the earth." The ten original buildings grew to three hundred, and another hundred "minor pavilions and shelters of a less important character" were built by concessionaires and exhibitors in the Midway Plaisance, a tract about 600 feet wide and a mile long.[3]

On October 19, 1892, Muybridge entered into a contract to construct a building at his own expense for lecturing purposes, to give lectures there on the science of animal locomotion, and to sell photographs, or "mechanically printed illustrations thereof," and "Zoöpraxiscopic Fans." The building was to be completed by the first day of March 1893, two months before the opening of the exposition. Bonds to the amount of $6,000 were given by Muybridge to secure the contract.[4]

In due course, a "commodious theatre" was erected for Muybridge's purposes in the Midway Plaisance and was designated the "Zoopraxographical Hall." Along with the jaw-breaking name, which surely must have deterred many fairgoers from entering, it had the distinction of being the world's first commercial motion-picture theatre. The chaste, white building, in the classical style featured at the exposition, measured about 50 x 80 feet. A Roman porch with monumental columns broke the façade. The exterior was finished with plaster rustication giving the impression of stonework. Three little banners flew from flagpoles on the roof when performances were given, quite as in Shakespeare's time.[5]

The fact that the Zoopraxographical Hall faced the "Moorish Palace," the "Persian Concession," and the Natatorium, and was backed by the "Street in Cairo," took nothing away from the seriousness of what went on inside. An announcement put out by the Fine Arts Commission set the tone:

WORLD S COLUMBIAN EXPOSITION
DEPARTMENT OF ZOOPRAXOGRAPHY

By invitation of the FINE ARTS COMMISSION of the World's Columbian Exposition, Mr. EADWEARD MUYBRIDGE will give at intervals, from May to October, 1893, in the Zoopraxographical Hall of the Exposition, a series of Lectures on the Science of Animal Locomotion, especially in relation to Design in Art.

These Lectures will be given under the auspices of the United States Government BUREAU OF EDUCATION, and will be based on the electro-photographic investigation of the movements of animals, made by Mr. Muybridge for the UNIVERSITY OF PENNSYLVANIA.

[3] Ibid.
[4] *World's Columbian Exposition, Concession Agreements*, Chicago, 1892, III, 41-60.
[5] *Descriptive Zoöpraxography*, p. 2.

From the investigations of Mr. Muybridge — which were commenced in 1872 — originated the Science of ZOOPRAXO-GRAPHY, and the lectures and demonstrations on this subject have been given by the Author at nearly all the principal institutions of Science, Art and Education in the United States and in Europe.

It is a subject of the most profound importance to the Scientist and the Artist, and has been universally recognized as of the greatest interest to the general public.

Although it is probable that the present series of Lectures may not be unworthy the attention of the Philosopher, they will be free from technicalities, and adapted not merely for the instruction, but also for the entertainment of popular and juvenile audiences.

The illustrations will comprise a selection of the consecutive phases of movements by Men, Women, Children, Horses, Dogs, Cats, Wild Animals, and Birds, photographed while they were running, jumping, boxing, dancing, galloping, trotting, kicking, flying, or engaged in other muscular exercises. They will be projected by the electric light on a large screen, and after an analysis, the successive phases will be combined, and put in motion with the semblance of actual life by the ZOOPRAXISCOPE.

The difference between a true and false impression of animal movements will be demonstrated by illuminated projections of the works of many eminent Painters and Sculptors of Ancient and Modern Times.

For a synopsis of the Lectures, and arrangements for the admissions of Associations, Colleges, Art Schools, and other special audiences, address

Newton H. Carpenter, Secretary
Art Institute
Chicago, Illinois, U.S.A.[6]

[6] In Scrapbook, dated January 1893.

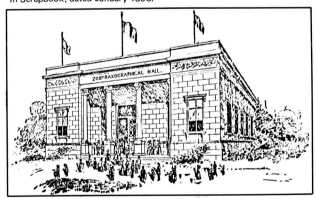

149. The Zoopraxographical Hall, built for Muybridge at the World's Columbian Exposition in Chicago, 1893. Here, for a brief period, Muybridge presided over the first commercial motion-picture theater in the world — a child of his own creation.

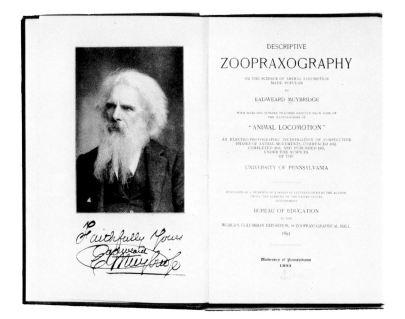

150. Title page of *Descriptive Zoopraxography* 1893,
intended by Muybridge as a popular presentation
of his professional work to date
and prepared for sale at the
World's Columbian Exposition.

151. The Midway Plaisance, *World's Columbian Exposition,* Chicago 1893. Muybridge's "Zoopraxographical Hall" is the building in the lower left corner. The photograph was taken from the ferris wheel, perhaps by Muybridge himself.

There is some evidence that, after an opening flurry in May, the gate receipts from the Zoopraxographical Hall were not sufficient to make Muybridge's enterprise a commercial success.[7] In competition with the barkers, hootchy-kootchy dancers, and wax museums, Ferris wheel, the Lustgarten of Old Vienna, and the Volcano of Kilauea, Muybridge must have had rather a hard go of it with his educational theater:

In the presentation of a Lecture on Zoopraxography the course usually adopted is to project, much larger than the size of life upon a screen, a series of the most important phases of some act of animal motion — the stride of a horse, while galloping for example — which are analytically described. These successive phases are then combined in the Zoopraxiscope, which is set in motion, and a reproduction of the original movements of life is distinctly visible to the audience.

With this apparatus, horse-races are reproduced with such fidelity that the individual characteristics of the motion of every animal can readily be seen: flocks of birds fly across the screen with every movement of their wings clearly perceptible; two gladiators contend for victory with an energy which would cause the arena to resound with wild applause, athletes turn somersaults, and other actions by men, women and children, horses, dogs, cats and wild animals, such as running, dancing, jumping, trotting and kicking, are illustrated in the same manner. By this method of analysis and synthesis the eye is taught how to observe and to distinguish the difference between a true and a false impression of animal movements. The Zoöpraxiscopical exhibition is followed by illuminated copies of paintings and sculptures, demonstrating how the movement has been interpreted by the Artists of all ages; from the primitive engravers of the cave dwelling period, to the most eminent painters and sculptors of the present day.[8]

Despite its intrinsic and historical importance, the Zoopraxographical Hall and its committed photographer-researcher-lecturer-author were in heavy contrast to the buzzing, booming attractions of the Midway Plaisance. The moral crusader Anthony Comstock was objecting to the "vile, licentious foreign dances" — the belly dances in the Turkish manner which the general public found fascinating — and threatened to indict the exposition's commissioners for "keeping a disorderly house."

If the gate receipts were disappointing, so were the sales of "Suggestive Tracings from 'Animal Locomotion,' " fifty engravings illustrating the phases of animal locomotion and mounted on cardboard disks in the manner of phenakistascope disks. A portfolio of these was intended to sell for five dollars. Single disks mounted on handles were sold separately as fans. Plates

from *Animal Locomotion* were also on display, and many visitors seem to have filled out subscription blanks for these, but they often failed to make payment for their purchases upon delivery. Muybridge turned this matter over to a New York firm of attorneys and then lost interest in pursuing it.[9]

Muybridge's work earned for him a Certificate of Honor from the commissioners,[10] but what he termed "that large and important class of students, known as the general public," and strenuously courted in 1893, was diverted elsewhere. Times had changed. A new tempo was required to hold the popular audience. Muybridge sensed it and left Chicago in October when his contract was fulfilled.

Leland Stanford, although now unable to walk without assistance, visited the World's Columbian Exposition for a few days in April. According to his biographer, probably he was afflicted by "hardening of the arteries or plain old age." In early May he was back at his Palo Alto home. "Thereafter he went out driving quite regularly and, as was his wont, frequently visited his stock farm, where he loved to watch the horses in training." On June 20, in his seventieth year, he succumbed to "paralysis of the heart."[11] In September, Muybridge again sought the return of his belongings, writing to the executors of Stanford's estate:

Gentlemen:

When I completed my investigations of animal locomotion at Palo Alto, I left in the building occupied by me, several boxes containing apparatus and personal property belonging to me. They were left there by permission of Mr. Stanford.

I have now occasion to use some of the articles and shall feel obliged if you will deliver all the boxes to the order of Mr. John T. Doyle, and oblige

Yours faithfully
Eadweard Muybridge

Among other goods left by me at Palo Alto, were
1 large white box containing a 24 x 24 camera.
4 boxes of size about 30 inches long x 15 inches, containing some landscape and other negatives, stereoscopic views of California and other effects.
A framework and gearing being a model for a Zoopraxiscope, a small Camera with plate holder and 6 lenses.
A canvas tent in a tarred canvas cover, size of bundle about 24 x 18 inches.
Some other bundles containing a photographic tent, and framework and poles for the same, etc.
And some boxes of miscellaneous articles.

[7] Maps of the fairgrounds shows that another enterprise was on the site of Muybridge's theater after, if not before, the six months' contract was completed.

[8] *Descriptive Zoöpraxography,* p. 2.

[9] Edward N. Dickenson, attorney, to Muybridge, March 21, 1895; in University of Pennsylvania Library.

[10] In Scrapbook.

[11] Clark, pp. 468-469.

*The probability is that Charlie or Tom, or perhaps McLean will
know all about them, they were left in the little house near
McLean's boarding house, but I believe were afterwards moved
over to the great barn.*

Eadweard Muybridge

Chicago, 5th Sept. 1893.[12]

Presumably it was in response to this petition that the items were
eventually given into the possession of Muybridge's lawyer in San
Francisco, John Doyle, who had a country home adjacent to the
Palo Alto Farm.

The one positive outcome of Muybridge's experience at Chicago
was the publication of another book. This was his *Descriptive
Zoöpraxography.* Its subtitle, *The Science of Animal Locomotion
Made Popular,* was indicative of the author's desire to reach the
aforementioned "large and important class of students." The title
page further described the book as a "Memento of a Series of
Lectures Given by the Author under the Auspices of the United
States Bureau of Education at the World's Columbian Exposition,
in Zoopraxographical Hall, 1893." A brief and compact work, it
contains a preface describing the method of presentation used by
Muybridge in the Zoopraxographical Hall and an introduction
giving the history of his photographic study of motion from 1872
to 1885. The author then acknowledges his obligations to the
guarantors and faculty commission in Philadelphia, and offers a
lucid 33-page essay on his "Studio, Apparatus and Method of
Working" which concludes with "condensed definitions of various
gaits." Three appendixes outline Muybridge's course of lectures
and provide tracings of figures in a series of circles as arranged for
the Zoöpraxiscope.

In this concentrated, well-written overview of his investigations
of animal locomotion, Muybridge is for the first time the sole
author involved in presenting his work. He shows a flair for
literary structure and organization, and the ability to communicate
succinctly what he has done, how he has done it, and the
importance of what he has done for science and art. The book
prefigures the two popular and summary volumes that he was to
undertake at the end of the century, *Animals in Motion* and *The
Human Figure in Motion.*

The last decade of the nineteenth century, during which
Muybridge considered himself virtually retired from active
research and photography, was a time of abundant activity on
the part of those many workers who were to develop the
motion picture industry of the twentieth century. It was
inevitable, as Muybridge himself knew, that his method would
be superseded and that more advanced techniques would be

found for the analysis and synthesis of motion. Although he was
not in the competitive arena so far as these turn-of-the-century
advances were concerned, he was aware of the progress being
made and of many of the men who were contributing to it. Among
these was the inventor Thomas Alva Edison.

Edison was interested in producing a commercially feasible
machine for showing motion pictures. Muybridge lectured in
Orange, New Jersey, on February 25, 1888, and two days later
seems to have sought out Edison in his workshop at West Orange
for the purpose of showing him some of the *Animal Locomotion*
plates and discussing the "practicability of using [the
Zoöpraxiscope] in association with the phonograph."[13] In
May, Muybridge sent a copy of the *Prospectus and Catalogue of
Plates* to Edison, who made a note: "Tell him to make the
selection for me." The receipt for $100 sent to the Photogravure
Company still exists in the Edison archives, along with a letter
of November 28 from Muybridge giving assurance that the plates
had been sent. In *The Edison Motion Picture Myth,* Gordon
Hendricks maintains that Edison's impetus for work on his
"Kinetoscope" followed rather than preceded the arrival of the
Muybridge pictures.[14] We know that Edison hoped to have
the machine in operation at the World's Columbian Exposition,
but this "new nickel-slot kinetoscope was not available in time
for commercial use at the Fair."[15] Muybridge must have awaited
with interest the introduction of the Kinetoscope, which
utilized for the first time, as he wrote, "a strip of ribbon
containing a number [of] figures in a straight line (instead of
being arranged on a large glass disc)."[16]

Had the Kinetoscope been displayed at Chicago, Muybridge
would still have had the satisfaction of being the only
commercial exhibitor of projected motion pictures at the time.
This continued to be the situation until 1896.[17]

[12] In Bancroft Library.

[13] *Animals in Motion,* p. 15 (in Dover edition). The Scrapbook contains a
clipping of an article by Antonia and W. K. L. Dickson, "Edison's Invention
of the Kineto-Phonograph," in *The Century,* June 1894, reporting Edison's
interest in the "synchronous attachment of photography with the
phonograph." Apparently not in Muybridge's hand is a note: "Suggested by
[William] Friese-Greene to Edison in the first place." Although Muybridge
seems to have discussed this with Edison in 1888, he does not give himself
credit for the idea. (For Dickson reprint see chap. 34, n. 7.)

[14] Berkeley and Los Angeles: University of California Press, 1961.

[15] Ibid., p. 141.

[16] *Animals in Motion,* p. 16 (in Dover edition).

[17] Jean Vivré, *Traité Général de Technique du Cinéma* (Vol. I of *Historique
et Développement de la Technique Cinématographique*), Paris: Editions
B. P. I., 1945, p. 58. Vivré's synoptic tables of the history and development
of the cinema are useful in sorting out the facts in this complex field.
Thomas Armat and F. Charles Jenkins, American inventors, collaborated on
a machine to project Edison's kinetographic reels. They joined with Edison
in 1895/6 to produce the "projectory Kinetoscope" which was marketed as
the "Vitascope" in 1896.

PART SEVEN:
Retrospection and Retirement

30. Last Lecture Seasons (1894~1896)

Muybridge now settled his affairs in Chicago and Philadelphia as best he could, and resolved to return to England for an indefinite period. He had several projects in mind. For one, he intended to capitalize on his experience at the exposition by offering his Chicago lectures in a more popular form at home. For another, he was planning to bring out a popular book — two books, as it turned out — on animal locomotion.

His address in the fall of 1894 was Hampton Wick, Middlesex, the home of his maternal grandparents.[1] By the spring he had moved across the Thames to Kingston, where from "The Chestnuts" he issued a brochure announcing a lecture season "from October next until March 1896." The topic was to be "The Motion of the Horse and other animals, in Nature and in Art."[2] This he promised to illustrate with 40 new zoopraxiscopic projecting disks.

For lectures during this season he charged a fee of ten guineas. The amount covered his lecture fee, the salary of an assistant, traveling expenses, and the cost of the oxy-hydrogen light for the Zoöpraxiscope. For lectures booked after the regular tours were arranged, transportation expenses from the point of departure were asked in addition to the fee. So popular did the lectures prove that in a circular letter dated October 1, 1895, Muybridge announced that he could accept no further engagements for the remainder of the year and none thereafter before February 1896, when he expected to commence planning for the 1896/7 season.[3]

In the circular letter Muybridge expressed his gratification that so many invitations had come from colleges and institutions where he had previously lectured. He promised them both the results of his electrophotographic investigations at the University of Pennsylvania and the zoopraxiscopic illustrations made for his lectures at the World's Columbian Exposition. He was offering old wine in new bottles, and it apparently was relished by his audiences. The intended 1896/7 tour, however, was never begun. A legal dispute with the Photogravure Company of New York erupted and called him back to the United States in 1896.

During the months of 1894 and 1895 when he was not traveling and lecturing, Muybridge began work on his new book. The manuscript, at first called "The Motion of the Horse and other animals, in Nature and in Art," after the title of his lectures, was far enough along by the summer of 1895 for him to lay the scheme before a London publisher.

The publisher proposed to bring out the work in two volumes — one on bipedal motion, one on quadripedal motion — and offered Muybridge 25 percent of the income from sales. This did not seem attractive enough to him, and he wrote to his friend Jesse Burk, at the University of Pennsylvania, that he would offer the university or the guarantors the drawings, plates, copyright, and manuscript for the book if they would publish it. He added: "I would go round and sell it on *their* a/c; and attend to all matters connected therewith, on an equitable commission, — say about one third, or 40%."[4]

[1] Letters of this period are written from Hampton Wick, Middlesex.

[2] Sent in May 1895 from Kingston; in Scrapbook.

[3] Announcement, October 1, 1895; in Scrapbook.

[4] August 5, 1895. All letters cited in this chapter are in the University of Pennsylvania Library.

This offer was not accepted, and evidently Muybridge had anticipated that it would not be, having learned that Pepper had resigned and that Charles Harrison was now the administrative head of the university:

I have had a very great notion to write to Mr. Harrison expressing my very humble tribute . . . but I am in much doubt whether he will appreciate it. Had "Animal Locomotion" turned out a splendid financial, in addition to a brilliant scientific success, I should undoubtedly have done so, but I am not very high in favor with my guarantors, and perhaps shall not be until they have recouped the thousand dollars or so they are each of them out of pocket as contributors to the world's knowledge, and the university's honor. I have done my best and if I did not succeed in making the work pay for itself, I cannot bring myself to believe that I am to blame.[5]

Perhaps the guarantors would have been content, had not the Photogravure Company threatened them with a suit for printing and storage expenses related to the unsold stock of *Animal Locomotion* still in the company's keeping.

Muybridge then wrote to Samuel Dickson, one of the guarantors, "at some length . . . about the fraudulent designs of the Printing Company of New York," and asked that Dickson try to have the suit postponed until he could come to the United States and attend to it.[6] He did not see how the guarantors could be repaid if the suit should go by default.[7] Further, the Photogravure Company apprently intended to destroy both the plates and the negatives for *Animal Locomotion* if the suit did not come out in the company's favor. In that event he could not finish the book. It was essential that he recover the negatives if he could, and this required that he cancel the proposed lecture season and travel again to the United States.

Muybridge informed the guarantors that he was willing to do everything in his power to bring about a desirable settlement of the affair with the Photogravure Company if they would cover his expenses and grant him authority to act in their behalf. The guarantors agreed to do so.[8]

This last American trip ended Muybridge's career as a public lecturer.

[5] Ibid.

[6] Confidential letter to Burk, August 7, 1895.
[7] Letter to Burk, August 5, 1895.
[8] Various related correspondence, June 9-25, 1896.

31. The End of *Animal Locomotion* (1896)

In February 1896, Muybridge established himself in Boston, both to be near the scene of the legal squabble over *Animal Locomotion* and to work on his new book in the Boston Public Library.[1]

At first the guarantors were inclined to let the Photogravure Company's suit go by default, but Muybridge pointed out to them that they could not then hope to get any further return of their money from the sale of the plates. He had already written to Dickson along these lines, from England, asking whether it was really advisable "for the Guarantors to permit this sacrifice, or for the University to allow such a disastrous termination of a work which is recognized as a standard authority on the subject, and known to the world over as being published under its auspices."[2]

While he was in Boston, a critical situation arose. The Photogravure Company passed into bankruptcy. Muybridge then appealed by telegram to his old friend and supporter, Dr. William Pepper: "Since writing saw opposing lawyer, sheriff removed plates, expenses running up. Can make no progress without cheque and authority."[3] When Pepper learned that the plates had actually been removed from the university's New York depository and placed, along with the negatives, in storage at the Garfield Trust Company, he made one of his characteristic gestures of personal generosity and agreed to pay the Photogravure Company's bill himself, stating in a letter to H. Galbraith Ward, the university's lawyer in New York:

I suppose I shall never get over my foolish habit of ruining myself for the University interests. I cannot help it, however. We are building for the future, and after all it does not much matter what happens to individuals. . . . I undertook my patronage of Muybridge, believing that it would promote the general recognition of the University. I believed also that it would lead to an important piece

[1] Letter to Dr. William Pepper, June 24, 1895. All letters and papers cited in this chapter are in the University of Pennsylvania Library.
[2] Confidential letter to Burk, August 7, 1895.

[3] June 12, 1896.

of useful work being done under scientific control. It has been expensive, but I think both results have been obtained. My associates do not seem to care to go further. I feel that it may help the University to be able to send presentation copies of these plates to important people from whom we seek concessions. Of course we shall never receive a dollar, and the advance, I suppose must be regarded as a further contribution.[4]

Pepper met with Muybridge in New York to outline the conditions of this gift. Upon his additional payment of $500 to Muybridge, the latter was to "agree to transfer, assign and make over" to Pepper all his interest whatever in "the impressions, or so called 'plates' of 'Animal Locomotion' to the number of thirty-three thousand, or thereabouts." This was to be contingent upon the other living guarantors' transferring their interests in the plates to Pepper, subject to the condition that "if in the future Dr. Pepper shall receive from the disposal of any portion of said plates, any return in money, the money so received shall be applied, first to reimburse him for the advances now made, and then further shall be distributed equally among the guarantors until the amount advanced by them shall have been refunded, when any further sum so received shall be paid to Eadweard Muybridge if he shall be at that time living."[5]

This proposal by Pepper was accepted by the guarantors. It relieved Muybridge of all indebtedness on his part that might be assumed to be due the guarantors or the university in any matters connected with his investigations of animal locomotion under the university's auspices. Pepper had wished Muybridge to make a transfer to him not only of the 33,000 plates, but also of the photographic negatives. Muybridge refused to assign the negatives until the agreement was changed to read: "It is also agreed that the negatives of said plates shall be placed in possession of Dr. Pepper, with permission to print from them such further

[4] June 15, 1896.
[5] Agreement, guarantors with Muybridge, June 9, 1896.

impressions therefrom as he shall consider advisable." Dickson, Harrison, and Coates signed the agreement on June 9. To this Muybridge affixed his signature also. Then Pepper sought to add a further statement: "It is understood that the within includes a transfer to Dr. Pepper absolutely of the negatives as well as the plates." Muybridge put his signature to this addition only when he had been assured by the lawyer, Ward, that as the photographer he was the absolute owner of the negatives. Ward closed the matter with Pepper in these words: "It does not amount to an absolute transfer of the negatives to you. They remain Muybridge's [with] you having the right to print from them as many plates as you think advisable, subject to the other terms of the agreement."[6]

By June 17, Pepper had paid all bills due the printers and given Muybridge his check for $500. Then the Garfield Trust Company refused to release the plates and negatives on the grounds that they had been deposited by the Photogravure Company. Disclaimers had to be obtained by Ward from the president and receiver of the bankrupt company before Muybridge was allowed to oversee the packing of the 28 crates of material, which were finally sent on to Pepper in Philadelphia.

There were left about 40 complete sets of *Animal Locomotion*. Occasional orders for the complete set or portfolios of 100 plates came in, and such orders were filled from the stock held by Pepper. Many single plates were also sold or were given away.

It was a source of great regret to Muybridge that the University of Pennsylvania itself had not found a way to buy a complete set of *Animal Locomotion*. In 1894 he left a personal copy, consisting of eleven bound volumes, in two boxes in the cellars of the university library, hoping that some means might be found by which it could be acquired.[7]

[6] Letter, Ward to Pepper, June 15, 1896.
[7] Letter to Burk, August 5, 1895.

32. Last Endeavors: *Animals in Motion, The Human Figure in Motion*, and After (1897–1904)

In the fall of 1897, Muybridge completed negotiations with the London firm of Chapman and Hall for the publication of two books in which he planned to summarize his work in motion photography. The contracts, signed on January 3, 1898, provided for payment to Muybridge of one percent of the trade price of the books for the first 100 copies sold and an additional one percent for each further hundred, up to 20 percent. The arrangement was later altered so that he received 12 percent of the trade price on sales of the first book and 15 percent on the second.

The first book, *Animals in Motion*, a handsome quarto of 264 pages, 9½ x 12 inches, was published late in 1899. Subtitled *An Electro-Photographic Investigation of Consecutive Phases of Animal Progressive Movements*, it illustrates these movements in about 100 plates, comprising more than 1,600 of the photographs of animals taken at Palo Alto and Philadelphia. The printing, on good coated stock, was by the relatively new halftone process.

In the sections of analysis Muybridge presents a distillation of what his instantaneous pictures have taught him about animal locomotion. For each of the eight systems of progressive motion analyzed, he supplies graphic notations of his own devising — chartlike symbols of the footfalls — which clarify the patterns of support and propulsion "employed by an animal during the execution of any of its regular gaits." Coupled with the photographs, these reveal various "laws" of motion. For example, there is the law of the regular system of limb movements used by all quadrupeds in the walk: "the support is thrown, during the stride, twice on the laterals, twice on the diagonals, twice on two fore-feet and one hind-foot, and twice on two hind feet and one fore-foot; eight different systems of support." Following this analysis of the stride, Muybridge compares various actual movements with renderings in works of art, ancient and modern. In an instance of the walking stride, for example, he finds that "the position of the limbs of the reindeer, in the well-known etching by some prehistoric artist, is precisely the same as [if it were] photographed from nature." He finds the equestrian statue of Marcus Aurelius in the Piazza del Campidoglio, Rome, "a remarkable instance of the failure of a sculptor to express his obvious intention." Meissonier's *1814* is cited as a "true" impression. Thompson's *Roll Call* is "a careful study of the walk."[1]

Muybridge's ability to marshal his scientific and artistic evidence and to present it cogently is evident in *Animals in Motion*. He achieves the credibility of the scholarly writer, whose role he thoroughly relishes.

The frontispiece of *Animals in Motion*, an awesome portrait taken by the London Stereoscopic and Photographic Company, shows a new Muybridge. The deeply sunken, serious, almost disillusioned eyes smolder under wisps of white eyebrows. A full beard floats down over his chest, increasing the look of noble sadness. The signature, "Faithfully Yours, Eadweard Muybridge," has the flourish of a final statement. Nearing seventy, he has aged markedly and seems to show signs of illness or despair.

In the preface Muybridge achieves a peak of lucid autobiographical statement. Beginning with his first work for Stanford in 1872, he traces both the method and the results of his several attempts to photograph animals in motion. He tells of his development of the Zoöpraxiscope to reproduce "complete and recurring acts of motion," and describes it as the "first apparatus ever used, or constructed, for synthetically demonstrating movements analytically photographed from life" and, "in its resulting effects," as the "prototype of all the various instruments which, under a variety of names, are used for a similar purpose at the present day."[2]

One sees that Muybridge is deeply concerned with putting on record the history of the contributions he has made. He does this with great objectivity, detailing the procedures employed in his several accomplishments and noting the dates when they were reviewed and commented upon by others. Among other episodes, he tells of his visit to Edison in February 1888 for the purpose of discussing "the practicability of using [the Zoöpraxiscope] in association with the phonograph, so as to combine, and reproduce simultaneously, in the presence of an audience, visible actions and audible words," and adds: "At that time the phonograph had not been adapted to reach the ears of a large audience, so the scheme was temporarily abandoned."[3]

Muybridge puts on record his version of the steps which led from the Zoöpraxiscope to the modern motion picture — first the Zoöpraxiscope (1879), then Marey's use of the single lens in photographing moving figures onto a strip of sensitized material,

---

[1] *Animals in Motion*, pp. 30, 34-35 (in Dover edition).

[2] Ibid., p. 15.

[3] Ibid.

as with the "photographic gun" (1882), and then Edison's use of the celluloid ribbon in the Kinetoscope (1893). He does not regard the Lumière brothers' Cinématographe (1895) or the Armat-Jenkins-Edison Vitascope (1896) as crucial advances in method over the preceding instruments, although he must have known and seen the results of their commercialization.

He concludes the preface with a description of the University of Pennsylvanian project and an explanation of his desire to republish his findings in popular form because of the "great cost of printing and manufacturing" which had restricted the sale of *Animal Locomotion.*[4]

Excellent notices of *Animals in Motion* appeared in British journals and newspapers. Muybridge must have enjoyed the harvest of clippings — from the chief newspapers in London, Manchester, Glasgow, and Edinburgh, and from the *Illustrated London News,* the *British Journal of Photography, Nature,* and *The Field,* among others. The notices were carefully dated and saved for the scrapbook in which he would eventually compile documents of his life's work.

"There is now no room for speculation or controversy about the motion of animals," wrote the reviewer for the *Scotsman* of June 1, 1899. "Every phase is demonstrated with an accuracy which, while it warns the artist that there are some movements that ought not to be painted, gives him an easy guide to pictorial effect." The reviewer in the *Athenaeum* of October 6, 1900, wondered no more "that Mr. Muybridge — first to enter upon the matter in a thorough-going way with the advantages which instantaneous photography of an ultra-sensitive kind offers — has devoted his life to it." The *British Journal of Photography,* July 14, 1899, noted: "The work of this eminent photographer was at one time very imperfectly appreciated and understood; but modern critics appear more disposed to rate it at its just value."[5]

Thus *Animals in Motion* won welcome critical recognition and eventually, as evidenced by its sale through several reprintings, a considerable popular audience. The response to the first book must have encouraged Muybridge as he completed the second, which Chapman and Hall published in 1901.

In similar format, *The Human Figure in Motion* — subtitled *An Electro-Photographic Investigation of Consecutive Phases of Muscular Actions* — contains a varied selection from the *Animal Locomotion* photographs of men, women, and children, clothed and unclothed. Muybridge's introductory comments do not differ substantially from those in *Animals in Motion* except in

[4] The price of *Animals in Motion* was 20 shillings.
[5] From clippings of reviews in the Scrapbook.

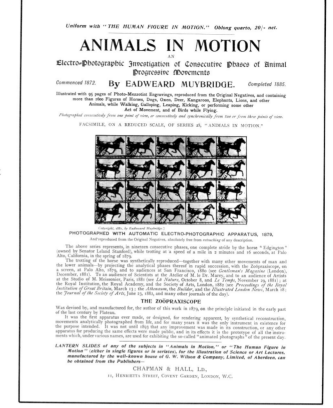

152. Prospectus for Muybridge's 1899 *Animals in Motion.*

one instance. In the first book he seems to be concerned with putting on record the position of the Zoöpraxiscope as a "prototype" machine. In *The Human Figure in Motion* he is more forward-looking, more cognizant of his successors:

It may, however, as a matter of record, be admissible to say that, as photographic analyses of changes incidental to motion of any kind commenced with this investigation by the author, so was the zoöpraxiscope the first instrument ever constructed or devised for demonstrating, by synthetical reconstruction, movements photographed from life, and for many years it was the only apparatus in use for that purpose.

Farther on, he states:

In the progress of physical science and mechanical construction it has, as might naturally be supposed, had to relinquish to its

In one volume.   Oblong quarto.   Twenty shillings net.

THE HUMAN FIGURE
IN MOTION

An Electro-Photographic Investigation of Consecutive
Phases of Muscular Actions

Commenced 1872.   **By EADWEARD MUYBRIDGE.**   *Completed 1885.*

Illustrated with 127 pages of Photo-Mezzotint Engravings, reproduced (absolutely
free from retouching) from the Original Negatives, and containing more
than 2700 Figures of Men, Women, and Children—nude, semi-
nude, or in diaphanous clothing—Photographed in
Seriates while engaged in
Walking, Running, Jumping, Dancing, Wrestling, Cricketing, or
executing other Games or Labours incidental
to everyday Life.

*Selected from the Larger Work of the Author, "Animal Locomotion," published under
the auspices of the University of Pennsylvania, copies of which, or parts thereof,
were subscribed for by nearly every University, and all the Principal Libraries,
and Science and Art Schools of Europe and America.*

153. Prospectus for Muybridge's 1901 *Human Figure in Motion.*

*younger rivals its former unique position; but it was not until
1893, or more than thirteen years after it was first used,
that any improvements in its construction or in its effects on the
screen were made public. The improvements in the modern
instruments are due to the invention of celluloid, as a substitute
for glass, for receiving and exhibiting the photographic images.*[6]

Retirement and relinquishment were the appropriate life
tasks for Muybridge at this time. He had made his demonstration
to the world. He had retired from the active arena of photography.
He knew that science must progress. He let go of his method for
photographing moving objects and his zoopraxisgraphic method
for portraying motion when it was appropriate to do so.

Reviews of *The Human Figure in Motion* reflected the new
terminology of the commercial motion picture. The *Graphic*, of

[6]Pp. 6, 61 of original edition.

London, on December 28, 1901, commented: "Mr. Muybridge
gives us a sort of *biograph* of the movements of men, women,
and children, draped and undraped, in all sorts of action,
and during every phase of such action." "Biograph" had become
a popular name for the motion picture as projected in the
Bioscope, Vitascope, or Cinématographe. So rapid had been the
advance in the production and distribution of the commercial
motion picture in the last five years of the nineteenth century
that the general public was now familiar with the outlandish trade
names of the new projectors and processes. A summary statement
appeared in the *Scotsman* of November 18, 1901:

*There has been a complete revolution in photographic methods
since the first publication of Mr. Muybridge's studies of
animal locomotion. In these days of cinematographs and
bioscopes it is difficult to imagine the difficulties involved in
their production or the intense interest that their publication
aroused. Yet in spite of all the improvements in apparatus, Mr.
Muybridge's researches in this direction have remained classical,
and there is no similar collection of studies that compare in
completeness with his work.*[7]

The day was to come when the facts about Muybridge's
pioneering effort were lost sight of and when his reputation
was pushed into obscurity by later workers in the field. Some
of this occurred during his lifetime, some long after his death. A
contemporary instance, when Jules Fuerst spoke before the
Camera Club in London, was reported in the *Standard*, November
5, 1897. Fuerst began his lecture on the Lumière Cinématographe
by noting the tremendous interest in chronophotography that
had grown out of the analysis of movement by Muybridge, Marey,
and the astronomer Janssen. He went on to ascribe the initial
success in the "reconstitution" of movement to Edison's
Kinetoscope and to the Cinématographe. Muybridge was mentioned
only as a contributor to the analysis of movement.[8]

Benjamin Carter, the borough librarian at Kingston-on-Thames,
was a close friend of Muybridge and was helping him prepare the
collection of clippings and documents that, arranged in the scrapbook, would provide a record of his career. For some time
Carter had been disturbed by the fact that many claimants were
beginning to put themselves forward, or were being put forward
by others, as the true inventors of the cinema. Now Carter
brought Fuerst's lecture to the attention of Muybridge and urged
him to answer it. At first, secure in his long period of public
acclaim, Muybridge rather enjoyed the spectacle of the struggling

[7]From clippings of reviews in the Scrapbook.

[8]Clipping in Scrapbook. The *Standard* may have been a Surrey newspaper.

claimants. In this attitude Carter thought him to be unjustifiably aloof. Finally, upon the urging of his friend, Muybridge wrote to the editor of the *Journal of the Camera Club.*

SIR: If a recent lecture at the Camera Club was correctly reported in **The Standard,** *of 5th Nov., I have no doubt of one of the statements made by the lecturer causing you and some of the other members of your club considerable astonishment.*

The paragraph reads as follows — "The reconstruction of that movement — that was to say the synthesis — was then considered a very distant problem. Towards 1893 appeared the Edison Kinetoscope, which realized the synthesis."

The "then" presumably refers to a date previously mentioned — 1874 — at which time a photographic investigation of animal movements had been announced in California.

During the last few years, numerous gentlemen in Europe and America have put forth claims to have been the first to demonstrate by synthesis the results of photographic analysis.

Having many years ago, practically retired from the field of photographic investigation, I have taken no part in this controversy. Since, however, the statement is gravely made to a body of scientific men assembled in your rooms, that an apparatus for showing "Animated Photographs" — so called — was not "invented" until about five years since, I thought it a not inappropriate occasion to send you, for the information of such members of your Club as care to take the trouble to read them, a few quotations in regard to some demonstrations of a similar character which were made so long ago that one may reasonably be excused for having forgotten all about them.

To this letter Muybridge attached extracts from newspaper accounts of his accomplishments from 1878 to 1888. These the editor printed with the letter as an answer to Fuerst and any other photographers who may have forgotten this pioneering work.[9]

With this statement clearly made, and the evidence put on record, Muybridge withdrew from professional concerns. He spent his last years in his native place, comfortably surrounded by friends and relatives, and occupied with reading and gardening. His Hampton Wick cousins kept one another informed about him: "Edward is looking older than when I saw him two years ago. He is thin, and put me in mind of the pictures I have seen of Wesley." Or, again: "I have not seen Eadweard Muybridge for some time although the girls see him. . . . He is well, and wears a long white beard. He has taken up residence with Kate Plow Smith and George Lawrence. . . . They now live in Liverpool Road,

Kingston."[10] From that address Muybridge penned an occasional informative letter to a newspaper. On March 28, 1902, the *Standard* printed his comments on "Primitive Vision and Colour Blindness." On May 22 of that year his letter on "The Tablet of Mena" appeared in *The Times.*

In 1904 Muybridge had reached the age of seventy-four years. In a photograph taken in Kingston we see a well-groomed elderly gentleman. Although there are signs that his health is failing, he appears to be well cared for, too. Time was dealing with him kindly, for all the strains of previous years.[11]

On March 14 he wrote his will. To Catherine Edith Plow Smith, the cousin Kate with whom he made his home, Muybridge bequeathed his books and a life income from all money on deposit in his name. To George Lawrence he bequeathed his gold watch, lantern, cameras, lenses, plates, lantern slides, and all the remainder of his photographic apparatus, except that the Borough of Kingston was to have his "Zoöpraxiscope and negatives and plates concerned with the investigation and demonstration of Animal Locomotion." These were to be deposited for the benefit of the borough "in the Kingston Museum when erected and in the meantime in the Kingston Public Library." After Kate's death "all such money . . . on deposit" in Muybridge's name was willed to "the Mayor, Corporations and Burgesses for the time being of the said Borough of Kingston-upon-Thames" on condition that it be "invested by them at their discretion and the income thereof be applied in the purchase by them from time to time of artistic and scientific books for the Reference Department of the said Kingston Public Library."[12]

On May 8, Muybridge died in Kingston while digging the ground for a model of the Great Lakes in his garden. His body was cremated and his ashes were buried at Woking. The resting place of Muybridge's ashes is marked by a brown marble slab, about fifteen inches square, incised with these words: "In Loving Memory / of / Eadweard Maybridge / Died May 8th 1904 / Aged 74 Years." The misspelling of his last name consorts with a misspelling of his first in the crematorium register: "Edward James Muggeridge / know as / Eudweard Muybridge."

[9] Issue of November 9, 1897; in Scrapbook.

[10] Rachel Rickard (née Smith) to Elizabeth Selfe, November 6, 1894, and Sydney Smith to Norma Selfe, January 4, 1903; in Selfe correspondence.

[11] This presumably last photograph is in the Bancroft Library.

[12] Last Will and Testament of Eadweard Muybridge, March 14, 1904; photostat copy obtained by Janet Leigh, in Haas collection.

PART EIGHT:
Man in Motion

33. Toward a Semi-Centennial Estimate (1904-1931)

The years directly preceding and following the death of Eadweard Muybridge were the pioneering age of the modern motion picture. The introduction of the flexible film strip opened up commercial possibilities that sent technicians and inventors into a race to devise machines by which motion pictures could be made and projected for profit.

For a few years Edison's peep-show Kinetoscope was a world-wide wonder, with its 40-foot strips of flexible film produced in the "Black Maria" studio in West Orange, New Jersey; but only one customer at a time could watch these nickel-in-the-slot performances. Around 1895, new projection machines appeared: the Lumière Cinématographe, the Skladowsky Bioscope, and the Armat-Jenkins-Edison Vitascope. These machines were capable of serving large audiences, and presently film shows were being produced for them. Also bitter patent suits were being fought, particularly by Edison, as many "inventors of the cinema" asserted their claims. Meanwhile the use of flexible film led to the successful photographing of ever longer episodes of movement.

Muybridge's glass disks had contained a very limited number of images; the sequence of projected images was repeated with each complete turn of the disk. Edison's Kinetoscope increased the duration, though only by a matter of seconds. As the public responded to these brief episodes, film shows grew in number, length, and variety. As Kenneth Macgowan expressed it:

Railroad trains, ocean waves, and card games lost their charms. Vaudeville turns disappeared. . . . News events — foreshadowed

by the shot of the German Emperor reviewing his troops — grew more and more popular, along with short travelogues, and very short science films. Camera men made advertising pictures. Tricks of lens and shutter spawned more elaborate fantasies. Comic episodes grew into rudimentary story films of several scenes. The discovery of what the skills of editing and camera work could do finally led to the ten-minute drama.[1]

By 1910, a New York newspaper could declare that a "large part of the population" was "moving-picture mad." The commercial motion picture was out of its infancy.

On a September day in that year the Surrey town of Kingston-on-Thames was celebrating the opening of a new place of entertainment, the "Picture Theatre." The doors opened to an audience thirsting for the 586 feet of *Ben the Stowaway*, the 978 feet of *She Slept Through It All*, and the 444 feet of *Fixing the Flirts*. To lend dignity to the occasion, honored guests were on hand. The mayor had been asked to prepare a brief ceremonial address. This he did, with the help of the borough librarian, Benjamin Carter. Their collaboration, delivered by the mayor before the first reel of film was set going, provided a surprise. Kingston, the mayor stated, could "claim the honor of having given birth to the inventor of moving pictures, in the person of Mr. Eadweard Muybridge."[2]

At this point a photograph of the venerable Muybridge —

---

[1] *Behind the Screen,* New York: Delacorte Press, 1965, p. 87.

[2] *Surrey Comet,* September 1910; in Scrapbook (added by Carter).

solemn and grizzled — was flashed upon the screen. Perhaps the young persons in the audience cared little about the shadowy old man whose visage appeared before them, but the mayor's remarks could stir memories in some of the older townsfolk:

Mr. Eadweard Muybridge was born at Kingston-on-Thames in 1830, migrated to the States in early life and entered upon a commercial career. In the year 1872, whilst in charge of the General Photographic Survey of the Pacific Coast in California, he first interested himself in moving pictures, and the Governor [Leland Stanford] and another millionaire having had a bet as to whether a horse had all four legs off the ground at the same moment, and it being impossible to ascertain the precise facts, Mr. Muybridge was asked if he could demonstrate it by the aid of photography. The point in question was settled satisfactorily by the taking of a rapid succession of photographs of a trotting horse, and this investigation led to the publication of a work, "The Trotting Horse" ["The Horse in Motion"], which caused a sensation throughout the scientific and artistic world. Mr. Muybridge then arranged a lecturing tour with a lantern, and used, for illustrative purposes the German toy, the Zoëtrope. The University of Pennsylvania came to his assistance and created "a chair" and arranged a studio for Mr. Muybridge, where he fixed up a battery of cameras, electrically connected. The cameras — consisting of two sets of twelve and one of twenty-four — were arranged so that the subject to be photographed could be taken at the same time from three different points of view, each movement being taken by a different camera on extremely rapid wet plates — the exposure, at times, being only one 6,000th part of a second. The shutters of the cameras were operated by means of thin thread stretched across the path of the human being or animal, the record of whose movements was to be taken. Thus, in the case of a horse jumping an obstacle an impression was obtained upon the plates in rotation, and the whole, when thrown upon the screen by means of Mr. Muybridge's apparatus, gave a realistic impression of what movements actually take place.

In order to project the pictures upon the screen so that they would appear to move, Mr. Muybridge invented a machine which he named "The Zoöpraxiscope," which is claimed to be the first instrument ever constructed or devised for demonstrating by synthetical reconstruction, movements originally photographed from life; and for many years it was the only apparatus used for that purpose. The first exhibition was given in the autumn of 1879, when oxy-hydrogen was used for projection. Mr. Muybridge was on friendly terms with Mr. T. A. Edison, and when the phonograph arrived Mr. Muybridge wrote to Mr. Edison suggesting the possibilities of the two inventions and said one might even go so far as to give a whole opera by combining these two things. Mr. Edison replied that he thought there were great possibilities, but other things were so pressing he could not give it attention at present.[3]

[3] Ibid. The statement that Muybridge worked with "extremely rapid wet plates" at Philadelphia is erroneous.

In concluding his remarks, the mayor read from a letter by Thomas S. Weaver which had recently appeared in the American *Film Index.* Weaver had met Muybridge in Boston in 1882 and become interested in "the man and his peculiar work." He wrote:

These pictures attracted a great deal of attention among scientific and sporting men, and among artists. Mr. Muybridge proved by them that the conventional drawing of the horse in motion was altogether wrong, as the horse did not use his feet and legs in the way artists had represented them, that dogs did not travel exactly as horses in the succession of steps with their feet, and that, except in jumping, no animal ever had all his feet off the ground at one time. The artists made fun of his ideas, and tried to draw their horses "after Muybridge" but soon became convinced that he was right, and the horse has been drawn on Muybridge lines ever since. These experiments were before the introduction of the flexible film for the camera, and before rapid photography had been developed. Mr. Muybridge lived to see the motion picture a wonderful thing, and I have often thought how much he must have enjoyed the development of his crude idea in general lines, rather than confined to the study of the gaits of animals.[4]

As additional support for his claim that Eadweard Muybridge was indeed the inventor of motion pictures, without whose previous work the Kingston audience would not have been assembled for the entertainment of the day, the mayor noted that Muybridge's books, lantern slides, and press cuttings, which on his death in 1904 were bequeathed to the borough of Kingston, had been placed on exhibition at the Public Library. One may suppose that the audience, young and old, after surrendering to the excitements of the cinema, left the theater standing taller for their knowledge that all these wonders had their origin with "not only an Englishman, but a Kingstonian, and a descendant of an old Saxon family."

One guest, the reporter for the *Bioscope,* slipped away from the Picture Theatre to the library, following his hunch that he might find data for a surprising human-interest story. The sudden claim that Muybridge was the inventor of motion pictures did not square with the film history that the reporter knew. The name of Muybridge, since his retirement in the 1890s, had faded from public notice, and men connected with the film industry were claiming to be the true fathers of the thriving new form of entertainment. The most prominent were Robert W. Paul and William Friese-Greene in England, the Lumière brothers in France, and Edison in the United States.[5] These were living claimants who could and did speak out for themselves.

[4] Ibid.

[5] James Card, "Problems of Film History," *Hollywood Quarterly,* IV

At the library the *Bioscope* man met Benjamin Carter, who had suggested the tribute to Muybridge at the opening of the theater. The reporter confessed to Carter that he had often read of Muybridge, but in his mind the name had "always hitherto been connected with San Francisco, California." Now he saw the scrapbook of hundreds of clippings from over the world, reviewing Muybridge's work in landscape photography, instantaneous motion photography, and the projection of motion, covering the years from 1868 to 1902. Here also were files of the landscape photographs, volumes of the motion photographs taken at Palo Alto Farm and the University of Pennsylvania, and Muybridge's projection machine of 1879, the Zoöpraxiscope, still in working order.

Convinced by Carter's presentation, the reporter notified his journal of two discoveries: first, that Eadweard Muybridge was an Englishman with a long history of experimentation in motion photography, and second, that he had constructed an apparatus by which animated pictures were first projected upon a screen. For the first time since his death, Muybridge's historical role in the development of the cinema was thus brought up for wide public notice. The claim of his being the inventor of motion pictures, sounded from Kingston and later amplified in the *Bioscope*,[6] only served to increase the number of contenders, but the position of the "Kingston Claimant" in film history was not to be established easily.

A two-volume biography of Edison, by Dyer and Martin, which came out in the same year that the Picture Theatre opened in Kingston, devoted a page or two to Muybridge. While the authors noted that positive prints were, sometime before 1880, mounted upon a modified form of zoetrope and projected upon a screen by Muybridge, they cautioned readers not to assume that anything like a "true illusion of movement" had been obtained. They then controverted their own position by quoting Sala's eyewitness account of the Muybridge showing of 1880: "Nothing was wanting but the clatter of hoofs upon the turf, and an occasional breath of steam from the nostrils, to make the spectator believe that he had before him genuine flesh and blood steeds."[7] Dyer and Martin were clearly more concerned about establishing preeminence in the development of the modern motion picture for Edison, whose "basic inventions," they wrote,

"practically constitute the art." Later research has substantially narrowed this claim,[8] but the "Edison myth" (started in 1894 by the Dicksons[9] and maintained by the Edison interests) fostered a persistent general belief in the story as Dyer and Martin told it in 1910.

In 1913 the role of Muybridge was described by Benjamin Carter in an article requested from him by the *Bioscope* and entitled "The Genesis of the Motion Picture."[10] Self-described as "the only moving picture paper in Great Britain and the leading journal in the world devoted to animated pictures," the *Bioscope* carried some weight. Carter stuck close to Muybridge's version of his career: rapid motion photography by the wet-plate process (1872-1879), development of a projecting machine (1879), and further work with the dry plate (in the 1880s). In a paragraph of personal reminiscence Carter stated:

It was during the preparation of [**Animals in Motion***] that certain people were spoken of in the Press as being inventors of the moving picture. The writer urged Muybridge to definitely settle the matter, if only for the sake of historical accuracy. But he was very reluctant to take action. He looked upon the invention of the motion picture as a mere incident in his work of investigation of animal movements for purposes of science and art. It was for this that he wished to be remembered; and he feared that the association of his name with the now popular moving picture would overshadow the work of which he was justly proud. He, however, eventually yielded, and in the preface to* **Animals in Motion** *he describes the genesis of the moving picture.*

Muybridge there claimed (as we have noted in the preceding chapter) that the Zoöpraxiscope was the "first apparatus ever used, or constructed, for synthetically demonstrating movements analytically photographed from life," and that it was the "prototype" of later instruments used for that purpose.[11] It was Carter who unwittingly introduced the term "invention."

Carter's line of argument was bitterly attacked by Edmund Seal Donisthorpe, son of Wordsworth Donisthorpe, an early motion-picture patentee.[12] He stated that his father had in 1876 "described the *first* machine for the photography of motion" and had obtained the first patent to "describe and claim the use of continuous film for that purpose." He further stated (correctly) that Muybridge "never claimed to have invented the first moving

1950, 279-288. Film historians have tended to take a nationalistic position in ascribing the "invention" of the motion picture to one or another of the claimants.

[6] In articles by Carter.

[7] Frank L. Dyer and Thomas C. Martin, *Edison: His Life and Inventions,* New York: Harper, 1910, II, 533 ff.

[8] Gordon Hendricks, *The Edison Motion Picture Myth,* Berkeley and Los Angeles: University of California Press, 1961.

[9] Antonia and W. K. L. Dickson, "Edison's Invention of the Kineto-Phonograph," *The Century,* June 1894, pp. 206-214.

[10] In the issue of March 20, pp. 845-849.

[11] *Animals in Motion,* p. 15 (in Dover edition).

[12] "The Genesis of Motion Photography," *Bioscope,* May 15, 1913, p. 503.

picture machine" and (incorrectly) that Muybridge "never made or used a machine of any kind" for the purpose under discussion.

In a subsequent article Carter gave up the idea of an "invention": "No one person can be said to have invented the moving picture."[13] Since he had discovered that Wordsworth Donisthorpe made "no provision in his specification for projecting the photograph on the screen," it followed that the Donisthorpe claim was somewhat narrowed, too.

The next year, three books offered estimates of Muybridge's contribution. F. A. Talbot, in *Moving Pictures*, called Muybridge the "father of animated photography." He added, however, that Muybridge's system "had no commercial possibilities. Its real value lay in the fact that it stimulated the ingenuity of a host of inventive brains towards the solution of animated photography."[14] John Rathbun's *Motion Picture Making and Exhibiting* took this line of reasoning: "While these experiments paved the way to future success, the Muybridge system was out of the question for practical work, for not only were all the pictures broadside views" — an incorrect statement — "but 16,000 cameras would be required for a commercial 1,000 foot reel."[15] Robert Grau's *The Theatre of Science* straddled the fence: "It appears to be an accepted fact that Muybridge's achievement was the basis for inventions that first produced motion pictures."[16]

In 1915 an American champion for Muybridge appeared. H. C. Peterson, director of the Stanford University Museum, working from first-hand materials about the Stanford-Muybridge experiments, entered the field with an article giving his version. After tracing the essential events with accuracy, Peterson added this coda:

From Muybridge's twenty-four negatives it is a long jump to the miles of film used to produce one play last year, or the 4,400,000 feet of negative that has been made by one company alone. His wildest dreams could not have pictured the expense account of the last year in motion picture work in this state [California] alone, with its $5,720,000 paid out by the various operating companies. He, and two assistants, produced the world's supply of motion picture negatives then. Today, eighty thousand people are necessary to handle the industry. He died a few years ago in England, an old man. He made possible the greatest aid to education that has ever been conceived. He created an entirely new and distinct industry. He made possible the

bringing of the horrors of war and the blessings of peace to our eyes with such terrible force that we stand aghast at the brutality of the one and the failure of the other. We look and marvel, But to the wizard who created it all not twenty people of the fifteen million who daily witness the production of motion pictures on the screen have ever heard the name MUYBRIDGE.[17]

Muybridge had been called the inventor and the father of motion pictures. Now Peterson called him a wizard and ascribed the new industry to him. The claim that Muybridge had "created an entirely new and distinct industry" was certainly overdrawn. He may have created the field, but not the industry. Nevertheless, written as it was for a popular audience, Peterson's article presented Muybridge to a new generation as a primary figure in motion photography.

Peterson's article also focused on a neglected figure in the Muybridge story. This was John D. Isaacs, the "young electrician connected with the Southern Pacific" who, according to Peterson, had been asked by Stanford to "devise a simple and less noisy shutter" for Muybridge. This was an aspect of the story that was to be amplified in the succeeding years.

Carter and Peterson may be credited with the major English and American statements in the first quarter of the twentieth century as to the importance of Muybridge's work in the early development of the modern motion picture. Numerous popular writers and film historians in the next few years took positions much the same as theirs. The following are illustrative:

Regarding Muybridge and Instantaneous Photography
(1) Muybridge "May be regarded as the father of instantaneous photographs" (Philadelphia *Public Ledger*, March 12, 1916)
(2) Muybridge "succeeded in developing instantaneous photography to the point which has not yet been surpassed" (Ben J. Lubschez, 1920)[18]

Regarding Muybridge in Relation to the Projection of Motion Photographs
(1) Muybridge "succeeded in taking instantaneous pictures and then projecting them upon a screen so that the idea of continuity of motion might be conveyed to the observers" (Homer Croy, 1918)[19]
(2) "Pictures attaining anything akin to action were thus projected on a screen for the first time" (Croy)

Regarding Muybridge and the Modern Motion Pictures
(1) Muybridge may be regarded as "the step-father of motion pictures" (*Public Ledger*, March 12, 1916)

[13]"The Genesis of the Moving Picture," *Bioscope*, July 17, 1913, pp. 202-3.

[14]*Moving Pictures: How They Are Made and Worked*, Philadelphia: Lippincott, 1914, pp. 12-16.

[15]Chicago: Charles C. Thompson, 1914, pp. 5-7.

[16]Chicago: Broadway Publishing Co., 1914, pp. 1-2.

[17]"The Birthplace of the Motion Picture," *Sunset,* San Francisco, November 1915, pp. 909-915.

[18]*The Story of Motion Pictures,* New York: Reeland, 1920, pp. 29-33.

[19]*How Motion Pictures Are Made,* New York: Harper, 1920, pp. 14-24.

(2) "A careful study of the experiments and research of any
of these inventors will convince one that Muybridge's
inventions led to the discovery of modern moving pictures"
(*Current Opinion*, July 1917)

(3) "They were really motion pictures made by photography
from real moving objects, and brought much nearer to the
present point of development than anyone had succeeded
in bringing them before" (Ben J. Lubschez, 1920)

Despite the ups and downs of reported opinion, the Kingston
Claimant's renown grew steadily between 1910 and 1925. His
status as the earliest consistent worker in instantaneous photography was conceded, but the degree to which his Zoöpraxiscope
gave him the right to be called the father of motion pictures
remained unsettled, particularly among persons within the industry.
Homer Croy did not think of the Zoöpraxiscope as a motion
picture machine at all. Ben J. Lubschez thought of it as producing
motion pictures but not in the modern sense of the term. *Current
Opinion* regarded Muybridge as having developed something
that "led to the discovery" of modern motion pictures. The
writer in the *Public Ledger* probably came closest to the generally
accepted position: Muybridge was the stepfather rather than
the father of motion pictures.

So things stood until 1926, when Terry Ramsaye, the editor of
an American trade magazine, the *Motion Picture Herald*, took
up the "debunking" fashion of the decade and dealt a blow from
which the Kingston Claimant has never fully recovered. In an
entertainingly written but biased two-volume history of the
motion picture, *A Million and One Nights*, Ramsaye declared
that Muybridge "had nothing to do with motion pictures at all."[20]

Claiming to have had access to private records in the files of
the Southern Pacific Railroad, Ramsaye asserted that Isaacs had
saved Muybridge's analytical photography from failure and
thus was responsible for his renown following the successful
experiments under Stanford's auspices. On the basis of this
evidence, and after discussions with Isaacs, Ramsaye was
persuaded that "a very small part, if any, in the creative work
of the hallowed race horse incident was Muybridge's."[21]

As to the Zoöpraxiscope, which he had not seen (and
apparently without seeing the accounts of its operation that
had been forthcoming in the public press from as early as 1879),
Ramsaye took an even stranger position. He credited it to
Meissonier (in 1881) and concluded that "obviously Muybridge

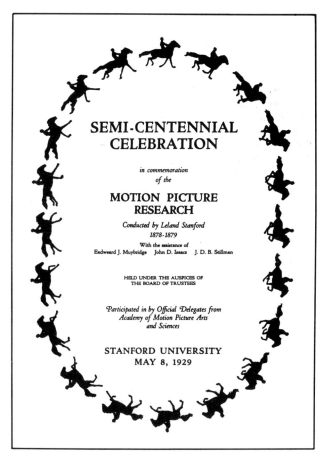

154. Semi-centennial celebration of Muybridge's 1879 motion
pictures. Leland Stanford, Jr., University.

had nothing to do with the development of this device."[22]

Not content with denying Muybridge's professional claims
to fame, Ramsaye occupied himself heavily with a negative
character analysis, finding Muybridge to be "without energy or
ambition," "about ready to give up," "past the creative age,"
a "lion hunter," "drunk with great names," and so on. Ramsaye
discoursed at length on Muybridge's unhappy marriage and in
a curiously ambiguous phrase described the shooting of Larkyns
as the "only aggressive act of Muybridge's life."[23]

[20] New York: Simon and Schuster, 1926, Vol. 1, p. 21.

[21] Ibid., The Private records appear to have been the depositions taken for
the Muybridge-Stanford lawsuit.

[22] Ibid., p. 41.

[23] Ibid., p. 33.

Although there are half a hundred demonstrably false-to-fact statements to be found in Ramsaye's 48-page chapter on Muybridge, these pages made very good reading. Popularistic film historians and journalists have been content to accept Ramsaye's highly colored and distorted account ever since.[24]

Two events closed the third decade following Muybridge's death with a somewhat soberer estimate of his accomplishments. One of these was the "Semi-Centennial Celebration of the Stanford Motion Picture Research," on the university campus at Palo Alto. The other was the placing of a memorial tablet to Muybridge in the Public Library at Kingston-on-Thames.

The Semi-Centennial Celebration, on May 8, 1929, was a cooperative venture of Stanford University and the recently established Academy of Motion Picture Arts and Sciences, which sent several representatives. To some extent, the celebration was planned as an answer to the glaring inaccuracies of Terry Ramsaye, although it was primarily intended to increase public awareness, particularly in the West Coast motion-picture industry, of Leland Stanford's patronage of the early research in California. The positions taken by Walter R. Miles, professor of experimental psychology at the university and chairman of the planning committee for the celebration, were these: (a) "Leland Stanford conceived the notion of taking photographs of horses in action"; (b) Stanford "secured Eadweard Muybridge, a photographer of San Francisco to attempt the photographs"; (c) Stanford paid Muybridge "for his services and kept insisting that further trials be made"; (d) Stanford "instructed Muybridge to provide a series of cameras to be operated in rapid succession"; (e) Muybridge "saw himself as a 'movie' cameraman engaged in a new and special branch of photography"; (f) John D. Isaacs was "secured to improve certain technical features connected with the timing of the consecutive pictures"; (g) Stanford "supplied living quarters for Muybridge and paid all expenses connected with securing the apparatus and with carrying on the investigation"; (h) Stanford "willingly permitted Muybridge to copyright the photographs"; (i) Stanford "appears to have felt well repaid for the cost and labor involved in securing his famous album of pictures and the sets which he used in his large zoëtrope"; (j) Stanford "turned to Dr. J. D. B. Stillman and secured him to make a study of those series of photographs which related to the motion of the horse"; and (k) the investigation was the "first scientific experiment

to be conducted on what is now Stanford University campus," and it was "only fitting that this important investigation should be celebrated by the University."[25]

The celebration included several interesting events. Louis Tolhurst lectured on the evolution of the motion picture. Samples of early films such as *San Francisco before the Fire* and *The New York Hat* were shown. At a commemoration assembly three addresses were presented: "The Stanford-Muybridge Research on the Portrayal of Motion," by Walter Miles; "The Debt of Motion Pictures to the Early Researcher," by Louis B. Mayer, vice-president of the Metro-Goldwyn-Mayer motion picture company; and "The Cost and Value of Research," by Alonzo E. Taylor, of Stanford. At a luncheon at the university president's house, Walter Miles again spoke, on "the Technique and Results of the Palo Alto Experiments." Materials relating to the history of the Stanford-Muybridge research were displayed at the Stanford Art Gallery, where the "later periods of motion-picture history were represented by objects contributed through the kindness of the Academy of Motion Picture Arts and Sciences." A tablet was unveiled in the Inner Quad, and a duplicate placed in the vicinity of Muybridge's Palo Alto Farm studio.[26]

At a concluding dinner given by the university trustees for the representatives of the Academy of Motion Picture Arts and Sciences, William C. De Mille spoke on "The University and the Future of Motion Pictures," the acting president of the university spoke on "The Relation of the University to Industrial Progress," and, as a surprise finale, Ray Lyman Wilbur, president of the university, who was on leave to serve as secretary of the U.S. Department of the Interior, appeared on a screen in a "talking-picture address" that had been delivered in Washington about a week earlier and recorded by the Fox Movietone Company. In its use of "new portable talking-picture equipment" devised by the Bell Telephone Laboratories, the event "made motion-picture history," according to Walter Miles. It was "probably the

[24] Card's "Problems of Film History" (n. 5 above) provides an analysis of the weaknesses of Ramsaye as a film historian, particularly with respect to Muybridge. See also Harlan Hamilton, "Muybridge's Contribution to the Motion Picture," *Film Comment*, Fall 1969, pp. 24-25.

[25] "Leland Stanford and Motion Pictures," *Stanford Illustrated Review*, June 1929, pp. 469-472.
[26] The tablet commemorated the "motion picture research conducted in 1878 and 1879 at the Palo Alto Farm," which provided "consecutive instantaneous exposures" by means of a "battery of twenty-four cameras fitted with electro-shutters." The "extensive photographic experiment portraying the attitudes of men and animals in motion" was said to have been "conceived by and carried out under the direction and patronage of Leland Stanford." The tablet stated further that "Eadweard J. Muybridge, photographer, carried out the investigation and showed that the photographs could be combined in projection to give the true appearance of motion"; that "John D. Isaacs, mechanical engineer, advanced the research by devising electrical equipment"; and that "J. B. D. Stillman, M.D., analyzed the photographs relating to the locomotion of the horse."

first time that an address prepared for a specific occasion outside of a theatre was brought to that occasion through the means of talking-pictures."

The celebration, and the various professional articles and popular newspaper accounts that preceded and followed it, undoubtedly helped to stimulate a reestimation of Muybridge's work in Philadelphia and even in Kingston. From Philadelphia, in February, had come George E. Nitzsche's article "Who Invented Moving Pictures?" It traced the origin of motion pictures to Philadelphia, and to Muybridge, who, "under the auspieces of the University of Pennsylvania, made modern moving pictures possible." Nitzsche also credited Muybridge with the first use of the moving picture in medical research, since he had taken instantaneous pictures of the movements of a dog's heart in action for Dr. Edward T. Reichert, a professor of physiology at the university.[27] Harry Leffman took exception to Nitzsche's claim that Muybridge had made moving pictures possible, declaring in an article: "Muybridge devised and carried out with great ingenuity and success the *analysis* of motion, but the present day screen-play is a *synthesis*."[28] He, in turn, was quickly challenged by L. F. Rondinella. In an article, "Muybridge's Pictures," Professor Rondinella reminded the world that he had been in charge of Muybridge's electrical apparatus and scientific records during the summers of 1884 and 1885, and took the position that Muybridge was equally successful in synthesis:

In view of the established fact that Muybridge was the first to project motion pictures upon a screen (in 1879) — that with the improved methods which he devised and used in his University work the scope and quality of his motion pictures were much enhanced (from 1885) — and that he operated the first theatre in which motion pictures were commercially shown (in 1893) — I think that there is **ample** *"justification for declaring Eadweard Muybridge the inventor of motion pictures."*[29]

Leffman noted that Heyl had projected a series of pictures "taken from living models and synthesized so as to reproduce the illusion of movement" in Philadelphia in February 1870, and hence before Muybridge, but neglected to explain that Heyl's

155. The plaque unveiled on July 11, 1931, in Muybridge's birthplace, Kingston-upon-Thames.

models were posed in different stages of the waltz and thus were not photographed in actual motion at all. On the other hand, he was right in asserting that a "claim that Eadweard Muybridge was the 'inventor' of motion pictures cannot be sustained." Yet, Rondinella was on firmer ground in basing his claim on the fact that Muybridge, for the first time, combined the

---

[27] *The Corn Exchange*, Philadelphia (published by the bank of that name), January-February 1929, pp. 1, 3. For further reference to medical photographs by Muybridge see H. L. Gibson, "The Muybridge Pictures of Motion," *Medical Radiography and Photography*, Rochester, N.Y., XXVI, no. 1 (1950).

[28] *Journal of the Franklin Institute*, Philadelphia, June 1929, p. 254. Leffman was an electrical expert at the university and an assistant to Muybridge.

[29] *The Camera*, October 1929, pp. 252-254.

projection with the showing of serial photographs taken while the subject was in actual motion. Both Heyl and Muybridge used combinations of previously existing processes and devices; hence neither could claim to be the inventor of what he did. Muybridge's particular combination of the analytically produced photograph and the synthesizing projection machine, however, directly prefigured the modern film industry and its techniques.

Kingston-on-Thames was now to achieve a "fitting memorial" for Muybridge. This came about from a visit by Will Day, well known as a collector of machines "illustrating the long series of discoveries culminating in the invention of the modern cinematograph."[30] Day spoke at the Public Library in late 1930. After tracing the evolution of the early educational toys that pictorially suggested movement, he made the claim that "William Friese-Greene, an Englishman, was the inventor of commercial cinematography, in 1888," while granting that "Eadweard Muybridge was the first man successfully to portray the movements of animals on the screen."[31] Like Rondinella, Day failed to indicate that Muybridge's strongest claim to fame was the fact of his having been the first to project onto the screen photographs instantaneously taken from life. This no one had achieved before him.

Day expressed the hope that the people of Kingston would "make every effort to provide a fitting memorial to their own townsman," whose researches had "contributed so much to their amusement and instruction." On July 11, 1931, ceremonies

[30] *Daily Telegraph,* London, August 12, 1929.
[31] *Surrey Comet,* November 1, 1930.

were held at the library to commemorate Muybridge's "achievements in the Arts and Science, and his benefactions to his native town." After an address by Will Day, the mayor unveiled a memorial tablet

EADWEARD JAMES MUYBRIDGE
A NATIVE OF KINGSTON-UPON THAMES
BENEFACTOR OF THIS PUBLIC LIBRARY
A SCIENTIFIC INVESTIGATOR OF
ANIMAL LOCOMOTION
WITH HIS CAMERA AND MACHINE
THE ZOOPRAXISCOPE
HE PRODUCED MOVING PICTURES
IN AMERICA IN THE YEAR 1880
AT PARIS IN 1881 AND BEFORE
THE ROYAL INSTITUTION IN 1882
FROM THESE INVENTIONS THE MODERN
CINEMATOGRAPH
HAS BEEN EVOLVED

The *Illustrated London News,* on July 18, devoted a page to "The Muybridge Tablet: Pioneer Motion Pictures of the '70's." After such fanfare, few in England could have been unaware of the name, work, and renown of the Kingston Claimant.

Most importantly, Muybridge's work itself seemed to continue to have meaning for the reading public during this period. By 1931, *Animals in Motion* was in its fifth printing, and *The Human Figure in Motion* was in its seventh. A minor event of significance, near the beginning of the period, was the appearance on the West Coast of a pirated, miniature edition of the *Panorama of San Francisco from California Street Hill* in 1911.

34. Centennial Estimate (1931–1972)

Any estimate of what has been written about Eadweard Muybridge since the 1920s must begin with the two chapters which concern him in George T. Clark's 1931 biography of Leland Stanford. In the chapter on "The Palo Alto Farm" Clark describes Stanford's interest in fast horses and their training, and the purchase and development of the farm, its world championship records, and its demise as a breeding establishment. In the chapter on "Animal Locomotion and Muybridge" he covers, from records available to him as former director of the Stanford University Library, the Stanford-Muybridge relationship from 1872 to 1883.

Highlights of Clark's position are these: (*a*) Stanford conceived

the idea of using photography to record the action of a horse; (*b*) the story of the bet is groundless, as Stanford was not a betting man; (*c*) the first attempt to get a photograph of Occident was made in 1872; (*d*) the photographer succeeded in getting a picture of a trotting horse with all feet clear of the ground, but the results were inconclusive; (*e*) a conclusive picture was taken in 1877; (*f*) Stanford conceived of increasing the number of cameras to illustrate various positions of the entire stride; (*g*) John D. Isaacs developed the electrical control device for the shutters of the multiple cameras; (*h*) Muybridge copyrighted the resulting pictures in his own name with Stanford's approval; (*i*) Muybridge devised a satisfactory projecting machine with which he showed the pictures in motion in 1879; (j) Muybridge delivered to Stanford a set of all the pictures, collected in an album, in 1881; (k) these pictures he copyrighted in his own name; (l) at Stanford's expense Muybridge was enabled to go abroad, where he exhibited his pictures in 1882; (m) Stanford assigned Dr. J. B. D. Stillman to the task of writing and supervising the publication of *The Horse in Motion*, based on Muybridge's findings; (n) the title page of that work did not carry Muybridge's name; (o) Muybridge instituted suits against the publisher and Leland Stanford; (p) the suits were dismissed; and (q) Muybridge and Stanford severed their relationship over these misunderstandings.[1]

Except for not noting the second attempt to photograph Occident in 1873, Clark's treatment seems basically fair, and some documentation exists to support each of the points. In some cases the persons giving evidence may not have been beyond the claim of vested interest. On the other hand, Clark is "restrained, efficient, and painstaking," as Ray Lyman Wilbur notes in his foreword. Muybridge's private life is not overemphasized (although unfortunately Clark in a footnote refers the reader to Ramsaye's book for details). Isaacs's role is restricted to the developing of the electrical control idea. The irritation of Stillman and Stanford over Muybridge's suit and its attendant claims is made clear. Clark's account, one might say, is the "official" Stanford University history of the Stanford-Muybridge years as they were understood in 1931. His restraint and careful documentation are in sharp contrast to Ramsaye's sensational narrative.

Other photography or motion picture historians in the thirties range between these extremes in their assessment of Muybridge's significance. Benjamin Bowles Hampton gives Isaacs credit for the row of cameras.[2] G. R. Doyle says that the results of Muybridge's zoetropic projection were convincing, but the method was cumbersome.[3] Gilbert Seldes mentions Muybridge as a photographer of horses, but assigns to Meissonier the credit for projecting the photographs.[4] Leslie Wood describes Muybridge's sequences as giving the "crudest semblance of movement," and credits Friese-Greene with the invention of the motion picture.[5] Robert Taft makes a very balanced presentation of Muybridge's work, pointing out that Heyl, although he

preceded Muybridge by nine years, did not have the "advantage of the 'instantaneous' views" of Muybridge, and that Muybridge deserves to be called the "father of motion pictures."[6] Charles G. Clark's position parallels that of Ramsaye.[7] M. Jackson-Wrigley and Eric Leyland claim that Muybridge's process was not intended for projection upon a screen, and that Friese-Greene should be credited with the development of the modern motion picture.[8]

Writers of the forties range in like fashion. C. L. Turner follows Ramsaye.[9] Beaumont Newhall does the same.[10] Bernard Alfieri calls the Zoöpraxiscope the "forerunner of the modern ciné projector," but dates it as of 1881.[11] An article in *Life* magazine credits the first motion picture to Thomas Eakins because he took pictures with a single-lens camera while working with Muybridge in Philadelphia.[12] An article in a Sacramento newspaper claims that city, accurately, as the birthplace of the motion picture.[13] An article in *Peninsula Life* claims Palo Alto as the birthplace.[14] Frederick M. Thrasher follows the modest line of George T. Clark.[15] Leslie Wood credits Muybridge with suggesting the use of the 24 cameras, and Meissonier with suggesting "Uchatius' machine" as the model for the Zoöpraxiscope.[16] Emanuel W. Robson mentions the Zoöpraxiscope but not Muybridge, and champions Friese-Greene as the inventor of the motion picture.[17] Martin Quigley, Jr., following Ramsaye's lead, debunks Muybridge's contribution as cumbersome and says that Muybridge was not in fact a pioneer in instantaneous

[1] Clark, pp. 341-379.

[2] *A History of the Movies,* New York: Covici, Friede, 1931, pp. 4-5.

[3] *Twenty-five Years of Film,* London: Mitre Press, 1936, p. xv.

[4] *The Movies Came from America,* London: Batsford, 1937, p. 16.

[5] *The Romance of the Movies,* London: Heinemann, 1937, p. 15.

[6] *Photography and the American Scene,* New York: Macmillan, 1938, pp. 408-9.

[7] Antonia and W. K. L. Dickson, *Edison's Invention of the Kineto-Phonograph,* Los Angeles: Pueblo Press, 1939 (a reprint of the article in *The Century,* June 1894).

[8] *The Cinema,* London: Grafton, 1939, pp. 7-9.

[9] *Chronological Outline of Film History,* New York, 1940 (published by the author), p. 1.

[10] In W. D. Morgan, ed., *The Compleat Photographer,* n.p., 1942, 1943, pp. 2660-2665.

[11] "The Birth of Action Photography: The Work of Eadweard Muybridge, 1834-1900," *Amateur Photographer,* February 17, 1943, pp. 106-7.

[12] Issue of May 15, 1944, p. 77. Eakins developed his own camera, a variation on Marey's photographic gun and not so reliable as the latter.

[13] Wilder Wilie, "Capital Is Birthplace of Motion Pictures," in the *Union,* Sacramento, May 27, 1945, p. 13.

[14] Theron G. Cady, "Peninsula — Birthplace of the Movies," *Peninsula Life,* August, 1946, pp. 10-11, 30-32.

[15] *OK for Sound,* New York: Duell, Sloan, and Pierce, 1946, p. 12.

[16] *The Miracle of the Movies,* London: Burke Publishing Co., 1947, pp. 67-70.

[17] *The Film Answers Back,* London: John Lane, 1947, p. 23.

photography and that Isaacs was, and that it was Marey who analyzed and synthesized the photographic results, in a projector which he got in Paris from Reynaud.[18] Robert O'Brien, in a colorful but unscholarly, Ramsayesque vignette characterizes Muybridge as the "Othello of the horsecars."[19] The most serious and balanced account of the decade appears in Joseph Maria Eder's *History of Photography*.[20] Eder, a German scholar, accepts Muybridge's own dates and own estimate of his work, and concludes that "Muybridge must be recognized as the real inventor of the projected animated photograph from life." An important contribution to the history of the motion picture came from France, Jean Vivié's extensive documentation of the history and development of cinematographic techniques.[21] But, while discussing Muybridge as a precursor in chronophotography, Vivié totally ignores his projection of sequential photographs in the Zoöpraxiscope. Another positive force in this period was the increasing interest of Beaumont Newhall in Muybridge and his work. Although Newhall dates the first picture of motion as 1873, he traces out an otherwise essentially accurate account, concluding with the judgment that "Muybridge projected pictures on a screen, anticipating motion picture photography."[22] An important event was the exhibition at Dorland House, London, in 1946, of materials and machines relating to the early motion picture. For this exhibition the Kingston Library lent the original Zoöpraxiscope, The then borough librarian, Harry Cross, reported: "It is a tribute to Muybridge's skill that the machine, electrically operated, worked without a hitch for the whole period the show was open — 11 a.m. to 7 p.m. each day, including Sundays."[23]

Serious Muybridge scholarship may be said to date from the fifties. It began with two extensive articles by George E. Nitzsche reviewing photographic and motion picture history in Philadelphia and Muybridge's part in it. Nitzsche had the advantage of personal acquaintance with many of the men who had been associated with Muybridge, and he had gathered an important collection of Muybridge relics on which he based his historical judgments. While not overlooking the earlier work in California, Nitzsche focused on Muybridge's methods and results as a significant contribution to research at the University of Pennsylvania, and noted that Muybridge gave the university credit for "enabling him to carry on his research work and perfect his experiments."[24] Seeing these experiments as probably having "a wider influence throughout the world than most modern inventions in the history of science," Nitzsche commented: "His [Muybridge's] motion picture became a valuable aid to education and science; made it possible to get a glimpse of the actual life of people in all parts of the world without leaving one's house; and developed into the greatest entertainment medium of all time."[25] Moreover, "Muybridge's experiments not only made modern movies possible, but they enabled both the artist and the scientist to study motion with accuracy." On the issue of who was the "inventor" of the motion picture, Nitzsche declared: "We may claim that honor for Muybridge, without denying credit from former investigators of the various problems involved."[26] He termed the Zoöpraxographical Hall at Chicago in 1893 the "first moving picture theatre in the world," and the photographs made for Dr. Reichert "one of the first uses of the movie in medical research." He noted that Muybridge consulted with Edison in 1888 on the possibility of combining the effects of the Zoöpraxiscope and the phonograph, and that "Edison made his first continuous movie on strip film using Muybridge's motion photographs of running horses."[27] As examples of later influence at Philadelphia, Nitzsche cited his own 1917 proposal to Henry Ford to "have a full movie made of Muybridge"; a 1925 proposal to "establish a school covering every phase of motion picture art" at the University of Pennsylvania; the inclusion in a 16 mm. sound film, made in 1940 for the two-hundredth anniversary of the university, of "a section devoted to the Muybridge experiments, which included

[18] *Magic Shadows,* Washington, D.C.: Georgetown University Press, 1948, p. 142.

[19] *This Is San Francisco,* New York: McGraw-Hill, 1948, p. 290.

[20] New York: Columbia University Press, 1945, pp. 500-505, 507, 717-718, 788; translation of *Geschichte der Photographie,* 2 vols., 4th ed., Halle, 1932.

[21] *Traité Général de Technique du Cinéma* (Vol. I of *Historique et Développement de la Technique Cinématographique*), Paris: Editions B.P.I., 1945, pp. 21-23; chart on pp. 44-45 omits Muybridge's Zoöpraxiscope

[22] *The History of Photography from 1839 to the Present Day,* New York: Museum of Modern Art, 1949, pp. 104-8, 110.

[23] To Janet Pendegast Leigh, n.d.; Haas collection.

[24] "Pennsylvania Pioneering in the Movies," *General Magazine and Historical Chronicle,* University of Pennsylvania, Autumn 1951, p. 43. For Nitzsche's 1929 article "Who Invented Moving Pictures?" see chap. 33, n. 29, above.

See also Beaumont Newhall, "The George E. Nitzsche Collection of Muybridge Relics," in *Medical Radiography and Photography,* XXVI (1950), 24-26. The collection includes "a number of Muybridge's original negatives and prints, as well as notes and apparatus he used in producing . . . *Animal Locomotion.*"

[25] "Philadelphia as the Birthplace of Moving Pictures," *Germantowne Crier,* Philadelphia, March 1950, p. 26.

[26] "Pennsylvania Pioneering in the Movies," p. 44.

[27] Confirmed by Hendricks in 1961 (see chap. 33, n. 8, above).

a series of modern films taken directly from the original Muybridge negatives" in his collection; and the gifts of his Muybridge relics to the George Eastman House in 1949. Nitzsche proposed that the alumni of the University of Pennsylvania "might do well to erect a monument, somewhere along our beloved Hamilton Walk, to the man who there, with the support of the University, for the first time in history succeeded in perfecting a practicable system for photographing motion."[28]

In 1950, three Eastman House scholars entered the arena in Muybridge's behalf. Beaumont Newhall studied the Nitzsche collection and concluded that Muybridge's work "bridges still and motion-picture photography" and that Muybridge "must be ranked as a pioneer [who] anticipated the moving picture."[29] H. L. Gibson reviewed Muybridge's *Animal Locomotion* and was full of "admiration for the thoroughness of his procedure and for the astounding variety of his human and animal studies." He noted that anatomists, biologists, physicians, and artists had never before "had the benefits of such a revealing tool as the special cameras he used." Gibson drew examples particularly from Muybridge's medical photography.[30] James Card performed an important service in reviewing film histories and exposing the "carefree character of film scholarship." He cited a number of false assumptions about Eadweard Muybridge held by Terry Ramsaye and Martin Quigley, Jr., for which corrective data were readily available. In setting a model for more careful film-history writing, Card demonstrated how, in Muybridge scholarship, "facts may be neatly twisted to prove a point."[31] A brief biographical sketch accompanied the Newhall article and, in the main, gave the facts of Muybridge's life accurately.[32] Three areas of confusion still existed: the date of his arrival on the West Coast was set as 1860; the date of the first photographs of motion for Stanford was sidestepped; and Meissonier was still credited with collaborating on the Zoöpraxiscope.

Kenneth Macgowan, following Card's lead, attempted to establish the story of the "invention of the tools of the motion picture."[33] This he did convincingly until he came to Eadweard Muybridge. Macgowan recognized that before "Marey had used his photographic gun or done more than record various stages of movement on a single plate, a photographer of California was using a battery of twenty-four separate cameras to take successive positions of horses and other animals in motion. More than that, he had projected his moving pictures before at least four audiences in San Francisco." In tracing the "confusions and contradictions" over Muybridge and his work, however, Macgowan left his role in motion picture history ambiguous.

In 1955, Helmut and Alison Gernsheim's *History of Photography* marked an advance in the objective treatment of Muybridge. It contained the best estimate thus far, presenting him with chronological accuracy and within the context of others working in the photography of motion.[34] The next year, Beaumont Newhall revised his earlier judgment. In "Muybridge and the First Motion Picture," working from records preserved in the scrapbook at Kingston, he pieced together a cogent account of Muybridge's career in California, Europe and Philadelphia.[35] He rejected Muybridge's 1872 date as unverifiable and accepted April 1873 as the month and year of the first photograph of Occident in motion. On Muybridge's use of the Zoöpraxiscope, Newhall concluded:

*Nobody had **reproduced** action, by taking a series of instantaneous photographs in rapid sequence and then projecting them intermittently on a screen before an audience. Yet this is exactly what Muybridge did. By every definition of cinematography, Muybridge's instantaneous photographic, magic lantern zoetrope was the first motion picture presentation in the world.*

Of the greatest importance for the understanding of Muybridge's historical contribution in the following years was the reprinting, by Dover Publications, of *The Human Figure in Motion* and *Animals in Motion*.[36] Pictorial artists and graphic designers became suddenly aware of Muybridge's work. The visual impact of the reprint volumes was supplemented by the useful, factual prefaces of Robert Taft and Lewis S. Brown, respectively, together with Muybridge's own text. The Dover reprints accomplished

[28] "Pennsylvania Pioneering in the Movies," pp. 41, 46. The proposal to Ford was interrupted by World War I and not realized. Nor were the other proposals; but an oil portrait of Muybridge by Mrs. Nitzsche hangs in the University of Pennsylvania Library as a memorial.

[29] Op. cit. (in n. 25, above).

[30] "The Muybridge Pictures of Motion," *Medical Radiography and Photography*, XXVI (1950), 18-24.

[31] "Problems of Film History," *Hollywood Quarterly*, IV (1950), 279-288.

[32] On cover 2 of the journal.

[33] "Coming of the Camera and Projector," *Quarterly Film, Radio, T.V.*, Fall 1954, pp. 1-15.

[34] London and New York: Oxford University Press, 1955, pp. 325-332; in rev. ed., New York: McGraw-Hill, 1969, pp. 435-440.

[35] *Image*, V (1956), 4-9. In 1952, I visited Kingston-on-Thames, studied the Scrapbook, and realized how important it would be to have a photocopy. This was suggested to Beaumont Newhall, who arranged to have the work done for the George Eastman House on microfilm, which was then shared with me, printed by my son, Peter Holland Haas, and returned. Newhall's subsequent study of the microfilm led to his writing several articles which were instrumental in changing the historical perspective on Muybridge.

[36] New York, 1955, 1957.

for Muybridge what no earlier historical or critical writing had yet done: because of the physical availability of the pictures and text, localized interpretations of his work and its importance were transcended, and the essential facts of his biography and the results of his motion investigations became known internationally.[37]

The 1960s saw a further expansion of scholarly work and general interest. Publications about Muybridge dealt, naturally, with his contribution to the development of motion pictures, but also with the general range of his photography and with its significance for the other visual arts. The decade began with Gordon Hendrick's detailed study, *The Edison Motion Picture Myth*. Tracing the history of the Muybridge-Edison relationship, Hendricks established the germinal importance of the Muybridge analytical photographs for Edison's development of the Kinetoscope and controverted the claim that Edison succeeded with motion picture projection before 1896.[38] Next, William Homer, in an article particularly valuable for its documentation, narrowed the claims of Fairfield Porter and others that Thomas Eakins rather than Muybridge worked out the basic principles of the motion picture.[39] In contrast, C. W. Ceram was content with unverified dates and judgments: Muybridge "never thought initially of using the analysis as a means of later synthesis" and "was quite unaware that he was doing something momentous when he projected his series of positives in San Francisco in 1879."[40] Kenneth Macgowan's *Behind the Screen* included many of the materials and judgments he had already used and expressed in his 1954 article, but with some notable changes of emphasis, playing down the bet, the murder of Larkyns, and the contribution of John D. Isaacs. These changes amounted to a questioning of Terry Ramsaye's account.[41] But on all points the most useful study published in this period was an article by Harlan Hamilton in 1969. Hamilton reviewed Muybridge research under several headings, and sifted out the errors and biases by going to primary sources for irrefutable evidence. He concluded that "Muybridge's main contribution to film as we know it today seems to be his zoopraxiscope"; that Muybridge did not invent the zoopraxiscope, which was not patentable since it "utilized so many ideas of other inventors"; and that Muybridge was "the first person in the world to devise a suitable means of taking a sequence of still pictures of animals *in motion* and successfully projecting them on a screen before an *audience* in such a way as to give the appearance of movement we are so familiar with in the movie houses of today."[42]

Assessments of Muybridge's accomplishments as a photographer took a fresh turn with an article on his Yosemite Valley photographs by Mary Hood and the present writer.[43] It combined biographical findings and observations on the photographs. Mary and William Hood's collection of copy-prints of nearly every known photograph of the valley by every major photographer who worked there in Muybridge's time permitted judgments about his accomplsihments as a photographer of this scenic region by fixing the vantage points that he chose and comparing his results with those of other photographers who had undertaken the same views. In 1964 the second edition of Beaumont Newhall's *History of Photography* appeared.[44] Newhall related Muybridge's early life briefly and in its essential details, still choosing 1873 as the date of the first action photograph for Stanford rather than 1872, and giving 1880 as the date for the first use of the Zoöpraxiscope rather than 1879. Newhall based his statements on his first reading and analysis of Muybridge's scrapbook. The Muybridge biographical entry in the 1966 *Encyclopaedia Britannica* was contributed by Gordon Hendricks. In what is for the most part a fair summary, Muybridge was called a "pioneer in cinematography." The year 1872 was accepted as the date of

---

[37] Strictly speaking, the welcome, indeed invaluable Dover books are not reprints, though for convenience so called. The text is from the 1899 and 1901 books, and it appears that plates from *Animal Locomotion* were photographed, 195 and 183, respectively, from the total of 781. Some of the quality of the plates has unavoidably been lost. The huge sheets of the *Animal Locomotion* plates, 19 1/8 x 24 3/8 inches, have very wide margins, however, and reduction of picture size has been avoided or kept at a minimum in Dover's 8 x 10 1/2 inch pages.

[38] Berkeley and Los Angeles: University of California Press, 1961. In a footnote (p. 6) Hendricks promised a monograph that would discuss Muybridge's work, "which seems to me to be the chief stimulus for the mechanical invention upon which the American motion picture is based." In 1974 his *Eadweard Muybridge: The Father of the Motion Picture*, New York: Grossman, was announced as forthcoming.

[39] William I. Homer, with the assistance of John Talbot, "Eakins, Muybridge, and the Motion Picture Process," *Art Quarterly*, Summer 1963, pp. 194-216. For Porter see Homer's *Thomas Eakins*, 1969, p. 116.

[40] *Archaeology of the Cinema*, New York: Harcourt, 1965, p. 81. Ceram is equally unaware as to which experiments were made in San Francisco, Sacramento, or Palo Alto.

[41] New York: Delacorte Press, 1965. Macgowan's changes came about through discussions with me at the University of California. I had by then begun my study of the Scrapbook.

[42] "'Les Allures du Cheval': Eadweard James Muybridge's Contribution to the Motion Picture," *Film Comment*, V, no. 3 (Fall 1969), 17-33.

[43] Mary V. Jessup Hood and Robert Bartlett Haas, "Eadweard Muybridge's Yosemite Valley Photographs, *California Historical Scoeity Quarterly*, XLII (March 1963), 5-26.

[44] *The History of Photography from 1939 to the Present Day*, New York: Museum of Modern Art.

his first instantaneous photograph for Stanford, but 1877 was erroneously accepted as the year when the "first successful sequential photographs of rapidly moving objects were taken," and 1878 erroneously as the year when "Muybridge devised a means for projecting those images cinematically, though the procedure had been anticipated by others." Rather than perpetuate the Stanford "bet" story, Hendricks used Muybridge's more moderate word, "wager," and ascribed Stanford's motivation for the photographic experiments to this.[45]

A less accurate account, trailing the Isaacs position of forty years earlier, was Arthur Knight's item about Muybridge under "Motion Pictures, Part I," in the same volume of the *Britannica.* It gave 1877 as the date when Muybridge, using the "photographic method devised by Isaacs," produced the "first real photographs of objects in rapid motion." Of course, Knight should have said either that 1872 was the first date of a photograph of a horse in rapid motion, or that 1878 was the date of the first use of the photographic method on which Isaacs collaborated. For an example of Muybridge's sequential photographs from an "early series," an 1887 picture was used — taken a decade after the first Palo Alto sequential photographs. Knight described the antecedents of the Zoöpraxiscope more fully than the Zoöpraxiscope itself, and thus bypassed its germinal importance for the development of the projected motion picture, giving credit to Edison, instead, for an optical effect no more advanced than Muybridge's and developed at a far later date: "The motion picture first emerged from the laboratories of abstract science on April 14, 1894, with the introduction of Thomas A. Edison's Kinetoscope, a coin-in-the-slot peep-show device that permitted individuals to glimpse about 15 seconds of film showing people and objects in wonderfully lifelike movement."[46] In 1969, Allan Marks, editor of the Da Capo Press, believing that the Dover reprints misrepresented the quality of the photographs, undertook to reproduce 100 plates from the original edition of *Animal Locomotion.* Because of the finer quality of their printing and their closer approximation to the original plates, these full-size illustrations served to show those who had no access to plates from the 1887 edition how masterful a photographer of motion Muybridge really was.[47]

In the early 1970s, Kevin MacDonnell's graphically deceptive

and highly inaccurate *Eadweard Muybridge: The Man Who Invented the Motion Picture* became the first book entirely devoted to Muybridge.[48] In happy contrast came Jean-Antony du Lac's superb full-size "photographic edition" of the 1877 *Panorama of San Francisco from California Street Hill,* as if to remind us again that the best evidence in Muybridge's behalf will always be his work itself.[49]

Harlan Hamilton noted a trend "to look at Muybridge from an aesthetic viewpoint and to be concerned with his influence on painting." An example of this influence was described by John Rothenstein in the catalogue of a retrospective exhibition of works by Francis Bacon:

Bacon's direct observation of nature . . . is casual; it is the photograph that serves as the window through which he looks at the world. . . . He even prefers, I think, to study the old masters through the medium of the photograph. But the photographs he uses most are those which he clips from the daily or weekly press. His studio is littered with hundreds of them and here too are Eadweard Muybridge's volumes **The Human Figure in Motion** *and* **Animals in Motion** *which he used to study at the Victoria and Albert Museum before he could afford to buy them. This remarkable Victorian classic showing nude men and women, as well as animals, in almost every conceivable posture, is to Bacon what his breviary is to a priest: he is able to find, in an instant, any one of the thousands of reproductions it contains. . . . Muybridge he uses to suggest themes or to help him to articulate correctly figures in motion he has imagined.*[50]

Aaron Scharf, in a 1962 essay, "Painting, Photography, and the Image of Movement," showed how painters of the late nineteenth century turned to the "images of the instantaneous camera to determine the truth of movement," and documented the influence of Muybridge's work on several of them.[51] Van Deren Coke, in 1964, prepared the catalogue for an exhibition of paintings and photographs which carried the demonstration of Muybridge's influence on painting, and on photography generally, into the twentieth century.[52] In a study of Eakin's *A May Morning in the*

[45] Chicago, XV, 1110.

[46] Ibid., pp. 898-901.

[47] Eadweard Muybridge, *Animal Locomotion, Volume 1, Males (nude),* New York. This work includes a photoreproduction of the *Prospectus and Catalogue of Plates.*

[48] Boston: Little, Brown, 1972. Aside from offering an undependable account of the subject's life and achievements, the book regrettably misuses a generous format to display Muybridge photographs in frequent disregard of the original dimensions and with backgrounds eliminated. For a detailed criticism see the letter by Anita Ventura Mozley in *Times Literary Supplement,* London, April 20, 1973, p. 446-447.

[49] San Francisco, 1973. This edition, limited to 50 numbered copies, consists of 13 photographs mounted on double-thick museum board.

[50] *Catalogue of Francis Bacon's Retrospective Exhibition at the Tate Gallery,* London, 1962.

[51] *Burlington Magazine,* May 1962, pp. 186-195.

[52] *The Painter and the Photograph,* Albuquerque: University of New

Park, Gordon Hendricks made clear the specific influence of Muybridge's photographs of 1878 on this painting.[53] In 1969, Aaron Scharf's *Art and Photography* extended the material presented in his 1962 article and provided a capstone demonstration of Muybridge's influence on the visual arts.[54]

The centennial of the Stanford-Muybridge investigations, in 1972, was marked by a memorable exhibition of Muybridge's accomplishments up to and through his association with Leland Stanford, together with fascinating objects relating to his life and to the Stanford family. The 136-page catalogue of the exhibition was particularly interesting because of its illustrations and materials on Muybridge's life, the technical aspects of the Palo Alto experiments, and the "philosophical toys" that were precursors of the Zoöpraxiscope.[55] Ever since the semi-centennial celebration in 1929 there had been increasing interest at Stanford University in the fact that important events in early motion-picture history had taken place on the site and under the sponsorship of Leland Stanford.

Most of the contemporaries of sponsor and photographer, of course, were gone. One remarkable woman, however, had bridged the generations, and from nearby Saratoga, where she lived until her death in 1958, she bombarded with carefully reasoned letters the university, the California State Library, Eastman House, and any writers who mentioned Muybridge in print, correcting misstatements about him. She was Janet Pendegast Leigh, daughter of William Wirt Pendegast, the lawyer who led Muybridge's defense at his trial. Janet Leigh was born on Christmas Day, 1874. She had been brought up by her widowed mother to love and respect Muybridge as her father had done, and to understand the principal issues of his personal life and professional career. She became a formidable antagonist of Terry Ramsaye. There is no doubt that her dedicated efforts helped greatly to adjust the focus of Muybridge research in the quarter century following the appearance of Ramsaye's book.

My own interest began before I met Mrs. Leigh. Splendid photographs made by Muybridge from Norton Bush paintings and inscribed to my great-grandfather were familiar objects in my childhood home.[56] My desire to know more about Muybridge

followed close upon research undertaken in the 1940s on the pioneer San Francisco photographer William Herman Rulofson.[57] A trip to Europe in the 1950s allowed for a visit to England. My first inquiry concerning Muybridge's birthplace was addressed mistakenly to the librarian in Stoke-on-Trent, rather than Kingston-on-Thames, from whom it brought a reply by way of Harry Cross, the former librarian in Muybridge's native town: "Mr. Haas is under the impression that this gentleman lived in Stoke-on-Trent, a fact I am unable to confirm. It is much more likely in view of Muybridge's well known association with Kingston-upon-Thames that you may be able to help Mr. Haas in this matter."[58] Sufficient to say, I shortly presented myself at the Public Library in Kingston, where Muybridge and his work began to take on detailed substance for me.

Harry Cross told me of Janet Leigh, who had supplied him with carbon copies of all her letters on Muybridge from halfway around the world. A few weeks later I called on Mrs. Leigh in California and our collaboration on a biography of Muybridge began. Through all the interruptions that followed, and even after her death (since she ultimately put all her Muybridge papers at my disposal), her commitment to the full telling of the story served as an inspiration to me.

In 1971 I met another remarkable woman concerned with the cause of Muybridge. Anita Ventura Mozley, a painter and also registrar and curator of photography at the Stanford University Museum of Art, had proposed a large-scale Stanford-Muybridge exhibition at the university, to open in October 1972. Our meeting began a second period of collaboration for me. We examined the Muybridge holdings at the university. We walked through the campus meadows to locate the exact site of the Muybridge studio. We went through the Stanford-Muybridge correspondence. We studied the Muybridge negatives (glass plates, often with his handwriting on them) and the bits of machinery constructed by Muybridge as models for the camera shutters or for the Zoöpraxiscope, and the paintings by Meissonier, Koch, and others that seemed to have a bearing on the coming exhibition. My rough draft of the present book provided Mrs. Mozley with a detailed chronology to use in planning the exhibition and its documentation, and in turn she constantly provided me with newly discovered materials.

The exhibition filled two large galleries. Facing across the first room were portraits of Eadweard Muybridge and Leland Stanford, the one a photograph, the other the painting by

Mexico Press, 1964, pp. 13-15, 35-36; expanded as *The Painter and the Photograph from Delacroix to Warhol*, 1972.

[53] "A May Morning in the Park," *Bulletin of the Philadelphia Museum of Art*, LX, no. 285 (Spring 1965), pp. 48-64.

[54] London: Allen Lane, Penguin Press, 1968, pp. 156-162.

[55] See chap. 18, n. 11, above.

[56] Norton Bush (1834-1894), a San Francisco artist, specialized in tropical landscapes and made three visits to Central and South America.

[57] "William Herman Rulofson," *California Historical Society Quarterly*, XXXIV (1955), 289-300, and XXXV (1956), 47-58.

[58] Cross to Haas, January 12, 1953.

Meissonier. The *Panorama of San Francisco from California Street Hill* was on curved walls along which spectators could pass to re-create Muybridge's 360-degree view of the city. Other walls held his monumental Yosemite photographs of 1872; the contents of Flora Muybridge's personal album of Muybridge's stereo views, along with Bradley and Rulofson photographs of her favorite actors and actresses; the Modoc War views; the Central American views; Muybridge's photographic copies of paintings of San Francisco; his 1877 "Electro-Photographic" snapshot of Occident, together with the newly discovered Koch painting of Occident which he had actually photographed; the negatives and prints from the series of 1878 called "The Horse in Motion"; and the glass-plate negatives of the eclipse of the sun, taken in 1880. It is safe to say that original prints of Muybridge's photographs had never before been seen in such variety and amplitude.

The second room contained mementoes of the Stanford family: Bonnat's portrait of Jane Lathrop Stanford, Carolus-Duran's portrait of Leland, Jr., and Thomas Hill's enormous canvas, *Palo Alto Spring,* showing the Stanford and Lathrop families on the lawn at Mayfield Grange. There were also young Leland's velocipede, his drawings, stuffed animals, and toy soldiers, and many more of the interesting and diverting things which he collected and with which his devoted parents surrounded him.

Optical toys and machines that foreshadowed the Zoöpraxi-scope were lent, from the Sol Lesser collection, by the Academy of Motion Picture Arts and Sciences. Standing in a niche was the Zoöpraxiscope itself — not the original machine, which is on permanent display in Kingston-on-Thames, but a working copy constructed around Muybridge's wooden model, parts of which had been discovered at the university, in the museum basement. Visitors could operate it, making a sequence of Muybridge's instantaneous photographs appear on the screen.

In 1973 the exhibition was taken to Sacramento and Los Angeles — appropriately, to the city where Muybridge began his motion studies and to the capital of the modern motion-picture industry.[59]

What of my own estimate of Eadweard Muybridge? When I began my biographical researches some twenty-five years ago,

[59] Three substantial articles appeared in the *Times,* Los Angeles, February 11, 1973: Arthur Knight, "Homage to Eadweard Muybridge: The Man Who Made Pictures Move"; Henry J. Seldis, "A Shatterer of Traditional Aesthetic Concepts"; and William Wilson, "Like Picasso — He Did Not Seek, He Found."
Thom Anderson of Los Angeles has an hour-length film, *Eadweard Muybridge — Zoopraxographer,* in preparation for broadcast on public television in 1975.

Muybridge was a shadowy figure. Subsequent research and a growing interest in nineteenth-century photography both in Europe and America have provided new information and a new framework for the Muybridge story. A reasonable picture of the man and his accomplishments now exists.

Muybridge's professional accomplishment in photography was threefold. First, his documentation of the American West (from Alaska to Central America, but particularly of California) is superior to that of any photographer working as his contemporary. Second, he was the first photographer to develop a practical system for taking a series of instantaneous photographs of an object in rapid motion, and these "analytical" photographs became the basis for whole new fields of scientific endeavor — for example, the study of locomotion and medical photography. Third, Muybridge was the first photographer to project images derived from his sequential, instantaneous photographs upon a screen, commercially, for the instruction and enjoyment of large audiences, and for this reason he may justly be considered the father of the modern motion picture and of the later industry which sprang up to develop the idea for mass markets. In each of these endeavors he was not only a pioneer figure in his own century, but also a major contributor to the twentieth century, whose artists, scientists, and film makers continue to express their indebtedness to Muybridge in their own work.

Behind this life of professional productivity and extraordinary accomplishment stands another Eadweard Muybridge calling across the years for assessment — Muybridge the individual, whose drives and capacities, temperament and character must have shaped his successes and his failures as a man, as well as his successes and his failures as a professional. After the lapse of more than a century, and because of Muybridge's extreme reticence about the details of his private life, most of what can be said about him must be conjectural. And yet some significant psychological patterns seem to appear in the events which are open to us.

Muybridge's overwhelming *drives* appear to have been to prove himself and to accomplish something of lasting value in the world which he could justly consider his worthy, personal contribution. This pattern can be traced from the time of his rejection of financial help from his grandmother and the promise to return to Kingston only when he was successful, and his early departure from England, on through his various business ventures as a successful dealer in books, to his enterprises as a novel and successful photographer, internationally famous lecturer, and author. What the unconscious or subconscious components of these drives were we will never know, but they must have been buried somewhere in his early family life and conditioned by the untimely death of his father, the seductive love of his mother, and the overwhelming personality, family authority, and material success of his maternal grandmother, Susannah Norman Smith. Whatever the balance of conscious, unconscious, or subconscious components was, Muybridge was vitally motivated for accomplishment throughout his life, and in his chosen work managed to achieve increasing satisfaction at each new and more complex stage of his career. The corn chandler's son did go out into the world and did accomplish something there of lasting value to the arts and sciences.

Muybridge's *capacities* must have been substantial to have supported his aspirations. The death of his father probably limited the amount of formal education he was able to achieve, yet he demonstrated, in the course of his life, an acquaintance with Greek and Latin, with modern European languages and literatures, with the history of art, and with scientific reasoning; substantial ability in writing and public speaking; more than ordinary competence in law and business practice; and the skillful management of a relatively new and promising medium, photography. Within each of the areas of his chosen activity, whatever the barriers he met along the way, his capacities seemed to have overcome them: economic insecurity, insufficient professional education, limited opportunity, boredom, personal loneliness, unhappy marriage, loss of patrons, threats to status, and historical distortions. These he overcame with hard work, fine craftsmanship, artistic sensitivity, and an ability to attract patronage and to organize scientific and artistic projects in novel and productive ways. As his life moved from phase to phase, his aspirations were fulfilled in increasingly complex projects. The move from bookseller to author was a vast one. The move from the application of photography in instantaneous photography to the organization of the Philadelphia project in animal locomotion was equally vast. The move from a limited knowledge of the arts to a major contribution to the arts was the capstone for a man who had learned to combine his capacities and his opportunities, and cut his losses, in order to fulfill the mission which he had discovered for himself far from the place of his birth.

One regrets never having actually seen Muybridge, the man, in real life. The accounts of his temperament and character which remain yield an ambiguous picture and to some degree belie the picture of success presented by his professional accomplishments. As a child he is inventive but mischievious; as a young man, aspiring, but rejecting of financial assistance; as a young business man, of good character, but "eccentric and wavering"; as a young photographer, talented and artistic, but full of silence and contempt for those he despises; as a husband, kind and affectionate, but capable of vengeance even to the point of justifying murder. In his work for Leland Stanford he sees himself as a principal researcher, whereas to Stanford he is merely an employee. In Europe he is modest and behaves in no way as a lion, yet Stillman and Stanford believe that success has gone to his head. The "quiet, good-natured old farmer" of California has become as "artistique au possible," with "traces of genius in his face." At Philadelphia he has a "brilliant scientific success," but is unable to make his work "pay for itself." In 1892 he visits Floredo Muybridge (who may well have been his own son), but disinherits him when he appears to be intellectually limited. In 1893, at the peak of his fame, he leaves the field of photography entirely to become an author. Shortly thereafter he retires to Kingston, resumes family life, and ultimately leaves a sizable income to a cousin and a sizable estate to the city of his birth.

It is clear that his belief in himself and his wish for fame sometimes led him to act in extreme ways. His persistence could become compulsive; his modesty could become vanity; his gentleness could become cold anger; his objectivity could become muddled with desire for self-justification. How much of his eccentric behavior was triggered by some tragic flaw of character and how much by the damage he sustained in the stage-coach wreck of 1860 we do not know. We do know that the impulse side and the control side of his personality were in conflict. Throughout his life close personal relationships seemed to be a threat. He was essentially a loner — friendships, family relationships, patrons, and business relationships tended to end in chaos and misunderstanding. On the other hand, each interpersonal failure seemed to spur him on to greater heights of professional performance. Interpersonal failure stimulated his need for accomplishment and success in the eyes of the world. He first catapulted himself from a business life to a professional life. From his professional successes he catapulted himself into the realm of the academic scientist. From the realm of science he catapulted himself once more into the broad realm of the arts, where he made successful applications of his findings to the visual arts and ultimately fulfilled his life in the role of author.

Each step on the ladder of fame brought him more relaxation, more security, and more humanity. But his personal life seems strangely limited along the way. Whether his drive for accomplishment narrowed his needs for a rich personal life, or whether his restricted personal life allowed his capacities to fulfill themselves in significant contributions to the world we shall never know.

What is certain is that Muybridge had two natures, and that these natures both express themselves in his finest work. In his "still" photographs (intended to document the scenery of Alaska, the West Coast, and Central America, and also the cities, private residences and possessions, and places of worship and recreation) some emotional qualities always come through, speaking either of the veiled and transient aspects of nature beneath the surface or of the spirit and dignity of the human beings who inhabit his world. In Muybridge's "motion" photographs (intended to document the movement of man and animal, and in which the emotional element inseparable from art was very rigorously excluded for the sake of scientific and technical discovery) his artist's impulse was also active, intentionally or not. The undraped figures, the domestic and wild animals, although recorded in their motions as objectively as possible, nevertheless speak to the viewer of the spirit of livings things as well.

Whether the photographs deal with the stillness of beauty or with unveiling the flow of movement, Muybridge has made an aesthetic gift to the world, for behind the emotionless lens was always the living photographer.

156. Eadweard Muybridge, 1830-1904.

Index